Workshop on Vision and Language 2015 (VL'15)

Vision and Language Meet Cognitive Systems

Held at EMNLP 2015

Lisbon, Portugal
18 September 2015

ISBN: 978-1-5108-1190-4

Printed from e-media with permission by:

Curran Associates, Inc.
57 Morehouse Lane
Red Hook, NY 12571

Some format issues inherent in the e-media version may also appear in this print version.

Printed by Curran Associates, Inc. (2015)

For permission requests, please contact the Association for Computational Linguistics at the address below.

Association for Computational Linguistics
209 N. Eighth Street
Stroudsburg, Pennsylvania 18360

Phone: 1-570-476-8006
Fax: 1-570-476-0860

acl@aclweb.org

Additional copies of this publication are available from:

Curran Associates, Inc.
57 Morehouse Lane
Red Hook, NY 12571 USA
Phone: 845-758-0400
Fax: 845-758-2634
Email: curran@proceedings.com
Web: www.proceedings.com

A WORKSHOP OF THE 2015 CONFERENCE ON
EMPIRICAL METHODS IN NATURAL LANGUAGE PROCESSING
(EMNLP 2015)

The Workshop on Vision and Language 2015 (VL'15)

VISION AND LANGUAGE MEET COGNITIVE SYSTEMS

Proceedings

September 18, 2015
Lisbon, Portugal

This workshop is supported by ICT COST Action IC1307, the European Network on Integrating Vision and Language (iV&L Net): Combining Computer Vision and Language Processing For Advanced Search, Retrieval, Annotation and Description of Visual Data.

http://ivl-net.eu/

COST is supported by the EU Framework Programme Horizon 2020

Preface

The Workshop on Vision and Language 2015 (VL'15) took place in the beautiful city of Lisbon, Portugal on September 18th 2015, as part of the 2015 Conference on Empirical Methods in Natural Language Processing (EMNLP 2015). The workshop was organized by the new European Network on Integrating Vision and Language, an initiative funded as a European COST Action under the Horizon 2020 programme supported by the European Commission.

The 2015 edition of the VL workshop is a successful continuation of the previous VL editions, where the VL workshops have the following general aims:

1. to provide a venue for reporting and discussing planned, ongoing and completed research that involves both language and vision; and

2. to enable NLP and computer vision researchers to meet, exchange ideas, expertise and technology, and form new research partnerships.

The flagship workshop's main purpose is to establish a strong inter-disciplinary forum which will ignite fertilizing discussions and ideas on how to combine and integrate established and novel techniques from different (but related) fields into new unified modeling approaches, as well as how to approach the problem of multi-modal data processing for NLP and vision from a completely new angle.

The call for papers for VL'15 soliciting both full research papers and short abstracts was issued in May 2015 and elicited a good number of high-quality submissions (23 in total), each of which was peer-reviewed by three members of the program committee. The interest in the workshop from leading NLP and computer vision researchers and the quality of submissions was high, so we aimed to be as inclusive as possible within the practical constraints of the workshop. In the end we accepted 13 full research papers, and 5 short abstracts.

The resulting workshop program packed a lot of exciting and diverse content into one day. We were delighted to be able to include in the program two great keynote speakers: Krystian Mikolajczyk and Marco Baroni. Our technical program combined 7 oral papers, and 11 poster presentations accompanied by short 5-minute poster spotlights.

The program also included a discussion session on future directions for the VL community and workshops, including plans for shared task competitions, summer schools, and expansions towards other related fields and research communities (e.g., information retrieval, data mining, digital humanities, Web search, cognitive science).

We would like to thank all the people who contributed to the organization and delivery of this workshop: the authors who submitted such high-quality papers; the program committee for their prompt and effective reviewing; our keynote speakers; the EMNLP 2015 organising committee, especially the workshops chairs, Zornitsa Kozareva and Jörg Tiedemann, and the publication chairs, Yuval Marton and Daniele Pighin; the participants in the workshop; and future readers of these proceedings for your shared interest in this exciting new area of research.

September 2015 *VL'15 Organizers*

Organizing Committee:

Anja Belz, *University of Brighton, UK*
Luísa Coheur, *INESC-ID, Portugal*
Vittorio Ferrari, *University of Edinburgh, UK*
Marie-Francine Moens, *KU Leuven, Belgium*
Katerina Pastra, *CSRI, Greece*
Ivan Vulić, *KU Leuven, Belgium*

Program Committee:

Ahmet Aker, *University of Sheffield, UK*
Yiannis Aloimonos, *University of Maryland, USA*
Marco Baroni, *University of Trento, Italy*
Raffaella Bernardi, *University of Trento, Italy*
Gemma Boleda, *University Pompeu Fabra, Spain*
Antoine Bordes, *Facebook Inc., USA*
Léon Bottou, *Microsoft Research, USA*
Elia Bruni, *Free University of Bolzano, Italy*
Yejin Choi, *University of Washington, USA*
Darren Cosker, *University of Bath, UK*
Simon Dobnik, *University of Gothenburg, Sweden*
Desmond Elliott, *CWI Amsterdam, The Netherlands*
Erkut Erdem, *Hacettepe University, Turkey*
Sergio Escalera, *Autonomous University of Barcelona, Spain*
Michel Galley, *Microsoft Research, USA*
Kristen Grauman, *University of Texas at Austin, USA*
Lewis Griffin, *University College London, UK*
Julia Hockenmaier, *University of Illinois at Urbana-Champaign, USA*
Yangqing Jia, *Google, USA*
Henry Kautz, *University of Rochester, USA*
Frank Keller, *University of Edinburgh, UK*
Douwe Kiela, *University of Cambridge, UK*
Polina Kuznetsova, *Stony Brook University, USA*
Pierre Lison, *University of Oslo, Norway*
Rebecca Mason, *Brown University, USA*
Cynthia Matuszek, *University of Maryland, USA*
John Philip McCrae, *University of Bielefeld, Germany*
Florian Metze, *Carnegie Mellon University, USA*
Rada Mihalcea, *University of Michigan, USA*
Margaret Mitchell, *Microsoft Research, USA*
Ray Mooney, *University of Texas at Austin, USA*

Vicente Ordonez, *University of North Carolina at Chapell Hill, USA*
Simone Paolo Ponzetto, *University of Mannheim, Germany*
Kate Saenko, *UMass Lowell, USA*
Carina Silberer, *University of Edinburgh, UK*
Alan Smeaton, *Dublin City University, Ireland*
Richard Socher, *MetaMind, USA*
Richard Sproat, *Google, USA*
Stefanie Tellex, *Brown University, USA*
Isabel Trancoso, *INESC-ID, Portugal*
Lucy Vanderwende, *Microsoft Research, USA*

Invited Speakers:

Marco Baroni, *University of Trento, Italy*
Krystian Mikolajczyk, *University of Surrey, UK*

Table of Contents

Conference Program

Friday, September 18, 2015

08:45–10:30 Session 1

08:45–09:00 *Opening Remarks*
Marie-Francine Moens

09:00–10:00 *Invited Talk 1: Grounding Distributional Semantics in the Visual World*
Marco Baroni

10:00–10:30 Poster Spotlights 1

10:00–10:05 *Visually-Verifiable Textual Entailment: A Challenge Task for Combining Language and Vision*
Jayant Krishnamurthy

10:05–10:10 *Computational Integration of Human Vision and Natural Language through Bitext Alignment*
Preethi Vaidyanathan, Emily Prud'hommeaux, Cecilia O. Alm, Jeff B. Pelz and Anne R. Haake

10:10–10:15 *Towards Reliable Automatic Multimodal Content Analysis*
Olli Philippe Lautenbacher, Liisa Tiittula, Maija Hirvonen, Jorma Laaksonen and Mikko Kurimo

10:15–10:20 *Lingusitic Analysis of Multi-Modal Recurrent Neural Networks*
Ákos Kádár, Grzegorz Chrupała and Afra Alishahi

10:20–10:25 *Defining Visually Descriptive Language*
Robert Gaizauskas, Josiah Wang and Arnau Ramisa

10:25–10:30 *Semantic Tuples for Evaluation of Image to Sentence Generation*
Lily D. Ellebracht, Arnau Ramisa, Pranava Swaroop Madhyastha, Jose Cordero-Rama, Francesc Moreno-Noguer and Ariadna Quattoni

10:30–11:00 *Coffee Break*

Friday, September 18, 2015 (continued)

11:00–12:15 Session 2

11:00–11:25 *Image Representations and New Domains in Neural Image Captioning*
Jack Hessel, Nicolas Savva and Michael Wilber

11:25–11:50 *Image with a Message: Towards Detecting Non-Literal Image Usages by Visual Linking*
Lydia Weiland, Laura Dietz and Simone Paolo Ponzetto

11:50–12:15 Poster Spotlights 2

11:50–11:55 *Visual Classifier Prediction by Distributional Semantic Embedding of Text Descriptions*
Mohamed Elhoseiny and Ahmed Elgammal

11:55–12:00 *Understanding Urban Land Use through the Visualization of Points of Interest*
Evgheni Polisciuc, Ana Alves and Penousal Machado

12:00–12:05 *Comparing Attribute Classifiers for Interactive Language Grounding*
Yanchao Yu, Arash Eshghi and Oliver Lemon

12:05–12:10 *Combining Geometric, Textual and Visual Features for Generating Prepositions in Image Descriptions (to appear in EMNLP 2015)*
Arnau Ramisa, Josiah Wang, Ying Lu, Emmanuel Dellandrea, Francesc Moreno-Noguer and Robert Gaizauskas

12:10–12:15 *From the Virtual to the Real World: Referring to Visible Objects Under Uncertainty in Real-World Spatial Scenes (to appear in EMNLP 2015)*
Dimitra Gkatzia and Verena Rieser

12:15–14:00 *Poster Session and Lunch*

Friday, September 18, 2015 (continued)

14:00–15:30	**Session 3**
14:00–15:00	*Invited Talk 2: The ImageCLEF 2015 Task on Scalable Image Annotation, Localization and Sentence Generation* Krystian Mikolajczyk
15:00–15:30	*Generating Semantically Precise Scene Graphs from Textual Descriptions for Improved Image Retrieval* Sebastian Schuster, Ranjay Krishna, Angel Chang, Li Fei-Fei and Christopher D. Manning
15:30–16:00	***Coffee Break***
16:00–18:00	**Session 4**
16:00–16:25	*Do Distributed Semantic Models Dream of Electric Sheep? Visualizing Word Representations through Image Synthesis* Angeliki Lazaridou, Dat Tien Nguyen and Marco Baroni
16:25–16:50	*A Weighted Combination of Text and Image Classifiers for User Gender Inference* Tomoki Taniguchi, Shigeyuki Sakaki, Ryosuke Shigenaka, Yukihiro Tsuboshita and Tomoko Ohkuma
16:50–17:15	*Coupling Natural Language Processing and Animation Synthesis in Portuguese Sign Language Translation* Inês Almeida, Luísa Coheur and Sara Candeias
17:15–17:40	*Describing Spatial Relationships between Objects in Images in English and French* Anja Belz, Adrian Muscat, Maxime Aberton and Sami Benjelloun

Friday, September 18, 2015 (continued)

17:40–18:00 Closing Remarks and Discussion

Visually-Verifiable Textual Entailment: A Challenge Task for Combining Language and Vision

Jayant Krishnamurthy
Allen Institute for Artificial Intelligence
2157 N. Northlake Way, Suite 110
Seattle, WA 98103
jayantk@allenai.org

Abstract

We propose visually-verifiable textual entailment as a challenge task for the emerging field of combining language and vision. This task is a variant of the well-studied NLP task of recognizing textual entailment (Dagan et al., 2006) where every entailment judgment can be made purely by reasoning with visual knowledge. We believe that this task will spur innovation in the language and vision field while simultaneously producing inference algorithms that can be used in NLP.

1 Introduction

It has long been acknowledged by the NLP community that extensive world knowledge and inference capabilities are necessary to perform basic language understanding tasks, such as reading a children's story (Minsky, 1975). Shallow knowledge representation techniques relying on only textual information have proven difficult to apply to complex inference problems because (1) much world knowledge is too obvious to be expressed in text, and (2) it is difficult to capture the complex structure of the real world within logical knowledge representations. Meanwhile, recent advances in computer vision have made it possible to train accurate object detectors (Russakovsky et al., 2014), suggesting that visual knowledge from images may be used to solve these natural language inference problems. However, many open problems must be addressed to successfully perform this combination, suggesting the need for a comprehensive challenge task to measure progress.

We propose that *visually-verifiable textual entailment* is a promising challenge task for combining language and vision. The task is to predict, given two texts, known as the text (T) and the hypothesis (H), whether the text *entails* the hypothesis ($T \vDash H$). T is said to entail H if, typically, a human reading T would infer that H is most likely true (Dagan et al., 2006). For example:

Text:	A man is flying a kite.
Hypothesis:	It is not raining

This example is an entailing pair because people typically do not fly kites in the rain. In visually-verifiable textual entailment, every entailment decision can be made purely on the basis of *visual* knowledge, i.e., knowledge that can be extracted from a large corpus of natural images. This criterion is satisfied by the above example – an image search for "man flying kite" returns no images where it is raining.

We believe that the task of visually-verifiable textual entailment is an exciting task for both the NLP and vision communities. From the NLP perspective, this task encourages the development of deep knowledge representation and inference techniques. These techniques may be able to solve more sophisticated inference problems than the shallow techniques – such as learning lexical substitution rules – currently in use (Giampiccolo et al., 2007). Recent work has also demonstrated the promise of using visual knowledge for entailment (Young et al., 2014). Furthermore, many NLP problems, such as coreference resolution and prepositional phrase attachment, can be posed as textual entailment problems; thus, this task provides a natural pathway for incorporating any developed techniques into downstream applications.

From the computer vision perspective, successfully performing this task requires developing accurate detection models of not just individual objects, but rather entire situations possibly unseen during training. The natural algorithm for visually-verifiable textual entailment is, given text T and hypothesis H, to first identify two sets of images, I_T and I_H, where the text and the hypothesis are true, respectively. Then, predict "en-

Proceedings of the 2015 Workshop on Vision and Language (VL'15), pages 1–3,
Lisbon, Portugal, 18 September 2015.

eating pizza		eating spaghetti		eating an apple	
holding pizza/a slice	3	enjoying spaghetti/meal	4	holding a fruit/apple	3
enjoying pizza	2	slurping spaghetti	2	thinking about things/apple	2
chewing pizza/food	2	holding a spoon/fork	2	posing with apple	2
consuming pizza	1	posing with spaghetti	1	biting apple	2

Table 1: Situation descriptions generated by Mechanical Turkers for three "eating" situations in preliminary data collection experiments. The descriptions are sorted by verb occurrence frequency.

tails" if $I_H \subseteq I_T$ and "not entails" otherwise.[1] Implementing this algorithm requires the ability to detect a wide variety of not just individual objects, but also attributes, relationships and events in images. Furthermore, it must be possible to compose these individual detectors in novel ways to form detectors for complete sentences. The variety problem has been partially addressed by webly-supervised algorithms for objects (Divvala et al., 2014; Chen et al., 2013) and subject-verb-object phrases (Sadeghi et al., 2015). The composition problem has also been examined, albeit with a very limited set of detectors (Matuszek et al., 2012; Krishnamurthy and Kollar, 2013). Progress on the proposed task requires improving on and combining these techniques.

2 Data Set

We propose to construct a data set for visually-verifiable textual entailment. As a starting point, we propose to focus on entailments between simple situations, given by a verb and optionally a subject and/or a direct object. This choice is motivated the fact that these situations are linguistically simple, yet can have complex entailments. For example, "eating an apple" $\models$ "holding an apple." However, "eating spaghetti" $\not\models$ "holding spaghetti;" rather "eating spaghetti" $\models$ "holding a fork." In the future, this data set can be expanded by including more complex language, e.g., prepositional modifiers.

To collect this data, we propose to use web image search and Mechanical Turk. First, we will manually identify a set of visual verbs and collect common arguments for them using a large corpus of syntactically parsed sentences. Combining these verb/argument pairs will produce a collection of situations. Second, we will feed these situations to an image search engine to retrieve multiple images depicting each situation. Third, we will construct a Mechanical Turk task for each image/situation pair, asking the worker to generate additional descriptions of the image. The design of this task will be tuned to generate more specific or general variants of the prompt situation (as in the example above). Because the generation occurs in the context of a particular image, not all of the generated situations will be entailed by the prompt situation. A final Mechanical Turk task will determine which situation pairs are entailments, thereby generating a data set with both positive and "near-miss" negative examples.[2]

We performed some preliminary experiments with this Mechanical Turk pipeline generating 18 situation descriptions for each of three "eating" phrases. The most frequent generations (sorted by verb) for each phrase are shown in Table 1. The resulting generations – though somewhat noisy – contain interesting structure: for example, both apples and pizza are held while being eaten. Apples are described with "biting," while spaghetti is described with "slurping."

3 Conclusion

We propose the task of visually-verifiable textual entailment as a challenge task for the field of combining language and vision. The object of this task is, given a text and a hypothesis, to predict whether the text entails the hypothesis. Crucially, the task design guarantees that each entailment decision can be made purely on the basis of visual knowledge. As a starting point, we propose to construct a data set of entailments between situations, i.e., verb/argument pairs, which appear to be the simplest case where nontrivial inference is required. Solving this entailment problem can require complex reasoning about real world situations, such as "eating pizza" $\models$ "holding pizza," whereas "eating spaghetti" $\not\models$ "holding a fork." We propose a data set collection methodology and present some preliminary data that demonstrates the potential of this task.

[1] This algorithm is unlikely to work in practice because it does not account for noise in the detections.

[2] If a binary yes/no entailment decision proves too ambiguous, we may also consider a ranking variant of the entailment task. In this variant, given a text and two hypotheses, the object is to predict which of the two hypotheses is more likely to be true.

Acknowledgements

We gratefully acknowledge Aria Haghighi, Oren Etzioni, Mark Yatskar and the anonymous reviewers for their helpful comments.

References

Xinlei Chen, Ashish Shrivastava, and Arpan Gupta. 2013. NEIL: Extracting visual knowledge from web data. In *2013 IEEE International Conference on Computer Vision (ICCV)*.

Ido Dagan, Oren Glickman, and Bernardo Magnini. 2006. The pascal recognising textual entailment challenge. In *Machine learning challenges. evaluating predictive uncertainty, visual object classification, and recognising textual entailment*, pages 177–190. Springer.

Santosh K Divvala, Alireza Farhadi, and Carlos Guestrin. 2014. Learning everything about anything: Webly-supervised visual concept learning. In *2014 IEEE Conference on Computer Vision and Pattern Recognition (CVPR)*.

Danilo Giampiccolo, Bernardo Magnini, Ido Dagan, and Bill Dolan. 2007. The third PASCAL recognizing textual entailment challenge. In *Proceedings of the ACL-PASCAL Workshop on Textual Entailment and Paraphrasing*.

Jayant Krishnamurthy and Thomas Kollar. 2013. Jointly learning to parse and perceive: Connecting natural language to the physical world. *Transactions of the Association for Computational Linguistics*, 1:193–206.

Cynthia Matuszek, Nicholas FitzGerald, Luke Zettlemoyer, Liefeng Bo, and Dieter Fox. 2012. A joint model of language and perception for grounded attribute learning. In *Proceedings of the 2012 International Conference on Machine Learning*.

Marvin Minsky. 1975. A framework for representing knowledge.

Olga Russakovsky, Jia Deng, Hao Su, Jonathan Krause, Sanjeev Satheesh, Sean Ma, Zhiheng Huang, Andrej Karpathy, Aditya Khosla, Michael Bernstein, et al. 2014. Imagenet large scale visual recognition challenge. *International Journal of Computer Vision*.

Fereshteh Sadeghi, Santosh K Divvala, and Ali Farhadi. 2015. VisKE: Visual knowledge extraction and question answering by visual verification of relation phrases. In *Proceedings of the IEEE Conference on Computer Vision and Pattern Recognition*.

Peter Young, Alice Lai, Micah Hodosh, and Julia Hockenmaier. 2014. From image descriptions to visual denotations: New similarity metrics for semantic inference over event descriptions. *Transactions of the Association for Computational Linguistics*, 2:67–78.

Computational Integration of Human Vision and Natural Language through Bitext Alignment

Preethi Vaidyanathan, Emily Prud'hommeaux, Cecilia O. Alm, and Jeff B. Pelz
Rochester Institute of Technology
(pxv1621|emilypx|coagla|jbppph)@rit.edu

Abstract

Multimodal integration of visual and linguistic data is a longstanding but crucial challenge for modeling human understanding. We propose a framework that uses an unsupervised bitext alignment method to integrate visual and linguistic data. We present an empirical study of the various parameters of the framework. Our results exceed baselines using both exact and delayed temporal correspondence. The resulting alignments can be used for image classification and retrieval.

1 Introduction

Modeling and characterizing human expertise is a major bottleneck in advancing image-based application systems. We propose a framework for integrating experts' eye movements and verbal narrations as they examine and describe images in order to understand images semantically. Eye movements can act as pointers to important image regions, while the co-captured descriptions provide conceptual labels associated with those regions.

Although successful when applied to scenic images in controlled experiments, many multimodal integration techniques do not transfer directly to scenarios requiring domain-specific expertise. Our approach is inspired by Yu and Ballard (2004), who combine NLP methods with eye movements to generate linguistic descriptions of videos, and Forsyth et al. (2009), who use image features to match words to the corresponding pictures. We expand here on earlier work (Vaidyanathan et al., 2015) exploring multimodal integration in medical image annotation.

Because an exact temporal match between the visual and verbal modalities cannot be assumed (Griffin, 2013), our framework integrates the two modalities without enforcing strict temporal correspondence. We use a bitext word alignment algorithm, originally developed for word alignment in machine translation, to align an expert's fixations on an image with the words in that expert's description of that image. The resulting alignments are then used to annotate image regions with corresponding conceptual labels, which in turn may aid image labeling and captioning applications. In this paper we discuss the parameters of our framework and their effects on alignment accuracy.

2 Data and Method

We eye tracked and voice recorded 26 dermatologists as they examined and described 29 dermatological images. From the narrations, we extract nouns and adjectives to create a temporally ordered set of linguistic units. To obtain the visual units, we cluster the fixations for all observers using mean shift clustering with a bandwidth (72 pixels) approximating the foveal size (Santella and DeCarlo, 2004). For each observer, we use these clusters to produce a temporally ordered sequence of visual units. Figure 1 shows a manually transcribed narrative, a scanpath for an observer, and clusters of fixations from all observers.

Prior research has established that there is a temporal lag between fixations and concept mentions (Griffin, 2013). Our method aligns visual and linguistic units without explicit assumptions about their temporal relationships. This is analogous to translating one language into another where the structural characteristics and word order of the two languages may be different. In our multimodal scenario, the observer's narrative description and fixations on an image represent a training pair. To create a sufficiently large parallel corpus, we use a 5-second sliding window over the pairs and add the linguistic and visual units within each window as a "sentence" to the corpus.

The sequences of visual units are substantially longer than the sequences of linguistic units. In order to balance the sequence lengths, we select

Proceedings of the 2015 Workshop on Vision and Language (VL'15), pages 4–5,
Lisbon, Portugal, 18 September 2015.

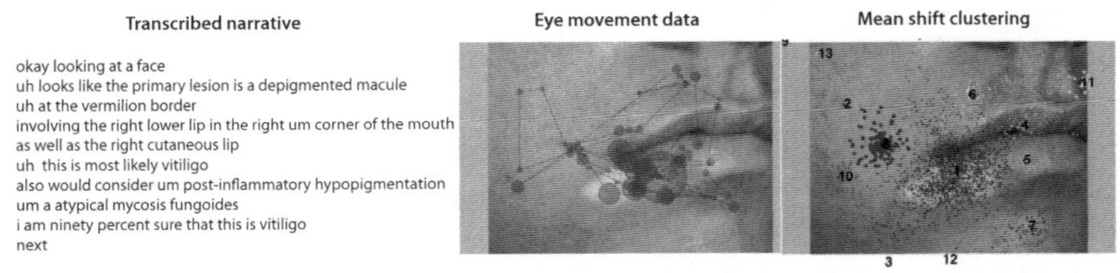

Figure 1: **Example of a multimodal data pair**. *Center*: Circle and circle size represent observer gaze location and duration, respectively. *Right*: Clusters shown with colors and/or shape and numerical labels.

	P (SD)	R (SD)	F1 (SD)
1-sec. delay	0.38 (0.1)	0.44 (0.17)	0.39 (0.1)
bitext alignment	0.45 (0.1)	0.56 (0.16)	0.49 (0.1)

Table 1: Comparison of performance for the 1-second delay baseline and our alignment method.

visual units in two ways, both preserving temporal order. In one method, the fixations are selected at random. In the other, the fixations are ranked and selected according to their duration.

We use the Berkeley aligner (Liang et al., 2006), an EM-based word aligner known for high accuracy and adaptability. The aligner is run on each visual-linguistic parallel corpus (one for each image), with the posterior threshold for decoding set to 0.1, a value empirically determined using a data subset. The resulting alignments for each corpus are evaluated against a set of reference alignments produced manually by an investigator experienced in analyzing dermatological images.

3 Results and Conclusions

We test the model on pairs of full narratives and fixation sequences. The alignment results are compared with two temporal baselines. One baseline assumes that an observer utters the word corresponding to a region at the moment the eyes fixate on that region. The second baseline assumes that there is a one-second delay (Griffin, 2013) between a fixation and the utterance of the word corresponding to that region.

Our alignment method yields strong performance in comparison to both baselines. As shown in Table 1, we achieve 7%, 10%, and 12% absolute improvement over the baselines in precision, F-measure, and recall, respectively. The results hold on a per-image basis as well, with the alignment approach yielding higher recall in all 29 images, higher F-measure in 28 images, and higher precision in 24 images. Using fixation length to select the visual units substantially improves the performance in comparison to the random selection process. Neither the size of the sliding window nor the ratio of visual to linguistic units affected alignment performance.

Both methods perform well on images with solitary lesions, and performance generally decreases as the number of lesions increases. Interestingly, the largest improvement of our aligner over the baseline occurs in images with multiple lesions, suggesting that a fixed temporal correspondence is particularly unlikely in more complex images.

In future work, we plan to use image segmentation algorithms to extract image features and a medical ontology to discover more complex relationships between image regions and semantic concepts. In addition, we will explore methods of alignment with soft temporal constraints to better model the relationship the two modalities.

References

P. Liang et al. 2006. Alignment by agreement. In *Proceedings of NAACL-HLT*, pages 104–111.

D. Forsyth et al. 2009. Words and pictures: Categories, modifiers, depiction, and iconography. In S. Dickinson, editor, *Object Categorization: Computer and Human Vision Perspectives*. Cambridge University Press, Cambridge.

P. Vaidyanathan et al. 2015. Alignment of eye movements and spoken language for semantic image understanding. *IWCS 2015*, page 76.

Z. Griffin. 2013. Why look? Reasons for eye movements related to language production. In J. Henderson and F. Ferreira, editors, *The interface of language, vision, and action: Eye movements and the visual world*. Psychology Press, New York.

A. Santella and D. DeCarlo. 2004. Robust clustering of eye movement recordings for quantification of visual interest. In *Proceedings of ETRA*, pages 27–34.

C. Yu and D. Ballard. 2004. A multimodal learning interface for grounding spoken language in sensory perceptions. *ACM Transactions on Applied Perception*, 1(1):57–80.

Towards Reliable Automatic Multimodal Content Analysis

Olli-Philippe Lautenbacher
Liisa Tiittula
Maija Hirvonen
Dept. of Modern Languages
University of Helsinki
firstname.surname
@helsinki.fi

Jorma Laaksonen
Dept. of Computer Science
Aalto University
jorma.laaksonen
@aalto.fi

Mikko Kurimo
Dept. of Signal Processing
and Acoustics
Aalto University
mikko.kurimo
@aalto.fi

Abstract

This poster presents a pilot where audio description is used to enhance automatic content analysis, for a project aiming at creating a tool for easy access to large AV archives.

1 Introduction

This poster presents a pilot study for a new interdisciplinary project which aims at creating an automated, time-aligned and language-based access to large archives of audiovisual documents. The idea is to facilitate the work of researchers who wish to pinpoint particular segments of AV material without having to browse through entire data sets. The project analyses human descriptions and film-viewing patterns in order to integrate that knowledge into an automatic content analyser. The pilot was set out to compare the results of the automatic and human methods available for content description.

2 AD *vs.* AMCA

Currently verbal content description for retrieving visual data is still scarce, although different methods exist: *human-made audio description* (AD) verbalizes visual information for visually impaired people (Maszerowska & al 2014) but is a slow and costly process. *Automatic Multimodal Content Analysis* (AMCA), on the other hand, consists of computer-driven detection of visual and auditory elements from multimedia (Rohrbach & al 2015; Viitaniemi & al 2015). AMCA is cost-effective and produces consistent output, but is still insufficient for high-level semantic analysis.

Our project combines these approaches to create an automatically produced narrative, but which is more informative than a mere list of descriptive concepts.

3 The pilot and its tools

We are now tackling our first pilot, a 15-minute excerpt from a documentary (*Helsinki, forever*, Peter von Bagh, 2008), a genre which the whole project will be concentrating on.

3.1 Automatic tools

A preliminary AMCA has already been made, based on earlier filmic contents, giving lists of descriptive concepts for each picture as an output. Consider the following example:

Screenshot from *Helsinki, forever*.

For this shot of 301 frames, the AMCA provides the following occurrence numbers for concepts:

Body_Parts (301); Man_Made_Thing (301); Outdoor (278); Legs (277); Building (254); Suits (245); Actor (184); Suburban (163); Person (141); etc.

Naturally, such concepts might seem counterintuitive for a human reading of an image, mainly because they do not inform us about the respective relevance of the various semantic elements retrieved from the picture. The AMCA concepts will thus need further filtering.

Another tool used for the visual description is automatic sentence-like caption generation per frame (Karpathy & Fei-Fei 2015), which will be combined with the abovementioned concept retriever. For the same shot, we now get for 97% of the frames:

a man in a suit and tie standing in front of a building

For the audio, an automatic transcription of the dialogue and voice-over can be made, using

Proceedings of the 2015 Workshop on Vision and Language (VL'15), pages 6–7,
Lisbon, Portugal, 18 September 2015. ©2015 Association for Computational Linguistics.

voice recognition (see Remes & al 2015). The output is a transcript that is coded on a confidence basis, informing the researcher on the degree of certainty of the recognized linguistic segments. A description of on-screen sounds, including automatic music recognition, could also enhance the validity of relevant concept retrieval.

3.2 Human input

In order to improve these automatic describers, three human ADs of the excerpt were ordered from professionals. The comparison of those ADs is important for the pilot since it reveals the characteristics they share in terms of visual element selection and lexical choices (identicality of referents and words, synonymy, level of abstraction etc.). For our example shot, the ADs are (translated from Finnish):

> AD1: "A nervous looking **man** [...] **stops** at the corner of the **bank** changing his *briefcase* from hand to hand and throwing glances *around him*."
>
> AD2: "A **man** [...] **stops** in front of a '**Bank**' sign looking confused and *hesitating*, holding a *briefcase* with both hands."
>
> AD3: "A black suited **man stops** at the door of the **bank** and *hesitates*. He looks *around*, fingering his portfolio."

Some words are identical in all ADs (**man**; **stops**; **bank**), some concepts are almost synonymous (*briefcase / portfolio; hesitating / nervous looking*), and some expressions reveal a "point of view" (at the corner of *x* / in front of *x* / at the door of *x*; changing *y* from hand to hand / holding *y* with both hands / fingering *y*). It appears that all descriptions are similar in terms of the thematised entities and actions, but the various lexical items used in referring to them invites to re-evaluate the idea that there is only one equivalent description per image. All in all, the pilot studies the semantic variability of the descriptions by both qualitative and quantitative comparative analyses.

These human descriptions will then serve to feed the AMCA, helping to filter its concept-suggestions in terms of relevance, adequacy and degree of precision. For instance, key word lists created in a corpus analysis enable us to compare the descriptions, harmonize the content words of AD and finally merge them with the concepts suggested by the AMCA.

Furthermore, we also use eye tracking (Kruger & al, 2015) in the pilot, to identify convergence patterns in the gaze positions of average viewers watching the excerpt. This "natural viewing" gives further insight into the relevance of the visual element selection made by the AD and the AMCA. Within the selected shot, we can notice that people tend to look at the most informative parts of the image (the man's face and the "Bank" sign) especially during the first seconds of their appearance on screen:

SMI heat maps (21 viewers) on the same shot.

4 Outcomes of the pilot

This poster presentation includes a demo video of each of these tools and their respective outputs. Later on, all the collected data from the excerpt will be integrated to the AMCA to enhance its output, which can be further enriched by new human input. Such a recursive machine learning process will lead, eventually, to a reliable automatic description tool for documentary films.

References

Andrej Karpathy and Li Fei-Fei. 2015. Deep Visual-Semantic Alignments for Generating Image Descriptions. CVPR 2015.

Anna Maszerowska, Anna Matamala and Pilar Orero (eds). 2014. *Audio Description: New perspectives illustrated*. Benjamins, Amsterdam, NL / Philadelphia, USA.

Anna Rohrbach, Marcus Rohrbach, Niket Tandon and Bernt Schiele. 2015. A Dataset for Movie Description. CVPR 2015.

Jan-Louis Kruger, Agnieszka Szarkowska, Isabela Krejtz. 2015. Subtitles on the Moving Image: an Overview of Eye Tracking Studies. *Refractory – a Journal of Entertainment Media*, vol. 25.

Ulpu Remes, Ana Ramírez López, Kalle Palomäki and Mikko Kurimo. Forthcoming. Bounded conditional mean imputation with observation uncertainties and acoustic model adaptation. *IEEE Transactions on Audio, Speech and Language Processing*.

Ville Viitaniemi, Mats Sjöberg, Markus Koskela, Satoru Ishikawa and Jorma Laaksonen. 2015. Advances in Visual Concept Detection: Ten years of TRECVID. In Ella Bingham et al. (ed.): *Advances in Independent Component Analysis and Learning Machines*, 1st edition. Elsevier, Amsterdam, NL.

Lingusitic Analysis of multi-modal Recurrent Neural Networks

Ákos Kádár
Tilburg University
a.kadar@uvt.nl

Grzegorz Chrupała
Tilburg University
g.a.chrupala@uvt.nl

Afra Alishahi
Tilburg University
a.alishahi@uvt.nl

1 Introduction

Recurrent neural networks (RNN) have gained a reputation for beating state-of-the-art results on many NLP benchmarks and for learning representations of words and larger linguistic units that encode complex syntactic and semantic structures. However, it is not straight-forward to understand how exactly these models make their decisions. Recently Li et al. (2015) developed methods to provide linguistically motivated analysis for RNNs trained for sentiment analysis. Here we focus on the analysis of a multi-modal Gated Recurrent Neural Network (GRU) architecture trained to predict image-vectors - extracted from images using a CNN trained on ImageNet - from their corresponding descriptions. We propose two methods to explore the importance of grammatical categories with respect to the model and the task. We observe that the model pays most attention to head-words, noun subjects and adjectival modifiers and least to determiners and coordinations.

2 Method

We used the IMAGINET model from Chrupała et al. (2015), trained on the MSCOCO dataset (Lin et al., 2014). It learns visually grounded meaning representations from textual and visual input and consists of two GRU pathways, TEXTUAL and VISUAL, with a shared word-embedding matrix. The inputs to the model are pairs of captions and their corresponding images. Each sentence is mapped to two sequences of hidden states: one by TEXTUAL and another by VISUAL. At each time-step TEXTUAL predicts the next word in the sentence from its current hidden state h_t^T, while VISUAL predicts the image vector from its last hidden representation h_{full}^V. The model is trained using a multi-task objective which combines cross-entropy loss for the word predictions and a mean squared error for the image predictions.

We focus our analysis on the hidden states and update-gate activations of VISUAL to assess the impact of syntactic structure on the learned meaning representations of sentences used to predict images. For each input sentence of length n, VISUAL produces n hidden activations $h_1^V, ..., h_n^V$ and n update-gate activations $z_1^V, ..., z_n^V$. We associate each word in the input sentence with their part-of-speech (POS) and dependency relation (DepRel) labels[1], and assess the contribution of the (word, POS, DepRel) tuples by estimating the following two scores:

1. d_{red} measures the distance reduction at each step by calculating the cosine distance between the current h_t and the last hidden state h_{full} and subtracting it from the previous distance: $d_{\text{red}}^t = d_{\text{red}}^{t-1} - cos(h_t, h_{\text{full}})$. The idea is to see how much each word brings the current state closer to, or further away from, the final interpretation.

2. z_{mean} assigns the average activation of the update-gate z at time step t to the tuple at positions t. The activation function for z is sigmoid, therefore it has values between 0-1. High values of z_{mean} indicate that the model places more importance on the previous tuples until $t-1$ than on the current one at t.

3 Results

We measure d_{red} and z_{mean} for every position in the first 5000 captions from the validation portion of MSCOCO and use them to analyze the importance of both POS and DepRel categories. We only report results on the grammatical categories that appear at least 500 times. Figure 1 demonstrates the d_{red} measurements for each word in an example sentence. A large distance between two adjacent

[1] We used the dependency parser from Martins et al. (2013) for both the POS and DepRel tags.

Proceedings of the 2015 Workshop on Vision and Language (VL'15), pages 8–9,
Lisbon, Portugal, 18 September 2015.

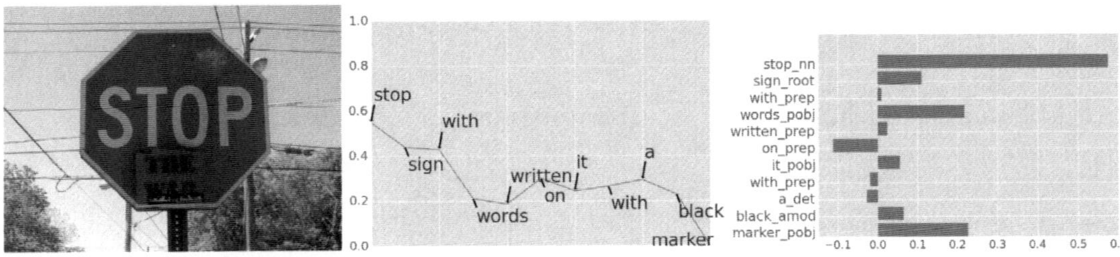

Figure 1: An example of the impact of each word in the sentence *Stop sign with words written on it with a black marker*, measured by d_{red}. Left: best retrieved image; middle: reduction of distance from h^V_{full}; right: d_{red} scores for each word.

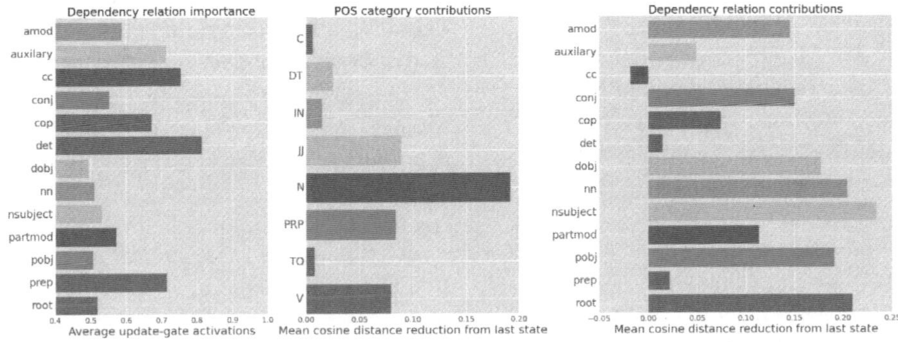

Figure 2: Importance of dependency relations as measured by z_{mean} on the left chart. Contribution of POS categories (middle) and DepRel categories (right) measured by d_{red}.

words signals the arrival of a highly informative word. Figure 2 shows the impact of both measures for each grammatical category. The low z_{mean} scores (left) for the roots, adjectival modifiers (amod), direct objects (dobj), noun compound modifiers (nn), noun subjects (nsubj), conjuncts (conj) and objects of prepositions (pobj) suggest that the model remembers words of these categories, while prefers to forget determiners (det), coordinations (cc), prepositions (prep) and auxiliaries. As indicated by the high d_{red} scores (middle graph), nouns (N), adjectives (JJ) verbs (V) and prepositions (PRP) provide the largest contribution to the meaning representations of the sentences, while determiners (DET) and conjunctions (C) provide the least. The d_{red} scores for DepRels are in line with the z_{mean} scores; they highlight the importance of nsubj, nn, amod, pobj and dobj.

4 Conclusions

We propose two measures to assess the impact of grammatical categories on sentence representations learned for predicting images. The observed patterns likely reflect the visual salience and informativeness of the lexical items associated with each category. They also provide insights into the details of the task e.g.: nouns came out significantly more important then other content word categories, indicating that predicting the correct entities is the most important aspect of the task.

References

[Chrupała et al.2015] Grzegorz Chrupała, Ákos Kádár, and Afra Alishahi. 2015. Learning language through pictures. *arXiv preprint arXiv:1506.03694*.

[Li et al.2015] Jiwei Li, Xinlei Chen, Eduard Hovy, and Dan Jurafsky. 2015. Visualizing and understanding neural models in nlp. *arXiv preprint arXiv:1506.01066*.

[Lin et al.2014] Tsung-Yi Lin, Michael Maire, Serge Belongie, James Hays, Pietro Perona, Deva Ramanan, Piotr Dollár, and C Lawrence Zitnick. 2014. Microsoft coco: Common objects in context. In *Computer Vision–ECCV 2014*, pages 740–755. Springer.

[Martins et al.2013] André FT Martins, Miguel Almeida, and Noah A Smith. 2013. Turning on the turbo: Fast third-order non-projective turbo parsers. In *ACL (2)*, pages 617–622. Citeseer.

Defining Visually Descriptive Language

Robert Gaizauskas[1] **Josiah Wang**[1] **Arnau Ramisa**[2]

[1] Department of Computer Science, University of Sheffield, UK
[2] Institut de Robòtica i Infòrmatica Industrial, Barcelona

{r.gaizauskas, j.k.wang}@sheffield.ac.uk aramisa@iri.upc.edu

Abstract

In this paper, we introduce the notion of *visually descriptive language* (VDL) – intuitively a text segment whose truth can be confirmed by visual sense alone. VDL can be exploited in many vision-based tasks, e.g. image interpretation and story illustration. In contrast to previous work requiring pre-aligned texts and images, we propose a broader definition of VDL that extends to a much larger range of texts without associated images. We also discuss possible VDL annotation tasks and make recommendations for difficult cases. Lastly, we demonstrate the viability of our definition via an annotation exercise across several text genres and analyse inter-annotator agreement. Results show reasonably high levels of agreement between annotators can be reached.

1 Introduction

Recent years have seen rapid growth in research integrating visual and textual modalities, including associating named entities in captions with faces in images (Berg et al., 2004), generating image descriptions (Kulkarni et al., 2011; Yang et al., 2011), text/image retrieval (Hodosh et al., 2013), story illustration (Feng and Lapata, 2010), and learning visual recognition of fine-grained object categories (Wang et al., 2009). This previous work concentrates on solving image-based tasks, and is heavily reliant upon datasets with pre-aligned images and texts, most of which have been manually collected and/or annotated. Thus, such image-centric texts are assumed to be at least partially, if not predominantly, 'visually descriptive' in nature. This raises some interesting research questions: (i) how much text out there without associated images is 'visually descriptive' and thus potentially useful for such image-based tasks? (ii) can these 'visually descriptive' text segments be identified automatically within documents which may consist of predominantly 'non-visual' text?

To be able to answer these questions, we first require a robust, inter-subjectively reliable definition of 'visually descriptive' text. Although previous work exists that models the 'visualness' of terms or concepts from images (Yanai and Barnard, 2005; Jeong et al., 2012), they are presented without an explicit definition apart from the intuitive notion that a visual term should exhibit some consistent visual characteristics across different objects. To our knowledge, the only work that explicitly proposes a definition for visually descriptive text is that of Dodge et al. (2012), where noun phrases within an image caption are classified as to whether or not they are depicted in the corresponding image.

In this paper, we propose a broader definition of *Visually Descriptive Language* (VDL). Our work differs from Dodge et al. (2012) in that our definition revolves around identifying text segments that express propositions that can be 'visually confirmed' rather than identifying 'visually concrete' noun phrase segments whose denotation can be located in an associated image. The consequences of this different definition are significant: (i) we are not restricted to mining VDL from texts with associated images, but can exploit any text, massively extending the volume of data that can be mined; (ii) we can gather larger, richer fragments of text than just noun phrases; (iii) we are not limited to the sort of language found in image captions or texts with embedded images (typically news), but can consider texts of any genre.

It is unlikely there is any one 'correct' definition of VDL. Rather, any proposed definition may be assessed in terms of how useful it is for some particular purpose and how easy it is to apply. Our purpose in defining VDL is to allow us to identify,

Proceedings of the 2015 Workshop on Vision and Language (VL'15), pages 10–17,
Lisbon, Portugal, 18 September 2015.

within a broad corpus of texts, segments that can be used to inform computational models useful in image interpretation and description. For example, co-occurrence in VDL of certain attribute values and object types, or of pairs of objects types, or of object types in particular semantic roles in relation to an activity or event type provide prior information that can be used in Bayesian models to help interpret or describe a new image. Corpora of VDL can also be used to learn language models for generating image descriptions, e.g. for the visually impaired. Other potential applications include identifying candidate text segments within a novel to be illustrated, automatic collection of joint visual-text training data, and automatic extraction of discriminative object descriptions for visual recognition (e.g. butterfly descriptions in Wang et al. (2009)).

1.1 Overview

The rest of the paper is structured as follows. Section 2 presents and discusses our definition of VDL. Section 3 describes possible VDL annotation tasks based on our definition and discusses and makes recommendations on difficult cases. To assess the viability of the definition, we have carried out a pilot annotation exercise on texts of different genres. Section 4 describes and analyses this exercise, including agreement statistics and insights on conflicting annotations. Finally, Section 5 offers conclusions and discusses future work.

2 Definition of VDL

Our intuition is that a segment of text is visually descriptive if we can determine what it says is true or false by visual sense alone. More precisely:

Definition. A text segment is *visually descriptive* iff it asserts one or more propositions about either (a) a specific scene or entity whose truth can be confirmed or disconfirmed through direct visual perception (e.g. (1)), or (b) a class of scenes or entities whose truth with respect to any instance of the class of scenes or entities can be confirmed or disconfirmed through direct visual perception (e.g. (2)).

(1) *John carried the bowl of pasta across the kitchen and placed in on the counter.*

(2) *Tigers have a pattern of dark vertical stripes on reddish-orange fur with a lighter underside.*

(3) * *Maria is thinking about what the future holds for her.* (Not VDL[1])

By *direct visual perception* we mean that:

1. An observer could determine the truth of the relevant proposition without intervening in the scene to acquire additional visual inputs. E.g. the truth of *John weighs 65 kg* might be determined visually by placing John on a scale and taking a reading; but if this scale and Johns standing on it are not part of the scene then this sentence is not VDL.
2. Any inference that needs to be carried out to confirm or disconfirm the proposition is such that it would typically be made by an observer drawn from the population of intended readers of the text without knowledge of the preceding textual content. For example, most observers of a scene that includes a boy sitting on the end of a dock holding a fishing rod whose line disappears into the water before him would infer without question that the boy is fishing, allowing them to confirm the truth of "The boy sat fishing on the dock" directly from the scene and without knowledge of earlier parts of the text in which the sentence is embedded. This example illustrates just how tightly coupled inference and perception are and that "what we see" is a product of both. Also, note how our definition is analogous to that of *textual entailment* where given a pair of textual expressions T and H "We say that T entails H if, typically, a human reading T would infer that H is most likely true" (Dagan et al., 2006); i.e. we rely on a judgement that would *typically* be made about what is going on in the scene.
3. An observer can visually identify any named entities. For example, in (1) we assume an observer knows who John is in this scene. This may only be possible because of knowledge obtained from other textual context, but we don't want to rule out the visualness of (1) on the grounds that not all the information that may be needed to identify John in the scene is present in (1).

By *asserts a proposition* we mean that text segments must express, explicitly or implicitly a predication, i.e. something that may be judged true

[1]We can neither confirm nor disconfirm through direct visual perception alone that Maria is thinking (she might be just staring into space), let alone know what she is thinking.

or false. Sentences or clauses with tensed verbs are candidates, as are noun phrases that predicate something of an entity. Thus, we rule out bare noun phrases (*the man*)[2], but include phrases such as *the tall man* or *a man wearing a green shirt*.

By *text segment* here we mean a phrase, clause, sentence or sequence of sentences, i.e. a sequence of contiguous words. One consequence of this constraint is that phrases like (4) are not VDL, since while they contain a mix of visual (*tall*) and non-visual (*well-educated*) attributes, they do not form a contiguous sequence of words which is visually confirmable as a whole. Since we frequently observed such cases, we want our scheme to accommodate them. We call such segments *impure visually descriptive language* (IVDL). To be IVDL a segment S_1 must contain discontinuous subsequences that if conjoined form a segment S_2 such that (a) S_2 is VDL, and (b) in context S_2 asserts a proposition that is entailed by the proposition S_1 asserts (this rules out conjoining of unrelated subsequences – see (5)). We annotate IVDL subsequences belonging to the same (discontinuous) segment with the same subscript indices.

(4) $\{$*the tall*$\}_1$, *well-educated* $\{$*man*$\}_1$

Condition (b) serves to rule out cases like:

(5) * $\{$*the tall*$\}_1$ *wardrobe beside the well-educated* $\{$*man*$\}_1$

as from (5) we cannot derive *the tall man*, since the predication it expresses is not entailed by those expressed by (5).

Note that IVDLs are distinct from *partially visual* segments such as (6) containing both visual and non-visual phrasal subcomponents:

(6) *As* $\{$*he walked by the lake*$\}$, *John thought about his dad.*

(6) contains a contiguous sub-segment that is VDL, unlike (4), which is IVDL.

3 Annotating VDL

We describe several possible VDL annotation tasks and provide recommendations on how to approach and annotate some difficult cases.

[2]*man* is undoubtedly a visually perceivable entity, but a list of such terms is available under the physical object synset in WordNet and we do not need a programme of text annotation to acquire them.

3.1 Possible Annotation Tasks

We distinguish two annotation tasks: *sentence-level annotation* and *segment-level annotation.*

Sentence-level annotation

We define a sentence-level annotation task as follows. Each sentence S in a document is assigned one of three values: (i) **0** if it contains no VDL; (ii) **1** if the entire sentence is VDL; (iii) **2** if it contains one or more proper sub-segments which are VDL, but the single segment comprising the whole sentence is not VDL. S=**2** may be further classified as **2P** (containing only pure VD sub-segments) and **2I** (contains pure and/or impure VD sub-segments). Variants of the task may be defined depending on whether VDL is taken to include pure VDL only, or to include both pure and impure VDL. In many texts there are significant numbers of impure VDL segments, so omitting them leads to the loss of a substantial quantity of potentially valuable VDL. On the other hand, including them requires substantially more annotation effort and is only likely to be useful if accurate automatic techniques for extracting pure from impure segments can be developed.

Segment-level annotation

Here the exact words comprising a VDL segment are annotated using a swipe and click annotation tool. Variants arise depending on whether one includes impure segments. Note that doing so requires the multiple sequences making up the pure non-contiguous subsequence of the segment to be selected and their association recorded. A simpler, but less informative, alternative is to give the full IVDL segment a distinct code, effectively deferring the task of identifying the pure subsequence in the impure segment. Another variant is to allow annotation to extend over multiple sentences (e.g. to gather action descriptions for interpreting video sequences instead of static scenes). Note that extending the scope of annotation to multiple sentences may affect the content of the annotations. Example (7) is a full single VDL segment in a multi-sentence annotation task.

(7) $\{$*John took a sip of coffee. He read the newspaper for a minute then took a second sip*$\}$

However, as a single-sentence annotation task, the second sentence will be impure as we cannot verify that the sip is a second one (i.e. (8)).

(8) $\{$*He read the newspaper for a minute then took a*$\}_1$ *second* $\{$*sip*$\}_1$

Note that sentence-level annotations may be inferred from segment-level annotations.

3.2 Guidelines for difficult cases

Inevitably, various difficult cases emerge during annotation. While it is to be expected that some areas of variation between annotators will unavoidably remain, consistency across annotators is increased and annotation decisions simplified if a standard approach is taken to various anticipated difficult cases. Because of space constraints, here we highlight only a subset of such cases and recommend ways to annotate them. The full set of guidelines, with extensive discussions and examples, is available online[3]. Below we proceed on the assumption that VDL is being annotated at the segment level, sentence-by-sentence.

Metaphors

In general, judgements that *A is like B*, *X appeared to be Y*, *C was as if D* etc., will not be VDL since the judgement of similarity underlying such statements is not something that is likely to be shared by an observer in viewing the entity to which they metaphor is applied. However, the expressions describing the entity to which the metaphor is applied and that supplying the metaphor may themselves be VDL.

(9) *the pews appeared to be* {*broad stairs in a long dungeon*}

(10) *he panted like* {*a big dog that has been running too long*}

Words with mixed visual/aural or visual/experiential meanings

Many words mix visual and aural or visual and experiential senses. For example, verbs like *shout*, *shuffle* and *pant* have an aural and a visual component, not necessarily in the same proportion. Verbs like *shudder* and *flinch*, adjectives like *sombre* and *insolent* (*insolent green eyes*) and adverbs like *deathly* (*deathly pale*) signal not just movement or appearance but also underlying emotional experience or response. Such words should be annotated if visual input alone is judged sufficient to allow a typical observer to unambiguously apply the words, e.g. {*a dreary housing estate*}.

[3] http://vdlang.github.io/

Temporal adverbials of frequency

Temporal adverbs of frequency (*often*, *sometimes*, *usually*) determine how frequently an activity takes place. These are considered VDL, because our imaginary observer could determine visually, over a period of time, how frequently the activity takes place and make an assessment of whether the temporal term applies. The exception is for adverbials that reference calendrical units (*On Tuesdays* {*Bob goes to the park for a picnic*}), because we cannot directly see that it is a Tuesday.

Temporal adverbials of duration

Temporal adverbs of duration determine how long an activity takes. They are marked as VDL where the duration is intuitively assessable as part of the viewing process ({*for a few minutes*}), but not marked when reference to a watch or calendar would be needed for precision or for tracking the extent of the activity (*in 9.58 seconds*, *for two weeks*).

Multiple visual perspectives

Sometimes a sentence may contain information that is visually confirmable, but only from more than one distinct perspective or frame of reference. For example, in (11), an observer could visually confirm that Billy was climbing a tree wearing his backpack. He or she could also visually confirm that the backpack contained various objects. But any position from which an observer could confirm the climbing would not simultaneously allow the visual confirmation of the contents of the backpack.

(11) {*Billy climbed the tree wearing his backpack*}, {*which contained his slingshot, some pebbles and a magnifying glass*}.

In such cases, we advocate annotating distinct VDL segments, one for each visual perspective or frame of reference, as in (11). The reason for this is that we want to derive models of VDL usage that can be used to help interpret or describe images or video that will be taken from a single perspective (at any given time point). Therefore descriptions that mix perspectives are more likely to be confusing than helpful.

Intentional contexts

For the most part, sentences expressing propositional attitudes will not be VDL. However, the sub-constituent that expresses the proposition towards which the speaker has an attitude may well

	Text	Type	|S|	S=1	S=2	VDL	IVDL	%Agree	Kappa	IoU
Oz	Ch7	Children's Story	95	0.13	0.51	51	47	0.76	0.73	0.65
	Ch9	Children's Story	78	0.12	0.42	38	23	0.72	0.69	0.62
Brown	A13	Sports Reportage	111	0.11	0.27	25	20	0.78	0.60	0.51
	A30	Culture Reportage	128	0.04	0.34	31	21	0.78	0.56	0.57
	G32	Biography	101	0.02	0.47	32	29	0.74	0.50	0.43
	L05	Mystery Fiction	151	0.21	0.31	65	20	0.87	0.79	0.63
	N13	Western Fiction	122	0.12	0.46	58	38	0.70	0.49	0.57
	P15	Romance Fiction	179	0.08	0.24	40	21	0.82	0.62	0.73

Table 1: Selected texts and results of the annotation experiment. Column **|S|** shows the number of sentences, columns **S=1** and **S=2** the average proportion of sentences labelled for each VDL type, and columns **VDL** and **IVDL** the number of segments marked as pure and impure VDL on average. Columns **% Agree** and **Kappa** show the inter-annotator agreement at sentence level, and **IoU** the agreement at segment level. Please refer to main text for more details.

be: *John believed that {Mary was playing in the garden}.*

Hypotheticals, modals, counterfactuals and subjunctives

Hypothetical or conditional propositions assert something to be the case provided something else is the case. We cannot literally see a conditional, so sentences expressing such propositions are not VDL. However, the antecedent and consequents of such propositions may be visual: *If {Jack sets the table} then {Will serves dinner}.*

Modal (including negation and future tense) and counterfactual sentences may be IVDL since while overall their truth value is not visually determinable, it relates to that of a visually descriptive segment derivable from them. For example, we cannot 'see' that *{James}$_1$ may {practice Tai Chi in the garden}$_1$*. But the truth of the derived sentence is visually determinable (and is key in possible worlds treatments of the semantics of modals).

Locational information

Locational information is in some cases visually determinable and other cases not. As a general rule any locational information that relies upon geopolitical naming, street plans or compass directions is not marked as VDL. Example (12) is VDL, whist examples (13) and (14) are not VDL.

(12) *{The Episcopal Church stood across the street}.*

(13) *The Episcopal Church was one block down Sussex Street.*

(14) *The Eiffel Tower is in the 7th Arrondissement in Paris.*

Note that although *The Episcopal Church* and *The Eiffel Tower* are named entities and thus visually identifiable according to our definition (see Section 2), locational information may require significant inference using world knowledge that is not part of the text, and thus may not be VDL. For example, we cannot necessarily confirm that someone is in a city called Lisbon based on visual perception alone.

Statements of purpose

Components of sentences that express an agents purpose in doing something should not be annotated as VDL: *{Billy climbed to the rooftop} to shoot at crows.*

Imperative and interrogative sentences

Imperative (e.g. (15)) and interrogative (e.g. (16)) sentences do not assert propositions and therefore, by our definition, cannot be VDL as a whole. However, they may contain components which are VDL, for example in (16).

(15) *Come out to the field and call us.*

(16) *How did {you escape from the beast}?*

Participial phrases

Participial phrases may express predications where they occur within a noun phrase (*{a man wearing a green shirt}*). However, in some cases participial phrases may be extraposed and function, not so much as a reduced relative clause as a sentence adverbial. In this case we annotate across phrasal boundaries, in order to capture the argument of the activity described in the participial phrase, i.e. the entity about which something visual is being predicated. For example in (17), where *John* is included as a VDL segment.

(17) {*Walking slowly across the ice, John*} thought about his mother.

Dialogues

Text segments that report dialogues do so using either direct (e.g. (18)) or indirect (e.g. (19)) quotation.

(18) *Dorothy said that* {*Toto was running away*}.

(19) *Dorothy said, "*{*Toto is running away*}*".*

In both cases we mark the segment spoken as VDL, if it is VDL. As a matter of convention we do not mark the words reporting who spoken even if we could determine visually whether the person reporting was speaking. This is because (a) these segments are of little interest, and (b) there are many verbs that express fine shades of meaning with respect to spoken utterances, many of which are not visually determinable (*reply*, *ask*, *exhort*, *assert*) and it is easiest just to rule them all out.

4 Results and Analysis

4.1 Experiments and Results

A small pilot annotation exercise was carried out to test the viability of our definition and annotation guidelines on a variety of text genres. As data we used two random chapters from The Wonderful Wizard of Oz and six samples from the Brown Corpus, selected randomly among five hand-picked categories (two news articles, one biography and three novels). As a pilot study, all texts were annotated by the authors at segment-level, the Oz texts by three annotators and the Brown texts by two, using the *brat rapid annotation tool*[4]. Sentence-level annotations are inferred from these segment-level annotations. We chose to annotate at segment level rather than sentence level as identifying VDL segments must be done mentally at sentence level anyway. Marking the segments directly with just a little additional effort will result in a more informative resource.

Table 1 shows the selected texts and an analysis of the resulting annotations. All texts are of similar length (mean 10,834, standard deviation 1,558 characters). Column **|S|** shows the number of sentences in each corpus. Columns **S=1** and **S=2** shows the average proportion of sentences labelled for each VDL type (VDL or partially VDL), and columns **VDL** and **IVDL** the number of *segments* marked as pure and impure VDL on average (rounded to the nearest integer). Percentage agreement (**% Agree**) and **Kappa** are computed at the sentence level. We also report an analysis of the annotation at the segment level: column **IoU** (Intersection-over-Union) shows the overlap of the annotations at word level; i.e. the ratio of words labelled by two annotators as visually descriptive to total number of labelled words by any annotator; at this point we did not distinguish between pure and impure VDL. Figures for the Oz data are averaged pairwise scores over the three annotators.

4.2 Analysis

As Table 1 shows, agreement values are consistently high among annotators and across all genres, supported also by high Kappa scores.

Results show what one would expect: children's stories contain many visual descriptions, hence the higher proportion of VDL sentences and annotator agreement. News articles and biographies contain less VDL than fiction, especially fully visual sentences (column **S=1**). In adult fiction, adventure novels are naturally more visually descriptive than romance, which tends to focus on the mental states and processes of the characters.

Regarding the segment-level analysis, the overlap (**IoU** column) is reasonably high among all texts, indicating that the majority of the visually descriptive phrases were correctly identified. Furthermore, examining the annotations reveals that most inconsistencies are a result of a mistake of just one of the annotators, rather than fundamental difference of opinion, so a revision phase would further increase the agreement.

4.3 Discussion

Further examination of the annotated data revealed some difficult cases in which annotators disagreed. We present and discuss a few example disagreements:

Word with mixed visual/experiential meanings

(20) {*Susan stared at him with hurt blue eyes*}$_1$.

(21) * {*Susan stared at him with*}$_1$ *hurt* {*blue eyes*}$_1$.

Here, *hurt* is used here as an adjective for eyes, which signals both the appearance of the eyes and

[4] `http://brat.nlplab.org/`

an underlying emotion within Susan. We believe that *hurt* can be accurately applied based on the appearance of Susan's eyes alone, and thus include it as part of the VDL segment.

Inference

(22) *{Rourke was talking on the phone when he came}$_1$ back.*

(23) * *{Rourke was}$_1$ talking {on the phone when he came}$_1$ back.*

As with the fishing example in Section 2, most observers may infer that Rourke is talking on the phone from a scene that involves him holding a phone by his ear while moving his mouth. Thus, we consider *talking on the phone* in this context as VDL.

Context

(24) *{The Lion went back}$_1$ a third time {and got the Tin Woodman}$_1$.*

(25) * *{The Lion went back a third time and got the Tin Woodman}.*

Without context, the annotator has no knowledge about the previous two attempts. Therefore, *a third time* is considered not VDL.

Visual observations over long periods

(26) *From the way {the wound in his head} was itching, Dan knew that it would heal.*

(27) * *From the way {the wound in his head} was itching, Dan knew that {it}$_1$ would {heal}$_1$.*

Although one is able to observe a wound healing, it is a very slow process that spans a long period, analogous to watching grass grow. To be able to confirm this proposition would require observation over a long period of time. Therefore, it is preferable not to annotate such cases as VDL.

Explicit naming of entities

(28) *{They go to school with a girl} named Gloriana*

(29) * *{They go to school with a girl named Gloriana}*

According to our definition an observer can visually identify any named entities. However, in this particular case, we cannot visually confirm that the name of the girl is Gloriana. Contrast this to *{They go to school with Gloriana}*, where Gloriana is a known named entity, and we can visually confirm the proposition asserted by the text segment.

Directional information

(30) *{He crossed the street and walked swiftly}$_1$ southward {to circle back to the Boulevard and}$_1$ north {a block to the open restaurant.}$_1$*

(31) * *{He crossed the street and walked swiftly southward to circle back to the Boulevard and north a block to the open restaurant.}*

It is stated in the guidelines that locational information that relies on compass directions should not be marked as VDL. Example (30) is thus the correct annotation.

Subjective opinions

(32) *They must be {dreadful beasts}.*

(33) * *{They}$_1$ must {be}$_1$ dreadful {beasts}$_1$.*

(34) * *They must be dreadful beasts.*

Here, the adjective *dreadful* should be considered VDL if it would typically be inferred by an observer given only visual input. Clearly *dreadful* also has an experiential sense, dependent on the subjective impression made on the observer. So the question is are a vast majority likely to agree that the beasts are dreadful? In this case, we accept (32) as valid, although a more complete version would be *{They}$_1$ must {be dreadful beasts}$_1$.*

Intensifier adverbials and Negation of entities

(35) *{The sides were so steep} that {none of them}$_1$ could {climb down}$_1$*

(36) *{The sides were}$_1$ so {steep}$_1$ that none of them could climb down*

(37) *{The sides were so steep that none of them could climb down}*

This is a difficult case where all three annotators annotated differently. Our guidelines did not address cases of adverbs such as *so* and *too*. Another issue that was not addressed in the guidelines is how to deal with the negation of entities (*none of them*). We hope to address these issues in future iterations of the guidelines.

5 Conclusion and future work

In this work we have offered a precise definition of Visually Descriptive Language (VDL), a notion with many possible applications at the intersection of language and vision, a subject of increasing interest. We have conducted a pilot annotation exercise, showing that the proposed definition and annotation guidelines can be used to successfully identify visual fragments in documents of different genres with good levels of agreement across annotators.

We believe that VDL is a useful concept to further stimulate research integrating language and vision. In the future we aim to further refine the proposed annotation guidelines, to explore the feasibility of adapting the annotation task for large-scale crowd-sourcing and to extract features and train models for automatically detecting visual fragments in new documents.

Acknowledgments

This work was funded by the ERA-net CHIST-ERA D2K 2011 VisualSense project (UK EPSRC EP/K019082/1 and Spanish MINECO PCIN-2013-047). This work was also partly funded by the Spanish MINECO project RobInstruct TIN2014-58178-R.

References

Tamara L. Berg, Alexander C. Berg, Jaety Edwards, Michael Maire, Ryan White, Yee-Whye Teh, Erik Learned-Miller, and David A. Forsyth. 2004. Names and faces in the news. In *Proceedings of the IEEE Conference on Computer Vision & Pattern Recognition*, pages 848–854.

Ido Dagan, Oren Glickman, and Bernardo Magnini. 2006. The PASCAL recognising textual entailment challenge. In *Proceedings of the First international conference on Machine Learning Challenges: evaluating Predictive Uncertainty Visual Object Classification, and Recognizing Textual Entailment*, MLCW'05, pages 177–190, Berlin, Heidelberg. Springer-Verlag.

Jesse Dodge, Amit Goyal, Xufeng Han, Alyssa Mensch, Margaret Mitchell, Karl Stratos, Kota Yamaguchi, Yejin Choi, Hal Daumé III, Alexander C. Berg, and Tamara L. Berg. 2012. Detecting visual text. In *Proceedings of the North American Chapter of the Association for Computational Linguistics (NAACL)*.

Yansong Feng and Mirella Lapata. 2010. Topic models for image annotation and text illustration. In *Human Language Technologies: The 2010 Annual Conference of the North American Chapter of the Association for Computational Linguistics*, HLT '10, pages 831–839. Association for Computational Linguistics.

Micah Hodosh, Peter Young, and Julia Hockenmaier. 2013. Framing image description as a ranking task: Data, models and evaluation metrics. *Journal of Artificial Intelligence Research (JAIR)*, 47:853–899.

Jin-Woo Jeong, Xin-Jing Wang, and Dong-Ho Lee. 2012. Towards measuring the visualness of a concept. In *Proceedings of the 21st ACM International Conference on Information and Knowledge Management*, CIKM '12, pages 2415–2418.

Girish Kulkarni, Visruth Premraj, Sagnik Dhar, Siming Li, Yejin Choi, Alexander C. Berg, and Tamara L. Berg. 2011. Baby talk: Understanding and generating image descriptions. In *Proceedings of the IEEE Conference on Computer Vision & Pattern Recognition*.

Josiah Wang, Katja Markert, and Mark Everingham. 2009. Learning models for object recognition from natural language descriptions. In *Proceedings of the British Machine Vision Conference*.

Keiji Yanai and Kobus Barnard. 2005. Image region entropy: A measure of "visualness" of web images associated with one concept. In *Proceedings of the 13th Annual ACM International Conference on Multimedia*, MULTIMEDIA '05, pages 419–422.

Yezhou Yang, Ching Teo, Hal Daumé III, and Yiannis Aloimonos. 2011. Corpus-guided sentence generation of natural images. In *Proceedings of the Conference on Empirical Methods in Natural Language Processing (EMNLP)*, pages 444–454. Association for Computational Linguistics.

Semantic Tuples for Evaluation of Image to Sentence Generation

Lily D. Ellebracht[1], Arnau Ramisa[1], Pranava Swaroop Madhyastha[2],
Jose Cordero-Rama[1], Francesc Moreno-Noguer[1], and Ariadna Quattoni[3]

[1]Institut de Robòtica i Informàtica Industrial, CSIC-UPC
[2]TALP Research Center, UPC
[3]Xerox Research Centre Europe

Abstract

The automatic generation of image captions has received considerable attention. The problem of evaluating caption generation systems, though, has not been that much explored. We propose a novel evaluation approach based on comparing the underlying visual semantics of the candidate and ground-truth captions. With this goal in mind we have defined a semantic representation for visually descriptive language and have augmented a subset of the Flickr-8K dataset with semantic annotations. Our evaluation metric (BAST) can be used not only to compare systems but also to do error analysis and get a better understanding of the type of mistakes a system does. To compute BAST we need to predict the semantic representation for the automatically generated captions. We use the Flickr-ST dataset to train classifiers that predict STs so that evaluation can be fully automated [1].

1 Introduction

In recent years, the task of automatically generating image captions has received considerable attention. The task of evaluating such sentences, though, has not been that much explored, and mainly holds on metrics such as BLEU (Papineni et al., 2002) and ROUGE (Lin and Hovy, 2003), originally proposed for evaluating machine translation systems. These metrics have been shown to poorly correlate with human evaluations (Vedantam et al., 2014). Their main problem comes from the fact that they uniquely consider n-grams agreement between the reference and candidate sentences, focusing thus only on the lexical information and obviating the agreement at the visual semantic level. These limitations are illustrated in Figure 1.

Vedantam et al. (2014) have proposed to address these limitations by making use of a Term Frequency Inverse Document Frequency (TF-IDF) that places higher weight on n-grams that frequently occur in the reference sentence describing an image, while reducing the influence of popular words that are likely to be less visually informative.

In this paper, we consider a different alternative to overcome the limitations of BLEU and ROUGE metrics, by introducing a novel approach specifically tailored to evaluate systems for image caption generation. To do this, we first define a semantic representation for visually descriptive language, that allows measuring to which extent an automatically generated caption of an image matches the underlying visual semantics of human authored captions.

To implement this idea we have augmented a subset of the Flickr-8K dataset (Nowak and Huiskes, 2010) with a visual semantic representation, which we call Semantic Tuples (ST). This representation shares some similarity with the more standard PropBank (Kingsbury and Palmer, 2002) style Semantic Roles (SRL). However, SRL was designed to have high coverage of all the linguistic phenomena present in natural language sentences. In contrast, our ST representation is simpler and focuses on the aspects of the predicate structure that are most relevant for capturing the semantics of visually descriptive language.

This ST representation is then used to measure the agreement between the underlying semantics of an automatically generated caption and the semantics of the gold reference captions at different levels of granularity. We do this by aggregating the STs from the gold captions and forming a Bag of Aggregated Semantic Tuples represen-

[1]System and data are made available here: `https://github.com/f00barin/semtuples`

Proceedings of the 2015 Workshop on Vision and Language (VL'15), pages 18–28,
Lisbon, Portugal, 18 September 2015.

Ref: A man sliding down a huge sand dune on a sunny day

SA: A man slides during the day on a dune.

SB: A dinosaur eats huge sand and remembers a sunny day.

System	1-gram	2-gram	3-gram	4-gram
A	0.47	0.29	0.16	0.11
B	**0.49**	**0.36**	**0.23**	**0.17**

Figure 1: The limitations of the BLEU evaluation metric: **SA** and **SB** are two automatically generated sentences that we wish to compare against the manually authored **Ref**. However, while **SB** does not relate to the image, it obtains higher n-gram similarity than **SA**, which is the basis of BLEU and ROUGE.

tation (BAST) that describes the image. We do the same for the automatically generated sentences and compute standard agreement metrics between the gold and predicted BAST. One of the appeals of the proposed metric is that it can be used not only to compare systems but also to do error analysis and get a better understanding of the type of mistakes a system does.

In the experimental section we use the ST augmented portion of the Flickr-8K dataset (Flickr-ST) as a benchmark to evaluate two publicly available pre-trained models of the Multimodal Recurrent Neural Network proposed by (Vinyals et al., 2014) and (Karpathy and Fei-Fei, 2014) that generate image captions directly from images. To compute BAST we need to predict STs for the automatically generated captions. This is sub-optimal because, ideally, we would like a metric that can be computed without human intervention. We therefore use the Flickr-ST dataset to train classifiers that predict STs from sentences. While this might add some noise to the evaluation, we show that the STs can be predicted from sentences with a reasonable accuracy and that they can be used as a good proxy for the human annotated STs.

In summary our main contributions are:

- A definition of a linguistic representation (the ST representation) that models the relevant semantics of visually descriptive language.
- Using ST we propose a new approach to evaluate sentence generation systems that measures caption-gold agreement with respect to the underlying visual semantics expressed in the reference captions.
- A new dataset (Flickr-ST) of captions augmented with corresponding semantic tuples.
- A new metric BAST (Bag of Aggregated Semantic Tuples) to compare systems. In addition, this metric is useful to understand the types of errors made by the systems.
- A new fully automated metric that uses trained classifiers to predict STs for candidate sentences.

The rest of the paper is organized as follows: Section 2 presents the evaluation approach, including the proposed ST representation, the human annotation process to produce a dataset of captions and STs and the proposed BAST metric computed over the ST representation. Section 3 describes in detail the proposed BAST metric. Section 4 describes the annotation process and the creation of the Flickr-ST dataset. Section 5 gives some details about the automatic sentence to ST predictors used to compute the (fully automatic) BAST metric. Section 6 discusses related work. Finally, Section 7 presents experiments using the proposed metric to evaluate state-of-the-art Multimodal Recurrent Neural Networks for caption generation.

2 Semantic Representation of Visually Descriptive Language

We next describe our approach for evaluating sentence generation systems. Figure 3 illustrates the steps involved in the evaluation of a generated caption. Given a caption we first generate a set of semantic tuples (STs) which capture the underlying semantics. While these STs could be generated by human annotators this will not be feasible for an arbitrarily large number of generated captions. Thus, in Section 5 we describe an approach to automatically generate STs from captions.

Ref: A man sliding down a hugh sand dune on a sunny day

Semantic Tuples (ST)

Predicate Agent Patient Locative

<SLIDE, MAN, NULL, DUNE (Spatial)>

<SLIDE, MAN, NULL, DAY (Temporal)>

Bag of Aggregated Semantic Tuples (BAST)

Single-Arguments

Participants (PA)	= {MAN}
Predicates (PR)	= {SLIDE}
Locatives (LO)	= {DUNE, DAY}

Arguments-Pairs

PA+PR	= {SLIDE-MAN}
PA+LO	= {MAN-DUNE, MAN-DAY}
PR+LO	= {SLIDE-DUNE, SLIDE-DAY}

Arguments-Triplets

PA+PR+LO	= {SLIDE-MAN-DUNE, SLIDE-MAN-DAY}

Figure 2: Bag of Aggregated Semantic Tuples.

In the second step of the evaluation we map the set of STs for the caption to a bag of arguments representation which we call BAST. Finally, we compare the BAST of the caption to that of the gold captions. The proposed metric allows us to measure the precision and recall of a system in predicting different components of the underlying visual semantics.

In order to define a useful semantic representation of Visually Descriptive Language (VDL) (Gaizauskas et al., 2015) we follow a basic design principle: we strive for the simplest representation that can cover most of the salient information encoded in VDL and that will result in annotations that are not too sparse. The last requirement means that in many cases we will prefer to map two slightly different visual concepts to the same semantic argument and produce a coarser semantic representation.

In contrast, the PropBank representation (SRL) (Kingsbury and Palmer, 2002) is what we would call a fine-grained representation which was designed with the goal of covering a wide range of semantic phenomena, i.e. cover small variations in semantic content. Furthermore, the SRL representation is designed so that it can represent the semantics of any natural language sentence whereas our representation focuses on covering the semantics present in VDL. Our definitions of semantic tuples are more similar to the proto-roles described by Dowty (1991).

Given an image caption we wish to generate a representation that captures the main underlying visual semantics in terms of the events or actions (we call them predicates), who and what are the participants (we call them agents and patients) and where or when is the action taking place (we call them locatives). For example, the caption "A brown dog is playing and holding a ball in a crowded park" would have the associated semantic tuple: [predicate = *play*; agent = *dog*; patient = *null*; locative = *park*] and [predicate = *hold*; agent = *dog*; patient = *ball*; locative = *park*]. We call each field of a tuple an argument; an argument consists of a semantic type and a set of values. For example the first argument of the first semantic tuple is a predicate with value *play*. Notice that arguments of type agent, patient and locative can take more than one value. For example: "A young girl and an old woman eat fruits and bread in a park on a sunny day" will have the associated semantic tuple: [predicate = *eat*; agent = *girl, woman*; patient = *fruits, bread*; locative = *park, day*].

Note also that we use italics to represent argument values and distinguish them from variables (over some well defined discrete domain) and words or phrases in the caption that we might regard as lexical evidence for that value. For example, the caption "A brown dog is playing and holding a ball in a crowded park" will have the associated semantic tuple: [predicate = *play*; agent = *dog*; patient = *null*; locative = *park*]. The word associated with the predicate *play* is playing, but *play* is a variable. In this case we are assuming that the domain for the predicate variable is the set of all lemmatized verbs.

Argument values will in most cases have some word or phrase in the caption that can be regarded as the lexical realization of the value. We refer to such a realization as the 'span' of the value on the caption. From the previous example, the span of the predicate is 'playing', and its value is *play*. Not all values will have an associated span, since as we describe below, argument values might have tacit spans which can be inferred from the information contained in the caption but they are not explicitly mentioned. In practice to generate the semantic representation we will ask human annotators to mark the spans in the caption corresponding to the argument values (for non-tacit values). We will define the argument variable to be a 'canonical' representation of the span. How this 'canonical' representation is defined will be described in more detail in the next section, where we discuss the annotation process.

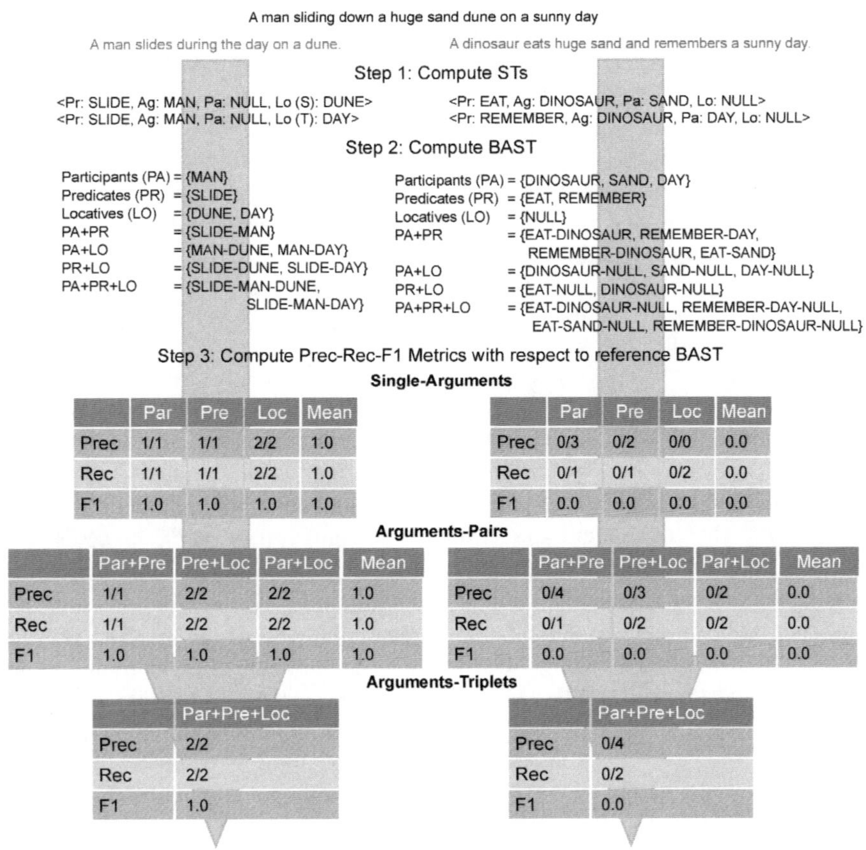

Figure 3: Computation of the BAST metric.

3 The Bag of Semantic Tuples Metric

As mentioned earlier, our semantic representation is 'coarser' than PropBank style semantic role annotations. Furthermore, there are two other important differences: 1) We do not represent the semantics of atomic sentences but that of captions that might actually consist of multiple sentences, and 2) Our representation is truly semantic meaning that resolving the argument value of a predicate might involve making logical inferences. For example we would annotate the caption: "A man is standing on the street. He is holding a camera" with [predicate = *standing*; agent = *man*; patient = *null*; locative = *street*] and [predicate = *hold*; agent = *man*; patient = *null*; locative = *street*]. This means that in contrast to the SRL representation, our semantic representation will not, in general, be 'aligned' with the syntax of the caption.

We now give a more detailed description of each argument type:

- The **Predicate** is the main event described by the sentence. We consider two types of predicates, those that describe an action and those that describe a state. Action predicates are in most cases expressed in the caption using verb-phrases. However, some action predicates might not be explicitly mentioned in the caption but can be naturally inferred. For example, the caption "A woman in a dark blue coat, cigarette in hand" would be annotated with the tuple: [predicate = *hold*; agent = *woman*; patient = *cigarette*; locative = *null*]. In the case that the predicate is indicating a state of being, there is typically a conjugation of the verb "to be", i.e. is, are, was. For example: "A person is in the air on a bike near a body of water."

- The **Agent** is defined as the entity that is performing the action. Roughly speaking, it is the answer to the question: Who is doing the action? For example: in the sentence "The man is sleeping under a blanket in the street as the crowds pass by" we have the predicate = *sleeping* with agent = *man*, and predicate = *pass* with agent = *crowd*. In the case of predicates that describe a state of being such as "A person is in the air on a bike near a body of water", we define the agent to be the answer to the question: Whose state is the predicate describing? Thus for the given example we would have agent = *person*.

- The **Patient** is the entity that undergoes a state of change or is affected by the agent performing some action. For example, the caption "A woman in a dark blue coat, cigarette in hand." would have: [patient = *cigarette*]. Unlike the predicate and agent, the patient is not always present, for example in "Two people run in the sand at the beach." The patient is never present with state-of-being predicates as: "A person is in the air on a bike near a body of water". When there is no patient we say that the argument value is *null*.

- The **Locative** is defined as the answer to the question: Where or When is the action taking place? So there are two main types of locatives, spatial locatives such as *on the water* and temporal locatives such as *at night*. Spatial locatives in turn can be of different types, they can be scenes such as *on-beach* or they can express the relative location of the action with respect to a reference object such as *under-blanket* in the caption "A man sleeping under the blanket". The locatives are actually composed of two parts: a preposition (if present), which expresses the temporal or spatial situation, and the main object or scene. Locatives, like the patient, are not always present. Thus the locative might also take the value *null*.

We could also consider a richer semantic representation that includes modifiers of the arguments, for example for the caption: "A brown dog is playing and holding a ball in a crowded park" we would have the associated semantic tuples: [predicate = *play*; agent = *dog*; agent-mod = *brown* patient = *null*; locative = *park*] and [predicate = *hold*; agent = *dog*; patient = *ball*; locative = *park*, locative-mod = *crowded*]. For the first version of the ST dataset, however, we opted for keeping the representation as simple as possible and decided not to annotate argument modifiers. One of the reasons is that we observed that in most cases if we can properly identify the main arguments extracting their modifiers can be done automatically by looking at the syntactic structure of the sentence. For example if we can obtain a dependency parse tree for the reference caption, extracting the syntactic modifiers of *dog* is relatively easy.

4 The Flickr-ST Dataset: Human Annotation of Semantic Tuples

We believe that one of the main reasons why most of the evaluations used to measure caption generation performance involve computing surface metrics is that until now there was no dataset annotated with underlying semantics.

To address this limitation we decided to create a new dataset of images annotated with semantic tuples as described in the previous section. Our dataset has the advantage that every image is annotated with both the underlying semantics in the form of semantic tuples and natural language captions that constitute different lexical realizations of the underlying visual semantics. To create our dataset we used a subset of the Flickr-8K dataset with captions, proposed in (Hodosh et al., 2013). This dataset consists of 8,000 images of people and animals performing some action taken from Flickr, with five crowd-sourced descriptive captions for each one. These captions are sought to be concrete descriptions of what can be seen in the image rather than abstract or conceptual descriptions of non-visible elements (e.g. people or street names, or the mood of the image).

We asked human annotators to annotate 250 image captions, corresponding to 50 images taken from the development set of Flickr-8K. In order to ensure the alignment between the information contained in the captions and their corresponding semantic tuples, annotators were not allowed to look at the referent image while annotating every caption.

Annotators were asked to list all the unique tuples present in the caption. Then, for each argument of the tuple, they had to decide if its value is *null*, *tacit* or *explicit* (i.e. an argument value that can be associated with a text span in the caption). For explicit argument values we asked the annotator to mark the corresponding span in the text. That is, instead of giving a value for the argument, we ask them to mark in the caption the evidence for that argument.

To create the STs that we use for evaluation we first need to compute the argument values. We assume that we can compute a function that maps spans of text to argument variables, and we call this the grounding function. Currently, we use a very simple mapping from spans to argument values: they map to lowercase lemmatized forms. Given the annotated data and a grounding function, we refer to the process of computing argument values for argument spans as projecting the annotations.

With our approach for decoupling surface (i.e. argument spans) from semantics (argument values) we can address some common problems in caption generation evaluation. The idea is simple, we can use the same annotation with different grounding functions to get useful projections of the original annotation. One clear problem when evaluating caption generation systems is how to handle synonymity, i.e. the fact that two surface forms might refer to the same semantic concept. For example, if the reference caption is: "A boy is playing in a park", the candidate caption: "A kid playing on the park" should not be penalized for using the surface form boy instead of kid. We can address this problem by building a grounding function that maps the argument span boy and the argument span kid to the same argument variable. We could automatically build such function using a thesaurus.

Another common problem when evaluating caption generation is the fact that the same visual entity can be described with different levels of specificity. For example, for the previous reference caption it is clear that "A person is playing in a park" should have a higher evaluation score than "A dog playing in a park". This is because any human reading the caption would agree that person is just a 'coarser' way of referring to the same entity. With our approach we could handle this problem by having a coarser grounding function that maps the argument span kid and the argument span person to the same argument value *human*. The important thing is that for any grounding function we can project the annotations and compute the evaluation, thus we can analyze the performance of a system in different dimensions.

Our goal is to define an evaluation metric that measures the similarity between the STs of the ground-truth captions for an image and the STs of a generated image caption. We wish to define a metric that is useful not only to compare systems, but also that allows for error analysis and some insight on the types of mistakes performed by any given system.

To do this we will first use the STs corresponding to the ground-truth captions to compute what we call a Bag of Aggregated Semantic Tuples representation (BAST). Figure 2 shows a reference caption and its corresponding STs and BAST. Notice that for simplicity we show a single reference caption, in reality if there are k captions for an image, we will first compute the STs corresponding to all of them. The BAST representation is computed in the following manner:

1. For the locatives and predicate arguments compute the union of all the corresponding argument values appearing in any ST. For the patient and agent we will compute a single set which we refer to as the *participants* set. We call this portion of the BAST the bag of single arguments representation.

2. We compute the same representation but now we look at pairs of argument values, meaning: predicate+participant, participant+locative and predicate+locative. We call these the bag of argument pairs.

3. Similarly we can also compute a bag of argument triplets for predicate+participant+locative

We can also compute the BAST representation of an automatically generated caption. This can be done via human annotation of the caption's STs or using a model that predicts STs from captions (such a model is described in the next section). Now if we have the ground-truth BAST and the BAST of the candidate caption we can compute standard precision, recall and F1 metrics over the different components of the BAST. More specifically, for the single argument component of the BAST we compute:

- Predicate-Precision: This is the number of predicted predicates present in the BAST of the candidate caption that where also present in the BAST of the ground-truth reference captions for the corresponding image. That is this is the number of correctly predicted predicates.

- Predicate-Recall: This is the number of predicted predicates present in the BAST of the ground-truth captions that were also present in the BAST of the candidate caption.

- Predicate-F1: This is the standard metric, i.e. the harmonic mean of precision and recall.

We can compute the same metrics for other arguments and for argument pairs and triplets of arguments. Figure 3 shows an example of computing the BAST evaluation metric for two captions.

5 Automatic Prediction of Semantic Tuples from Captions

To compute the BAST metric we need to have STs for the candidate captions, one option is to perform a human annotation. The problem is that collecting human annotations is an expensive and time consuming task. Instead we would prefer to have a fully automated metric. In our case that means that we need an automated way of generating STs for candidate captions. We show in this section that we can use the Flickr-ST dataset to train a model that maps captions to their underlying ST representation.

We would like to point out that while this task has some similarities to semantic-role labeling, it is different enough so that the STs can not be directly derived from the output of an SRL system, in fact our model uses the output of an SRL system in conjunction with other lexical and syntactic features.

Our model exploits several linguistic features of the caption extracted with state-of-the-art tools. These features range from shallow part of speech tags to dependency parsing and semantic role labeling(SRL). More specifically, we use the FreeLing lemmatizer (Carreras et al., 2004), Stanford part of speech(POS) tagger (Toutanova et al., 2003), TurboParser (Martins et al., 2013) for dependency parsing and Senna (Collobert et al., 2011) for semantic role labeling. We also tried using state-of-the art SRL system from Roth and Woodsend (2014), but we observed that Senna performed better on our dataset.

We extract the predicates by looking at the words tagged as verbs by the POS tagger. Then, the extraction of arguments for each predicate is resolved as a classification problem. More specifically, for each detected predicate in a sentence we regard each noun as a positive or negative training example of a given relation depending on whether the candidate noun is or is not an argument of the predicate. We use these examples to train an SVM that decides if a candidate noun is or is not an argument of a given predicate in a given sentence. This classifier exploits several linguistic features computed over the syntactic path of the dependency tree connecting the candidate noun and the predicate and features of the predicted semantic roles of the predicate.

	Model 1	Model 2
Participants (PA)	0.967	0.865
Predicates (PR)	0.703	0.808
Locatives (LO)	0.793	0.819
PA-PR	0.884	0.812
PR-LO	0.779	0.723
PA-LO	0.849	0.757
PA-PR-LO	0.815	0.704

Table 1: F1 score of the automatic BAST extractor taking as reference the manually annotated tuples for the sentences generated by the two models.

Table 1 shows the F1 of our predicted STs compared against manually annotated STs for the two caption generation systems that we evaluate in the experiments section.

6 Related Work

Our definition of semantic tuple is reminiscent in spirit to Farhadi et al. (2010) scene-object-action triplets. In that work, the authors proposed to use a triplet meaning representation as a bridge between images and natural language descriptions. However, the similarity ends there because their goal was neither to develop a formal semantic representation of VDL nor to provide a semantically annotated dataset that could be used for automatic evaluation of captioning systems. At the end, their dataset was created in a very simplistic manner by extracting subject-verb, object-verb and locative-verb pairs from a labeled dependency tree by checking for dependencies where the head and modifier matched a small fix set of possible objects, actions and scenes. As we have illustrated with multiple caption examples, the semantics of VDL can be quite complex and it can be very 'loosely aligned' with the syntactic (e.g. dependency structure) of the sentence. There has also been some recent work on semantic image retrieval based on scene graphs (Johnson et al., 2015), where they model semantic representation of image content to retrieve semantically related images.

BLEU has been the most popular metric used for evaluation, its limitations when used in the context of evaluation of caption quality have been investigated in several works (Kulkarni et al., 2013; Elliott and Keller, 2013; Callison-Burch et al., 2006; Hodosh et al., 2013). Another common metric is ROUGE which has been shown to have some weak correlation with human evaluations (Elliott and Keller, 2013). An alternative metric for caption evaluation is METEOR which seems to be better correlated with human evaluations than BLEU and ROUGE (Elliott and Keller, 2014). Recently a new consensus based metric was proposed by Vedantam et al. (2014), here, the main idea is to measure similarity of a caption to the majority of ground-truth reference captions. One of the limitations of metrics based on consensus is that they are better suited for cases when many ground-truth annotations exist for each image. We take a different approach, instead of augmenting a dataset with more captions, we directly augment it with annotations which reflect what are the most relevant pieces of information in the available captions.

Hodosh et al. (2013) propose a different metric for evaluating image-caption ranking systems and it can not be directly applied to evaluate sentence generation systems (i.e. systems that output novel sentences).

7 Experiments

7.1 The evaluated models

The evaluated models are two instances of the Multimodal Recurrent Neural Network described in (Simonyan and Zisserman, 2014a) and (Karpathy and Fei-Fei, 2014), that takes an image and generates a caption. content of the image in natural language).

This model addresses the caption generation task combining recent advances in Machine Translation and Image Recognition: it combines a Convolutional Neural Network (CNN) initially trained to extract image features, and a Long Short Term Memory Recurrent Neural Network (RNN-LSTM), which is used as a Language Model conditioned by the image features to generate the captions one word at a time.

Both networks can then be re-trained (or fine-tuned) together by back-propagation for the task of generating sentences. However, in this work we use the pre-trained models provided by Karpathy [2] for both the CNN and the RNN, which have been trained sequentially. is fed by the features extracted by the CNN during the training process).

The CNN used in our experiments is the 16-layer model described in (Simonyan and Zisserman, 2014b), which achieves state-of-the-art result in many image recognition tasks, provided by the authors of the paper, and we used the standard feature extraction procedure.

For the RNN-LSTM part, we have evaluated two models to generate two distinct sets of captions that then could be evaluated using the BAST metric. The architecture is the same in both networks but one is trained using the Flickr-8K (LSTM-RNN-Flickr-8K) train set, dubbed *Model 1* in the rest of the paper, and the other is trained using MicrosoftCOCO (LSTM-RNN-MsCOCO) training set, dubbed *Model 2*. Both networks can be downloaded from the NeuralTalk project web-page. Results for the two models using the existing metrics[3] can be seen in Table 2; notice that our installation reproduces exactly these results (third row).

7.2 BAST Metric Results

Figure 5 shows BAST scores for the two caption generation models, we show both results with the manually annotated STs and with the ones automatically predicted by the models. The first observation is that the automatically generated STs are a good proxy for the human evaluation. For all argument combinations, with the exception of locatives (where the differences between the two systems are small) both the BAST computed from automatic and manually annotated STs sort the two systems in the same way. Figure 4 shows some example images and generated captions with the extracted BAST tuples.

Another observation is that overall the numbers are quite low. Despite all the enthusiasm with the latest NN models for sentence generation the F1 of the system for locatives and predicates is quite

[2] We have used the open source project NeuralTalk `https://github.com/karpathy/neuraltalk` which makes it easy to use different pre-trained models for each network.

[3] Evaluation metrics other than BAST have been computed using the tools available at the MsCOCO Challenge website (Lin et al., 2014)

Dataset test	RNN	CIDEr	Bleu 4	Bleu 3	Bleu 2	Bleu 1	ROUGE L	METEOR
MSCOCO*	web ref.	0.666	0.220	0.317	0.461	0.646	0.469	0.205
MSCOCO*	Model 1	0.146	0.068	0.127	0.253	0.448	0.341	0.128
MSCOCO*	Model 2	0.666	0.220	0.317	0.461	0.646	0.469	0.205
Flickr-ST	Model 1	0.356	0.157	0.242	0.377	0.559	0.422	0.178
Flickr-ST	Model 2	0.208	0.101	0.179	0.316	0.528	0.374	0.145

Table 2: Results with current metrics for the two models described in the text. MSCOCO* is the subset of MSCOCO used in the NeuralTalk reference experiments. The first row are the results reported in the NeuralTalk project web-site.

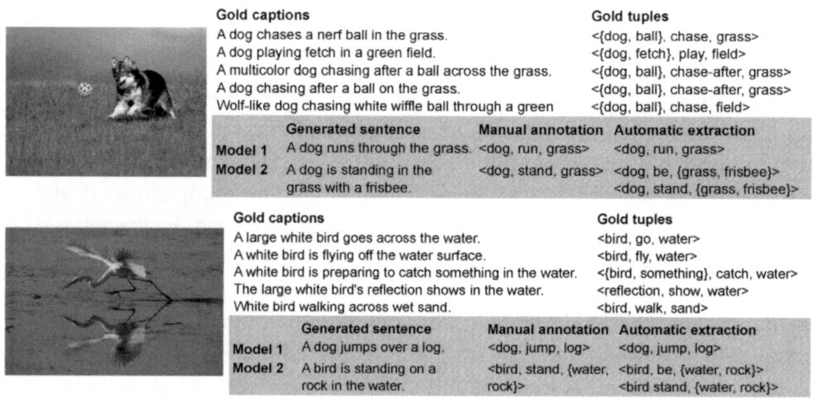

Figure 4: Example results of the two caption generation systems and BAST tuples.

modest, below 25%. Of all the argument types the participants seem to be the easiest to predict for both models, followed by locatives and predicates. This is not surprising since object recognition is probably a more mature research problem in computer vision and state-of-the-art models perform quite well. Overall, however, it seems that caption generation is by no means a solved problem and that there is quite a lot of room for improvement.

8 Conclusion

In this paper we have studied the problem of representing the semantics of visually descriptive language. We defined a simple, yet useful, representation and a corresponding evaluation metric. With the proposed metric we can better quantify the agreement between the visual semantics expressed in the gold captions and a generated caption. We show that the metric can be implemented in a fully automatic manner by training models that can accurately predict the semantic representation from sentences. To allow for an objective comparison of caption generation systems we created a new manually annotated dataset of images, captions and underlying visual semantics repre-

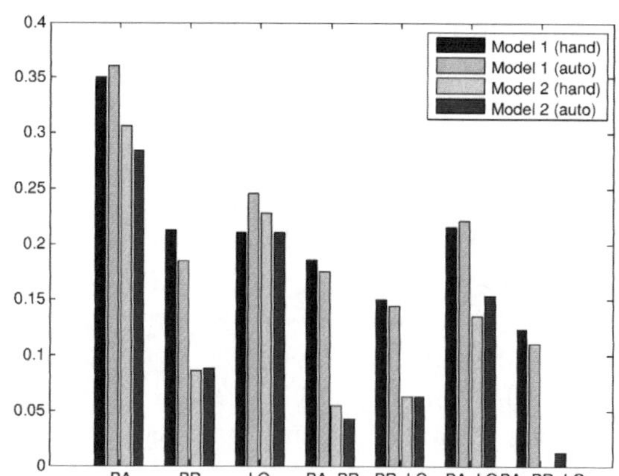

Figure 5: F1 score of the BAST tuples, manually and automatically extracted, from the captions generated by the two evaluated systems for the 50 annotated Flickr-8k validation set images.

sentation by augmenting the widely used Flickr-8K dataset.

Our metric can be used to compare systems but, more importantly, we can use the metric to do a better error analysis. Another nice property of our approach, is that by decoupling the realization of a concept as a lexical item from the underlying visual concept (i.e. the real world entity or event) our annotated corpus can be used to derive different evaluation metrics.

Acknowledgments

We thank the anonymous reviewers for their valuable comments. This work was partly funded by the Spanish MINECO project RobInstruct TIN2014-58178-R and by the ERA-net CHISTERA project VISEN PCIN-2013-047.

References

Chris Callison-Burch, Miles Osborne, and Philipp Koehn. 2006. Re-evaluation the role of bleu in machine translation research. In *EACL*, volume 6, pages 249–256.

Xavier Carreras, Isaac Chao, Lluis Padró, and Muntsa Padró. 2004. Freeling: An open-source suite of language analyzers. In *LREC*.

Ronan Collobert, Jason Weston, Léon Bottou, Michael Karlen, Koray Kavukcuoglu, and Pavel Kuksa. 2011. Natural language processing (almost) from scratch. *The Journal of Machine Learning Research*, 12:2493–2537.

David Dowty. 1991. Thematic proto-roles and argument selection. *language*, pages 547–619.

Desmond Elliott and Frank Keller. 2013. Image description using visual dependency representations. In *EMNLP*, pages 1292–1302.

Desmond Elliott and Frank Keller. 2014. Comparing automatic evaluation measures for image description. In *Proceedings of the 52nd Annual Meeting of the Association for Computational Linguistics: Short Papers*, volume 452, page 457.

Ali Farhadi, Mohsen Hejrati, Mohammad Amin Sadeghi, Peter Young, Cyrus Rashtchian, Julia Hockenmaier, and David Forsyth. 2010. Every picture tells a story: Generating sentences from images. In *Computer Vision–ECCV 2010*, pages 15–29. Springer.

Robert Gaizauskas, Josiah Wang, and Arnau Ramisa. 2015. Defining visually descriptive language. In *Proceedings of the 2015 Workshop on Vision and Language (VL'15): Vision and Language Integration Meets Cognitive Systems*.

Micah Hodosh, Peter Young, and Julia Hockenmaier. 2013. Framing image description as a ranking task: Data, models and evaluation metrics. *Journal of Artificial Intelligence Research*, pages 853–899.

Justin Johnson, Ranjay Krishna, Michael Stark, Li-Jia Li, David Shamma, Michael Bernstein, and Li Fei-Fei. 2015. Image retrieval using scene graphs. In *Proceedings of the IEEE Conference on Computer Vision and Pattern Recognition*, pages 3668–3678.

Andrej Karpathy and Li Fei-Fei. 2014. Deep visual-semantic alignments for generating image descriptions. *CoRR*, abs/1412.2306.

Paul Kingsbury and Martha Palmer. 2002. From treebank to propbank. In *LREC*. Citeseer.

Gaurav Kulkarni, Visruth Premraj, Vicente Ordonez, Sudipta Dhar, Siming Li, Yejin Choi, Alexander C Berg, and Tamara Berg. 2013. Babytalk: Understanding and generating simple image descriptions. *Pattern Analysis and Machine Intelligence, IEEE Transactions on*, 35(12):2891–2903.

Chin-Yew Lin and Eduard Hovy. 2003. Automatic evaluation of summaries using n-gram cooccurrence statistics. In *Proceedings of the 2003 Conference of the North American Chapter of the Association for Computational Linguistics on Human Language Technology-Volume 1*, pages 71–78. Association for Computational Linguistics.

Tsung-Yi Lin, Michael Maire, Serge Belongie, James Hays, Pietro Perona, Deva Ramanan, Piotr Dollár, and C. Lawrence Zitnick. 2014. Microsoft COCO: common objects in context. *CoRR*, abs/1405.0312.

André FT Martins, Miguel Almeida, and Noah A Smith. 2013. Turning on the turbo: Fast third-order non-projective turbo parsers. In *ACL (2)*, pages 617–622. Citeseer.

Stefanie Nowak and Mark J Huiskes. 2010. New strategies for image annotation: Overview of the photo annotation task at imageclef 2010. In *CLEF (Notebook Papers/LABs/Workshops)*, volume 1, page 4. Citeseer.

Kishore Papineni, Salim Roukos, Todd Ward, and Wei-Jing Zhu. 2002. Bleu: a method for automatic evaluation of machine translation. In *Proceedings of the 40th annual meeting on association for computational linguistics*, pages 311–318. Association for Computational Linguistics.

Michael Roth and Kristian Woodsend. 2014. Composition of word representations improves semantic role labelling. In *Proceedings of the 2014 Conference on Empirical Methods in Natural Language Processing (EMNLP)*, pages 407–413, Doha, Qatar, October.

Karen Simonyan and Andrew Zisserman. 2014a. Very deep convolutional networks for large-scale image recognition. *arXiv preprint arXiv:1409.1556*.

Karen Simonyan and Andrew Zisserman. 2014b. Very deep convolutional networks for large-scale image recognition. *CoRR*, abs/1409.1556.

Kristina Toutanova, Dan Klein, Christopher D Manning, and Yoram Singer. 2003. Feature-rich part-of-speech tagging with a cyclic dependency network. In *Proceedings of the 2003 Conference of the North American Chapter of the Association for Computational Linguistics on Human Language Technology-Volume 1*, pages 173–180. Association for Computational Linguistics.

Ramakrishna Vedantam, C Lawrence Zitnick, and Devi Parikh. 2014. Cider: Consensus-based image description evaluation. *arXiv preprint arXiv:1411.5726*.

Oriol Vinyals, Alexander Toshev, Samy Bengio, and Dumitru Erhan. 2014. Show and tell: A neural image caption generator. *CoRR*, abs/1411.4555.

Image Representations and New Domains in Neural Image Captioning

Jack Hessel
Computer Science Dept
Cornell University
jhessel@cs.cornell.edu

Nicolas Savva
Computer Science Dept
Cornell University
nss45@cornell.edu

Michael J. Wilber
Cornell Tech
Cornell University
mwilber@mjwilber.org

Abstract

We examine the possibility that recent promising results in automatic caption generation are due primarily to language models. By varying image representation quality produced by a convolutional neural network, we find that a state-of-the-art neural captioning algorithm is able to produce quality captions even when provided with surprisingly poor image representations. We replicate this result in a new, fine-grained, transfer learned captioning domain, consisting of 66K recipe image/title pairs. We also provide some experiments regarding the appropriateness of datasets for automatic captioning, and find that having multiple captions per image is beneficial, but not an absolute requirement.

1 Introduction

Describing the content of an image is an easy task for humans, but, until recently, had been difficult or impossible for computers. Recent work in computer vision has addressed this task of automatically generating the caption of an input image with promising results (Farhadi et al., 2010; Kulkarni et al., 2013; Ordonez et al., 2011; Karpathy and Li, 2014; Mao et al., 2014; Vinyals et al., 2014; Kiros et al., 2014; Donahue et al., 2014; Fang et al., 2014). Several state-of-the-art approaches couple a pre-trained deep convolutional neural network (CNN) for image representation with a recurrent neural network (RNN) to generate captions that describe image content.

We consider the possibility that the generation of these captions, however, is not heavily reliant upon the image representation input. For instance, if one was to train a RNN directly on image captions, one could learn a fair amount about the general language of image captions. Sutskever et al. (2011) demonstrate that RNNs are capable of producing diverse and surprisingly readable sentences, given a short starting sequence of seed words. Furthermore, non-neural memoization techniques like those proposed by Wood et al. (2009) and Gasthaus et al. (2010) are capable of producing very convincing language models for particular domains.

While it is clear that existing algorithms do discriminate based on image inputs, it is still unclear if the apparently highly specific generated captions are primarily a result of language modeling rather than image modeling. If it could be determined that either image modeling or language modeling is acting as the bottleneck in this multimodal setting, research efforts could be directed appropriately.

To examine the relative multimodal modeling capacities of existing neural captioning algorithms, we execute a series of experiments where we vary image representation quality produced from a fixed CNN, and examine how the output captions are affected.

For two existing datasets and a new domain we analyze here, our results suggest that caption quality does not scale well with increased classification accuracy of a fixed CNN. In fact, as the testing/validation accuracy of a CNN with fixed architecture increases, all seven caption evaluation metrics we consider appear to saturate at surprisingly low classification accuracies. While this does not prove that better image modeling algorithms could not produce better captions, it appears that many apparently fine-grained aspects of generated natural language are the result of surprisingly coarse grained visual distinctions.

For a fixed vision model, our results indicate that there is likely little room for caption improvement via gathering more training images alone. We further postulate that progress could be made

Proceedings of the 2015 Workshop on Vision and Language (VL'15), pages 29–39,
Lisbon, Portugal, 18 September 2015.

most quickly through the development of language modeling techniques that take better advantage of existing image representations. In particular, coupling our results with independent but consistent observations made by Karpathy and Li (2014) and Vinyals et al. (2014) regarding model modifications that lead to overfitting, it's very likely that overfitting language models to image features is still a big problem for many caption generation algorithms. Our analysis highlights what we believe to be an important question for these types of algorithms going forward: if better image representations contain useful, fine-grained information, is it possible to take advantage of that information without overfitting?

To supplement our analysis of image representations, we consider a new caption generating task: generating recipe titles based on images of food. The motivation for this new task results from the intuition that image representations might matter more in visually fine-grained domains, where algorithms must be able to discriminate between minute changes in the input images. We collect a dataset consisting of images of food coupled with recipe titles (e.g. "thai chicken curry") from `Yummly.com` for this purpose. When compared to captioning the coarse-grained ImageNet domain, the specificity of our food dataset calls for more subtle visual discrimination.

Instead of learning a food image representing CNN from scratch to derive representations, we apply transfer learning on a dataset of 101K food images. Using this approach, we significantly surpass current state-of-the-art performance for a classification task on this dataset, despite using a somewhat outdated deep architecture. We further demonstrate that this transfer learning process does indeed improve food captioning, though we observe a similar "flattening" of all linguistic evaluation metrics, after a point.

2 Related Work

2.1 Automatic Captioning

The model we choose to analyze in detail is the "Neural Image Captioning" (NIC) model detailed by Vinyals et al. (2014), though we believe the experiments we address here are relevant to researchers working on distinct but related models. In a similar fashion to Donahue et al. (2014) and Karpathy and Li (2014), NIC feeds a pre-classification representation of images produced by an architecture like GoogLeNet (Szegedy et al., 2014) or AlexNet (Krizhevsky et al., 2012) to a LSTM recurrent neural network (Hochreiter and Schmidhuber, 1997) for language generation. The RNN weights are usually trained on datasets consisting of pairs of images and several corresponding human-generated annotations, such as Flickr8k (Hodosh et al., 2013), Flickr30k (Young et al., 2014), or Microsoft COCO (Lin et al., 2014). The CNN is often pre-trained on a very large set of images such as ImageNet (Deng et al., 2009) and held fixed while the RNN is trained. For many existing captioning datasets, ImageNet is a convenient starting point, presumably because images in most modern captioning datasets are of similar objects.

More complicated caption generation models have also demonstrated success on several datasets. To the knowledge of the authors, Fang et al. (2014) hold the current best result (in terms of BLEU-4) on the MSCOCO official captioning test set, though Vinyals et al. (2014) reportedly outperform Fang et al. on 2/5 evaluation metrics detailed on the MSCOCO captioning leaderboard.[1] Their pipeline involves training a language model directly on captions and a discretized image representation consisting of a likely set of objects in that image. Switching from a fine-tuned AlexNet (Krizhevsky et al., 2012) to a fine-tuned VGG-net (Simonyan and Zisserman, 2014) improved BLEU-4 by 2.4 points, and METEOR by 1.4 points. Because their image representations were discrete, it's possible that their language models were less prone to overfitting. It's not immediately obvious that a similar improvement would occur for language models that operate on extracted vector representations of images like NIC, however.

In contrast to the previous approaches that provide their RNNs with a representation of an image only at the first timestep, Mao et al. (2014) propose an extension of a single-layer RNN, dubbed the "multimodal RNN," that feeds a representation of an image to the RNN at *every* word generation step. Finally, Kiros et al. (2014) propose a model that first uses a CNN and an RNN to embed an image and its corresponding caption in the same semantic space, and then feeds vectors from this space into a "language generating structure content neural language model", an extension of a

[1] `mscoco.org/dataset/`

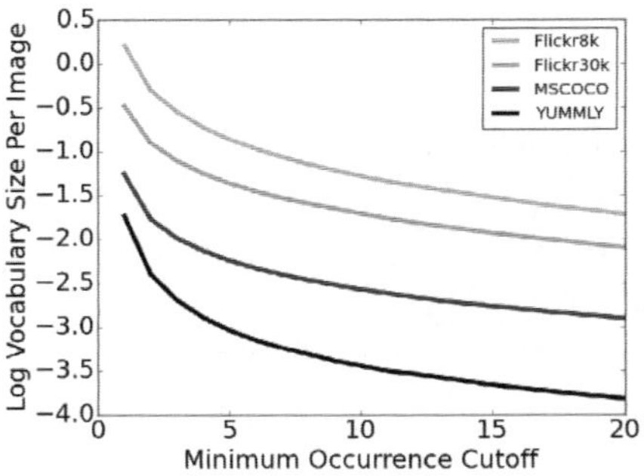

Figure 1: Word cutoff versus log-scale vocab size per image. This metric captures both dataset size and vocabulary size and shows that Yummly has the smallest vocabulary by a margin.

multiplicative RNN that "disentangles the structure of a sentence to its content."

Among models that directly input extracted features to a generating RNN, it is clear that image representations can be mishandled. Specifically, several authors note that passing image representations to the RNN at *every* timestep empirically leads to worse performance. While Karpathy and Li (2014) do not offer speculation as to why this is the case, Vinyals et al. (2014) briefly mention that this operation leads to over-fitting. These independent observations demonstrate that it is easy to overfit to image features.

2.2 Caption Evaluation Metrics

To evaluate captions, we use BLEU-{1,2,3,4} (Papineni et al., 2002) METEOR (Denkowski and Lavie, 2014) and CIDEr/CIDEr-D (Vedantam et al., 2014). BLEU-n is a precision measure over n-grams, whereas METEOR is a more sophisticated metric that involves the computation of an alignment between candidate and reference captions; both were originally conceived in the context of machine translation. CIDEr/CIDEr-D was created to evaluate captions of images and focuses on consensus, particularly in cases where there are multiple reference captions.

2.3 Recipe Title Prediction Tasks

To extend the scope of our investigation, we compile a dataset consisting of images of food coupled with recipe titles from `Yummly.com`. In this dataset, the title of a recipe is usually several words long and can be thought of as a "summary" of the image, rather than a direct description, as not all image content is described in the caption. The image associated with "garlic butter shrimp," for instance, contains shrimp, a bowl, a lemon, and a human hand, and the captioning algorithms must learn to pick out which items are important to describe. Furthermore, there is less grammatical structure present in this dataset.

We view this task as distinct from existing captioning tasks for three reasons. First, the captions within Yummly are both short and restricted; a caption in the Yummly setting has an average length of 4.5 words, which is very low compared to Flickr or MSCOCO settings (both have an average of 10 words per caption) and the vocabulary is very small (see Figure 1). Second, to address this data fully, models must learn very fine-grained visual distinctions. Compared to the broad ImageNet domain, the Yummly images generally consist of some food item on a plate, coupled with several words from a small vocabulary. Finally, this dataset contains a single caption for each image, thus the learning task is more difficult. Previous work (Hodosh et al., 2013) has emphasized the importance of having multiple captions per image in a caption ranking setting, though its unclear if similar observations extend to a generation setting.

While we are only aware of the work of Malmaud et al. (2015) that address food in a multimodal fashion, Bossard et al. (2014) compile the Food 101 dataset which generalizes and increases the scale of previous food image datasets (i.e. Chen et al. (2009), Yang et al. (2010)). Their dataset includes 101k images of 101 types of foods and the task they address is classification.

2.4 Choosing a CNN/RNN Architecture

While substantial improvements have been made in terms of classification accuracy on ImageNet using increasingly deep architectures, we rely on the canonical neural network described in Krizhevsky et al. (2012) to generate our representations in most of our experiments. The use of AlexNet in particular allows for more direct comparison with previous work (i.e. Bossard et al. (2014)) and faster training time when compared to other deep models. This is beneficial particularly because our experiments are not specifically designed to produce state-of-the-art results.

We perform 20 random parameter searches to determine decent parameter settings using the

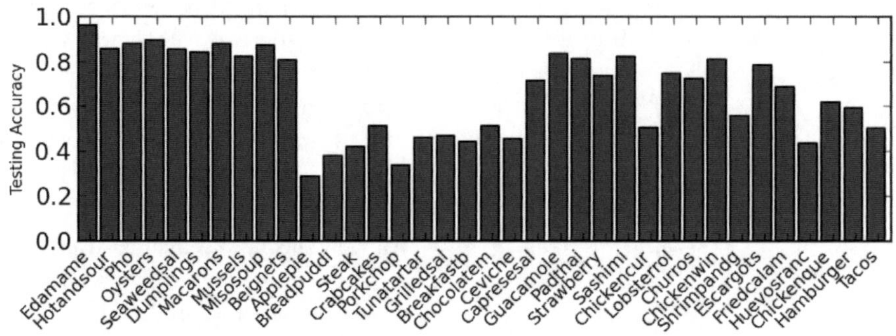

Figure 2: Transfer learned Food-101 CNN accuracy across various classes in the dataset, presented for easy comparison with Figure 6 in Bossard et al. (2014). In general, this model finds the same classes difficult to classify as the models described in previous work, suggesting that some types of fine-grained distinctions are difficult for many models.

Neuraltalk [2] library for all captioning experiments, selecting parameter settings resulting in the lowest validation set perplexity, unless specified otherwise. Settings we take as fixed include a minimum vocabulary threshold of 5, weight optimization using RMSprop (Tieleman and Hinton, 2012), and a hidden representation size of 256. We restrict our consideration to NIC because we believe it to be representative of the state-of-the-art in neural captioning. When we are evaluating models, we generate captions using a beam search of width 20. For the recipe title prediction evaluation, we include an end-of-caption token to avoid issues relating to predicted zero length captions; this has the result of artificially inflating evaluation metrics such that numerical cross-dataset comparisons are not valid.

2.5 Adapting the Food CNN through Transfer Learning

To represent food images properly, we find it appropriate to learn a model specific to the task of food recognition. Food-101 (Bossard et al., 2014) consists of only 101K images, which is a relatively low number of images to train a CNN from scratch. As such, we use a set of ImageNet-trained weights as initializations for our training of a CNN on the Food-101 classification task. This process is commonly referred to as transfer learning (Caruana, 1995; Bengio, 2012).

The intuition behind transfer learning in CNNs is that low-level features learned early on in the base network (which are generally observed to be color blob and Gabor features (Yosinski et al., 2014)) are useful to networks trained on diverse classification tasks. Initializing the weights of the network to weights successful in another classification task should allow training of the new network to converge faster and to a better local optimum than if random initializations were used.

In fact, for the Food-101 dataset, we achieve a rank-1 accuracy of 66.80% when using transfer learning, when compared with the 56.40% rank-1 accuracy reported by Bossard et al. (2014) using the same AlexNet architecture; class-by-class accuracies are given in Figure 2 for comparison with previous work. Our network is learned using only 100k iterations of the Caffe library at a reduced learning rate, whereas training from scratch required Bossard et al. 450k iterations. For our tuning process, we follow the guidelines and parameter settings specified by the transfer learning example distributed with Caffe.[3]

Once the network is tuned, we compute 4096 dimensional vector representations for each image in Yummly dataset by extracting the network activations in the final fully-connected layer.

3 Yummly Dataset: Description and Baselines

After establishing that a CNN could be transfer learned to classify images of dishes at state-of-the-art performance, we were able to shift our focus to caption generation in a food domain.

The food dataset we collect contains roughly 66K recipes, each consisting of a single image-

[2] `github.com/karpathy/neuraltalk`

[3] `https://github.com/BVLC/caffe`

Figure 3: Examples of the captioning system output on several images. The first row of images represents images that are well captioned. The second row represents different types of images the system believes to be sandwiches. The third row represents images that the system has captioned incorrectly.

recipe pair. This data was taken from `Yummly.com`, a website that aggregates and performs analysis of millions of recipes. Out of the 66K recipes, 6K are reserved for testing, 6K are designated as a validation set, and the remaining 54K are used for model training.

This dataset differs from the Flickr datasets and MSCOCO both in terms of vocabulary and in terms of image content. The vocabulary size per image is smaller than any of the other datasets by a wide margin (see Figure 1). While it's clear the vision task requires more subtle distinction when compared to ImageNet, because the average caption length is shorter, it's ambiguous as to whether or not the Yummly language generation task is particularly "fine-grained."

3.1 Baseline Results

Table 1 presents some baseline results using the algorithms listed. Common-3 predicts a reasonable ordering of the three most common words ("with chicken and") for all captions. Nearest neighbor predicts the caption of nearest neighbor in the transfer-learned 4096-dimensional embedding space. Common-Tri/Bi predict the most common tri/bigram in our dataset ("macaroni and cheese"/"ice cream") for all images.

Across the board, and particularly for BLEU-{2,3,4} scores, the caption generating programs outperform all baselines, which suggests the proposed task is adequately framed. However, it is worth noting that only roughly 300/6117 (roughly 5%) of generated captions are unique. This is rather low when compared with a representative result for Flickr8k, a dataset of similar size, where 200/1000 (roughly 20%) of generated captions are unique. It might be possible to re-frame the Yummly generation task as one of classification, however, it's not obvious how one might drive a fixed set of labels. In a later section we discuss whether or not only having one caption per image or other dataset features is a contributing factor to this result.

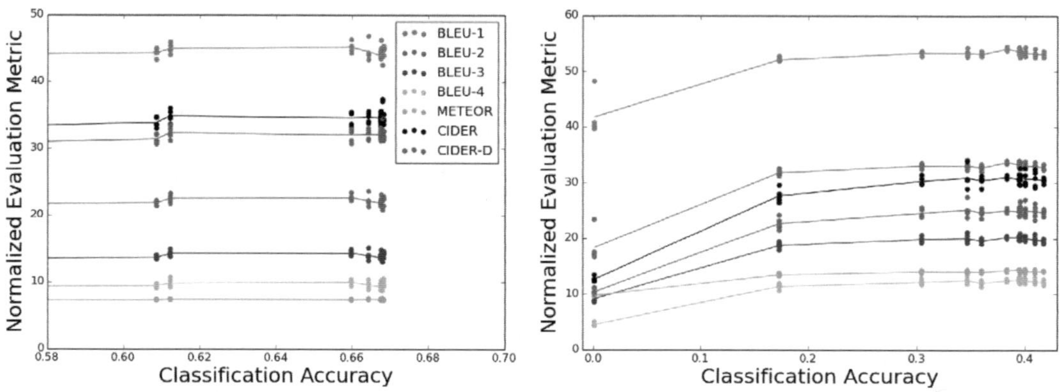

(a) Yummly: Transfer learned domain

(b) Flickr8k: Directly learned domain

Figure 4: Classification accuracy of CNN versus seven different normalized (100 is best possible) linguistic criteria for both the transfer learned (left) and directly learned (right) domains.

	B-1	B-2	B-3	B-4
Com-3	14.2	2.7	0.8	0.0
N-Neigh	20.5	2.5	0.6	0.0
Com-Tri	30.4	6.5	3.4	2.2
Com-Bi	35.4	8.9	5.2	0.0
Karpathy and Li (2014)	42.7	19.6	11.9	13.2
Vinyals et al. (2014)	46.2	23.1	14.8	10.2

Table 1: Yummly baseline BLEU-{1,2,3,4} scores for several baselines and two high performing language generation algorithms.

4 Image Representations

4.1 Experiment Descriptions

We vary image representation quality as follows: for the Flickr8k and Flickr30k datasets, we compute the representations given by snapshots of AlexNet taken mid-training on the ILSVRC2012 (Russakovsky et al., 2015) task. We use snapshots taken at intervals of 10k from 0k (random initialization) to 100k iterations. While this range of iterations is before the model has entirely converged, the rank-1 classification accuracy of the trained CNN over the ImageNet validation set increases from roughly 0% to over 40% during this time (after the model converges at 450k iterations, the rank-1 validation accuracy is 57%). From the standpoint of examining representation quality, this set of snapshots is important because this is likely where the network is learning most of its layer-by-layer abstractions, and the behavior of the network after 100k iterations can be extrapolated based on the data we analyze here.

In a similar fashion, for Yummly we compute representations generated by snapshots of the transfer learned network at intervals of 10k from 0k to 90k, though our starting point is a fully-converged CNN that produces 57% rank-1 accuracy on ImageNet's validation set.

We train 5 NIC models from a random initialization per CNN for Flickr8k and Yummly, and 2-4 NIC models per CNN for Flickr30k. Every data point described in the following section is the result of up to six days of parallel computation using a modern 4/8-core machine. It should be noted that test/validation accuracy of these CNNs is not monotonically increasing with snapshot number. While the trend is that training CNNs for more iterations results in higher accuracy, there is some noise. For instance, for the Food-101 transfer learned CNN, rank-1 test accuracy drops from 61% to 60% over the snapshots extracted at 10k and 20k iterations respectively, before abruptly jumping to 66% testing accuracy in the next 10k iterations.

4.2 Results

We evaluate predicted captions using seven caption evaluation metrics, namely, BLEU-{1,2,3,4}, METEOR, and CIDEr/CIDEr-D. Figure 4 shows our main results for both the directly learned and transfer learned domains. In both cases, all captioning metrics appear to level off early, and do not improve significantly with increased classification rate after a point. This suggests that weight settings for a fixed CNN with higher classification rates are unlikely to produce significantly better captions in terms of these seven evaluation metrics, after a point.

To quantify this lack of improvement, for each dataset we select a CNN that performs its associated visual classification task relatively poorly, and compare it to all better-classifying CNNs. For Flickr8k, for instance, we consider a CNN that produces 30.5% rank-1 accuracy on ImageNet's validation set, and compare its caption performance against that of 8 "better" CNNs that achieve between 34.6% and 41.7% accuracy; there are a total of 56 comparisons, in this case.

Though it is difficult to compute accurate statistics with only 5 observations in each group, we conduct three separate statistical tests, each with different variance/normality assumptions/efficiencies. The tests we perform are Students' t-test, Mann-Whitney U-test, and Welch's unpaired t-test.

In the case of Flickr8k, there are very few significant differences between the 30.5%-CNN and more accurate CNNs. In fact, in 14/56 cases (including half the time among BLEU-1/2 scores) the lower classifying CNN actually produced better captions. The results significant at the 5% level for any statistical test suggested that the 38%-CNN outperformed the 30.5%-CNN in terms of BLEU-1/2, and that the 39.5%-CNN outperformed the 30.5%-CNN in terms of METEOR.

The results for Flickr30k were very similar to the results for Flickr8k. In Figure 5 we present results from this dataset presented against CNN iteration number rather than CNN classification accuracy. We modify the presentation of our data simply to demonstrate that caption quality and iteration number (not just testing/validation accuracy) are also apparently independent after a point. No evidence of improvement was observed after the 30.5%-CNN, though only 2-4 observations per CNN could be made due to computational restrictions.

In total, in the directly-learned domain (Flickr8k/30k) all metrics appear to saturate after AlexNet reaches 30% classification accuracy over the ImageNet validation set. It is possible that training to convergence could result in slightly higher quality captions. However, our results indicate that efforts on ImageNet which result in less than a roughly 10% rank-1 classification

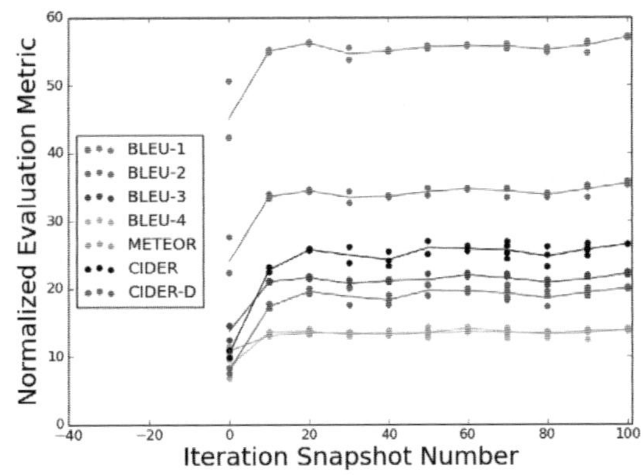

Figure 5: Caption quality versus CNN iteration (in thousands of iters) that representations were derived from. It is clear that a caption quality saturation happens very early on, and there is little to no improvement in captions as the CNNs are trained for more time.

accuracy increase for a fixed network are likely not worth undertaking if one's end goal is higher quality captions.

In the transfer learned domain, it is clear that domain adaptation improves caption quality, even after a small number of iterations. All statistical tests for all evaluation metrics indicate a highly significant difference ($p < .01$) between captions generated by a CNN trained directly on ImageNet, and one that has been transfer-learned using Food-101 for just 10K iterations (producing a rank-1 testing accuracy of 61.2% on that dataset). After a point, however, we observe the same independence of caption quality and classification accuracy.

It seems that "knowing more" about the image does not help the RNN generate more accurate captions after a point because the language patterns it learns are sufficient. This result is akin to prior work (e.g. Sutskever et al. (2011)) which demonstrates that RNNs are able to generate reasonable natural language, given a relatively weak seeding signal. The "weak" signal in this case is provided by image representations, rather than by a short sequence of starting words.

4.3 The Effect of Changing CNN Architectures

Our analysis thus-far has focused on a single image model, AlexNet, for extracting image representations. In this experiment, we compare the captions generated on Flickr8k when using an improved CNN. We train 15 NIC models based on features extracted from a fully converged AlexNet, and 15 NIC models based on features extracted form a fully converged 16-layer VGGNet (Simonyan and Zisserman, 2014). The former model produces a 57.1% rank-1 accuracy over ImageNet's validation set, while the later outperforms this mark, producing 75.6% rank-1 validation accuracy. The default train/valiation/test split of 6k/1k/1k images is used for training.

Our results are summarized in Table 2. In addition to the seven caption evaluation metrics we've used in previous experiments, this table also includes the proportion of the 1k generated captions that are unique, and the train/validation perplexities.

Counter-intuitively, we find that, despite producing 18% lower rank-1 validation accuracy across ImageNet's validation set, AlexNet generates *better* captions than VGG net by all evaluation metrics. Notably, the models using VGG features produce lower perplexity across the validation split. Because we used validation perplexity as a metric for hyperparameter selection, it's likely that the VGG net models are overfitting to the particular Flickr8k validation split we used. However, the AlexNet trained models do not suffer a similar performance degradation. Here, it appears that not overfitting to image features is more important than taking advantage of very detailed image representations.

Our results from this experiment illustrate that better image representations might actually cause models like NIC to become more prone to overfitting. It's possible, too, that the early saturation of caption quality observed in the previous sections could be primarily due to overfitting. Future work would be well suited to evaluate different methods of hyperparameter selection.

4.4 One caption per image?

We conclude with a final experiment to address one potential shortcoming of domains similar to Yummly, where one is only able to extract a single caption per image. Though Yummly differs from the other datasets we explore in several ways (caption length/vocab size) a fundamental question arises from its examination: for a fixed amount of training data, is it better to have more captions per image, or more images with single captions? In short, we hope to experimentally examine Hodosh et al.'s (2013) suggestion that having multiple captions per image is vital.

To address this question, we use Flickr30k, which provides five captions per image. We subset this dataset in two ways. In the first, we remove 4 captions randomly from each image in the training set, but keep all images (the "more images" method). In the second, we randomly remove 80% of training images, but keep all 5 captions for the remaining (the "more captions" method). This subsetting scheme is such that the overall number of image/caption pairs is the same between both methods, but the training data is of a different form.

We extract image representations from the ImageNet CNN at 100k iterations (which produces roughly 40% rank-1 classification accuracy over the ImageNet validation set) and train NIC on 6 random datasets constructed via the "more images" subsetting method, and 7 random datasets constructed via the "more captions" subsetting method. Finally, we generate captions and compare performance. A good hyperparameter setting for Flickr30k is borrowed from the random search conducted over the whole dataset experiments described in the previous section.

Our findings, summarized in Table 3, generally align with the accepted notion that having more captions and less images is better than having more images with single captions. For all seven evaluation metrics, the mean score for the models trained on the "more captions" datasets was greater than the mean score for the models trained on the "more images" datasets, and the results were significant at the 5% level for all three statistical tests in the case of BLEU-1 and BLEU-2. Interestingly, for CIDEr/CIDEr-D, the results were somewhat significant (all 6 p-values less than .15) but the results for METEOR were the least significant (all 3 p-values greater than .94).

The validation perplexity of the "more images" method is lower when compared to the more captions method, whereas the training perplexity is higher. Despite the fact that the output captions are better overall, this is an indication that having multiple captions per image can actually make NIC more prone to overfitting.

Finally, the NIC models trained on the "more caption" subsets produced higher proportions of unique captions on the test set. This suggests

	AlexNet	VGG
Top-1 ImageNet Val Acc	57.1%	75.6%
B-1	54.187	53.913
B-2	33.967	33.527
B-3**	20.640	20.007
B-4**	12.833	12.213
METEOR	14.559	14.559
CIDEr	32.416	31.362
CIDEr-D*	26.200	25.242
Proportion Unique***	20.5%	17.0%
Training Perplexity***	10.79	11.04
Validation Perplexity***	17.84	17.66

Table 2: Effect on caption quality when using the fully converged AlexNet and VGGNet on Flickr8k. Significance for all 3 statistical tests that there was a true difference between the subsetting techniques: $^{***}p < .001$, $^{**}p < .01$, $^{*}p < .05$

	More Captions	More Images
B-1**	55.167	54.243
B-2*	33.567	32.814
B-3	20.633	20.300
B-4	13.133	13.014
METEOR	13.105	13.096
CIDEr	21.428	20.418
CIDEr-D	16.350	15.550
Proportion Unique**	14.8%	9.96%
Training Perplexity**	14.69	16.01
Validation Perplexity*	25.86	25.33

Table 3: Evaluations for the NIC models trained on subsets of Flickr30k containing more captions (5 captions per image, 1/5 the total number of images) and more images (1 caption per image, all training images). Significance for all 3 statistical tests that there was a true difference between the subsetting techniques: $^{**}p < .01$, $^{*}p < .05$

that the single-caption per image feature of the Yummly dataset contributed to a lack of caption innovation.

Despite only having one caption per image, however, NIC was still able to produce good results on the single-captioned subsets. This indicates that quality captioning datasets can be built with only one caption per image. The number of additional images one needs to gather to compensate for this feature, however, is likely greater than the number of captions one would need to add to existing images.

5 Conclusion

We demonstrate the relationship between CNN classification accuracy and the quality of captions generated by a state of the art neural captioning algorithm. Training increasingly accurate image classifiers does not lead to better captions, after a point. This early saturation of caption quality is an indication that the performance of neural caption generating algorithms likely cannot be increased directly by producing more accurate CNNs. Furthermore, many of the apparently highly-specific generated captions output by models like NIC are likely due to language models capturing coarse grained information and generating corresponding plausible natural language sequences.

The role of overfitting to image features is difficult to quantify. On one hand, there is extra information contained in image representations that NIC, for instance, does not take advantage of, and even commonly overfits to. However, it's not clear that this extra, fine-grained information is even worth taking into account. The success of models that generate language based on discretized image representations (e.g. (Young et al., 2014)) demonstrates that algorithms are capable of state-of-the-art performance without consideration of rich, real-valued vector features. It's likely that these types of models are less prone to overfitting, as well.

6 Acknowledgments

We would like to thank Jason Yosinski for providing his AlexNet training snapshots/insights and Gregory Druck for his help with compiling the data collected from `Yummly.com`. We would also like to thank Serge Belongie, Lillian Lee, Abby Lewis, David Mimno, Xanda Schofield, the anonymous reviewers, and the students in the Spring 2015 iteration of CS6670 for their helpful discussions and comments.

References

Yoshua Bengio. 2012. Deep learning of representations for unsupervised and transfer learning. *Unsupervised and*

Transfer Learning Challenges in Machine Learning, Volume 7, page 19.

Lukas Bossard, Matthieu Guillaumin, and Luc Van Gool. 2014. Food-101 – mining discriminative components with random forests. In *European Conference on Computer Vision*.

Rich Caruana. 1995. Learning many related tasks at the same time with backpropagation. *Advances in neural information processing systems*, pages 657–664.

Mei Chen, Kapil Dhingra, Wen Wu, Lei Yang, Rahul Sukthankar, and Jie Yang. 2009. Pfid: Pittsburgh fast-food image dataset. In *Image Processing (ICIP), 2009 16th IEEE International Conference on*, pages 289–292. IEEE.

Jia Deng, Wei Dong, Richard Socher, Li-Jia Li, Kai Li, and Li Fei-Fei. 2009. Imagenet: A large-scale hierarchical image database. In *Computer Vision and Pattern Recognition, 2009. CVPR 2009. IEEE Conference on*, pages 248–255. IEEE.

Michael Denkowski and Alon Lavie. 2014. Meteor universal: Language specific translation evaluation for any target language. In *Proceedings of the EACL 2014 Workshop on Statistical Machine Translation*.

Jeff Donahue, Lisa Anne Hendricks, Sergio Guadarrama, Marcus Rohrbach, Subhashini Venugopalan, Kate Saenko, and Trevor Darrell. 2014. Long-term recurrent convolutional networks for visual recognition and description. *arXiv preprint arXiv:1411.4389*.

Hao Fang, Saurabh Gupta, Forrest Iandola, Rupesh Srivastava, Li Deng, Piotr Dollár, Jianfeng Gao, Xiaodong He, Margaret Mitchell, John Platt, et al. 2014. From captions to visual concepts and back. *arXiv preprint arXiv:1411.4952*.

Ali Farhadi, Mohsen Hejrati, Mohammad Amin Sadeghi, Peter Young, Cyrus Rashtchian, Julia Hockenmaier, and David Forsyth. 2010. Every picture tells a story: Generating sentences from images. In *Computer Vision–ECCV 2010*, pages 15–29. Springer.

Jan Gasthaus, Frank Wood, and Yee Whye Teh. 2010. Lossless compression based on the sequence memoizer. In *Data Compression Conference (DCC), 2010*, pages 337–345. IEEE.

Sepp Hochreiter and Jürgen Schmidhuber. 1997. Long short-term memory. *Neural computation*, 9(8):1735–1780.

Micah Hodosh, Peter Young, and Julia Hockenmaier. 2013. Framing image description as a ranking task: Data, models and evaluation metrics. *Journal of Artificial Intelligence Research*, pages 853–899.

Andrej Karpathy and Fei-Fei Li. 2014. Deep visual-semantic alignments for generating image descriptions. *arXiv preprint arXiv:1412.2306*.

Ryan Kiros, Ruslan Salakhutdinov, and Richard S Zemel. 2014. Unifying visual-semantic embeddings with multimodal neural language models. *arXiv preprint arXiv:1411.2539*.

Alex Krizhevsky, Ilya Sutskever, and Geoffrey E Hinton. 2012. Imagenet classification with deep convolutional neural networks. In *Advances in neural information processing systems*, pages 1097–1105.

Girish Kulkarni, Visruth Premraj, Vicente Ordonez, Sagnik Dhar, Siming Li, Yejin Choi, Alexander C Berg, and Tamara L Berg. 2013. Babytalk: Understanding and generating simple image descriptions. *Pattern Analysis and Machine Intelligence, IEEE Transactions on*, 35(12):2891–2903.

Tsung-Yi Lin, Michael Maire, Serge Belongie, James Hays, Pietro Perona, Deva Ramanan, Piotr Dollár, and C Lawrence Zitnick. 2014. Microsoft coco: Common objects in context. In *Computer Vision–ECCV 2014*, pages 740–755. Springer.

Jonathan Malmaud, Jonathan Huang, Vivek Rathod, Nick Johnston, Andrew Rabinovich, and Kevin Murphy. 2015. What's cookin'? interpreting cooking videos using text, speech and vision. *arXiv preprint arXiv:1503.01558*.

Junhua Mao, Wei Xu, Yi Yang, Jiang Wang, and Alan L Yuille. 2014. Explain images with multimodal recurrent neural networks. *arXiv preprint arXiv:1410.1090*.

Vicente Ordonez, Girish Kulkarni, and Tamara L Berg. 2011. Im2text: Describing images using 1 million captioned photographs. In *Advances in Neural Information Processing Systems*, pages 1143–1151.

Kishore Papineni, Salim Roukos, Todd Ward, and Wei-Jing Zhu. 2002. Bleu: a method for automatic evaluation of machine translation. In *Proceedings of the 40th annual meeting on association for computational linguistics*, pages 311–318. Association for Computational Linguistics.

Olga Russakovsky, Jia Deng, Hao Su, Jonathan Krause, Sanjeev Satheesh, Sean Ma, Zhiheng Huang, Andrej Karpathy, Aditya Khosla, Michael Bernstein, Alexander C. Berg, and Li Fei-Fei. 2015. ImageNet Large Scale Visual Recognition Challenge. *International Journal of Computer Vision (IJCV)*, pages 1–42, April.

Karen Simonyan and Andrew Zisserman. 2014. Very deep convolutional networks for large-scale image recognition. *arXiv preprint arXiv:1409.1556*.

Ilya Sutskever, James Martens, and Geoffrey E Hinton. 2011. Generating text with recurrent neural networks. In *Proceedings of the 28th International Conference on Machine Learning (ICML-11)*, pages 1017–1024.

Christian Szegedy, Wei Liu, Yangqing Jia, Pierre Sermanet, Scott Reed, Dragomir Anguelov, Dumitru Erhan, Vincent Vanhoucke, and Andrew Rabinovich. 2014. Going deeper with convolutions. *arXiv preprint arXiv:1409.4842*.

Tijmen Tieleman and Geoffrey Hinton. 2012. Lecture 6.5-rmsprop: Divide the gradient by a running average of its recent magnitude. *COURSERA: Neural Networks for Machine Learning*, 4.

Ramakrishna Vedantam, C Lawrence Zitnick, and Devi Parikh. 2014. Cider: Consensus-based image description evaluation. *arXiv preprint arXiv:1411.5726*.

Oriol Vinyals, Alexander Toshev, Samy Bengio, and Dumitru Erhan. 2014. Show and tell: A neural image caption generator. *arXiv preprint arXiv:1411.4555*.

Frank Wood, Cédric Archambeau, Jan Gasthaus, Lancelot James, and Yee Whye Teh. 2009. A stochastic memoizer for sequence data. In *Proceedings of the 26th Annual International Conference on Machine Learning*, pages 1129–1136. ACM.

Shulin Yang, Mei Chen, Dean Pomerleau, and Rahul Sukthankar. 2010. Food recognition using statistics of pairwise local features. In *Computer Vision and Pattern Recognition (CVPR), 2010 IEEE Conference on*, pages 2249–2256. IEEE.

Jason Yosinski, Jeff Clune, Yoshua Bengio, and Hod Lipson. 2014. How transferable are features in deep neural networks? In *Advances in Neural Information Processing Systems*, pages 3320–3328.

Peter Young, Alice Lai, Micah Hodosh, and Julia Hockenmaier. 2014. From image descriptions to visual denotations: New similarity metrics for semantic inference over event descriptions. *Transactions of the Association for Computational Linguistics*, 2:67–78.

Image with a Message: Towards detecting non-literal image usages by visual linking

Lydia Weiland, Laura Dietz and **Simone Paolo Ponzetto**
Data and Web Science Group
University of Mannheim
68131 Mannheim, Germany
{lydia, dietz, simone}@informatik.uni-mannheim.de

Abstract

A key task to understand an image and its corresponding caption is not only to find out what is shown on the picture and described in the text, but also what is the exact relationship between these two elements. The long-term objective of our work is to be able to distinguish different types of relationship, including literal vs. non-literal usages, as well as fine-grained non-literal usages (i.e., symbolic vs. iconic). Here, we approach this challenging problem by answering the question: 'How can we quantify the degrees of similarity between the literal meanings expressed within images and their captions?'. We formulate this problem as a ranking task, where links between entities and potential regions are created and ranked for relevance. Using a Ranking SVM allows us to leverage from the preference ordering of the links, which help us in the similarity calculation for the cases of visual or textual ambiguity, as well as misclassified data. Our experiments show that aggregating different features using a supervised ranker achieves better results than a baseline knowledge-base method. However, much work still lies ahead, and we accordingly conclude the paper with a detailed discussion of a short- and long-term outlook on how to push our work on relationship classification one step further.

1 Introduction

Despite recent major advances in vision and language understanding, the classification of usage relationships between images and textual captions is still an open challenge, which is still to be addressed from a computational point of view. Relationships between images and texts can be classified from a general perspective into three different types, namely literal, non-literal and no-relationship. Literal relations cover captions and/or longer corresponding texts that have a descriptive character with respect to the associated image. Non-literal refers instead to images and captions having a relationship that arouses broad associations to other topics, e.g., abstract topics.

The class of non-literal relationships itself can be further divided: *Symbolic photographs* are a common example of non-literal relations. Pictures of this kind can be used without any further explanation on the basis of common socially-mediated understanding, e.g., a heart as a symbol of love, an apple and the snake as an symbol of original sin, or the peace symbol. *Social media* typically use another type of language and sometimes can only be understood by insiders or people, who attended to the situation the photo has been taken, e.g., "Kellogs in a pizza box", with a photo showing a cat sleeping in a pizza box. Without the image, it would have been only clear to those who know Kellogs that a cat is meant by this caption. To the ordinary reader, this would rather suggest a typo and thus, cereals in the pizza box. Those types of relationships can often be found on Flickr, e.g., in the SBU 1M dataset (Ordonez et al., 2011).

A third category is the one of *Media icons* (Perlmutter and Wagner, 2004; Drechsel, 2010), which is typically focused on hot, sensitive, and abstract topics, which are hard to depict directly. Pictures of this kind are often used by news agencies, politicians, and organizations, e.g., a polar bear on an ice floe for global warming. This type of non-literal relationship uses a combination of descriptive parts and language beyond a literal meaning, which assumes fine-grained domain and background knowledge, e.g., the ice floe melting as a result of global warming. When knowledge of this kind is not readily available to the reader, it can be

Proceedings of the 2015 Workshop on Vision and Language (VL'15), pages 40–47,
Lisbon, Portugal, 18 September 2015.

Figure 1: Caption: "A girl with a black jacket and a blue jeans is sitting on a brown donkey; another person is standing behind it; a brown, bald slope in the background."

Figure 2: Non-literal caption: "Deforestation to make way for palm oil plantations has threatened the biodiversity of Borneo, placing species such as the orangutan at risk.". Literal caption: "Two orangutans hugging each other on a field with green leaves. A wooden trunk lays in the background.". Photograph: BOSF I VIER PFOTEN

still acquired by reading associated articles or, in general, by getting to know further facts about a topic. This way the readers are able to create the association of the topic to the image-caption pair.

In our work, we aim at developing methods for automatic understanding of relations between natural language text and pictures *beyond literal meanings and usages*. In particular, we ultimately aim to automatically understand the cultural semantics of iconic pictures in textual contexts (i.e., captions, associated texts, etc.). Far from being an abstract research topic, our work has the potential to impact real-world applications like mixed image-text search (Panchenko et al., 2013), especially in cases of ambiguous or abstract topics in textual queries. Even if current state-of-the-art search engines perform very well, not every search query is answered with what a user expects, e.g., in cases of ambiguity or image and text pairs with non-literal meaning. Being able to assess if a caption and an image are in literal, non-literal, or no relationship can have positive effects to search results. Another, more specific use case is the training of image detectors with the use of captions, which are available in large amounts on the World Wide Web. Training image detectors requires image-caption pairs of the literal class, so being able to reliably identify such instances will arguably produce better, more reliable, and precise object or scene detection models. This is particularly of interest in the news and social media domain, where customizing image detectors for trending entities is of high interest.

Most of the datasets used for training and testing methods from natural language processing, computer vision, or both, are focusing on images with literal textual description. When humans are asked to annotate images with a description, they tend to use a literal caption (cf., e.g., Figure 1). However, captions in real world news articles are devised to enhance the message and build bridges to a more abstract topic, thus have a non-literal or iconic meaning – cf., e.g., the caption of Figure 2 on deforestation in combination with an image showing the orangutan mother with her baby in an open field without trees. Note that image-captions of this kind are typically designed to arouse an emotive response in the reader: in this case, the non-literal usage aims at leading the reader to focus on an abstract topic such as the negative impacts of palm oil plantations. In contrast, the literal caption for this image would rather be "Two orangutans hugging each other on a field with green leaves. A wooden trunk lays in the background." The literal image-caption pair, without further background knowledge, does not trigger this association.

Existing methods from Natural Language Processing (NLP), Computer Vision (CV) do not, and are not meant to find a difference between the same images being used in another context or the same textual contexts depicted with other viewpoints of an abstract topic. In the case of image detection there is no difference between the image with the literal or non-literal caption – it is still the same image, classified as e.g., orangutans. Only when the caption is incorporated into the prediction process, we are able to identify the image-caption pair into the appropriate usage classes, either in a coarse-grained (i.e., 'literal' versus 'non-literal') or fine-grained (e.g., 'media icons' versus 'symbolic photographs').

Spinning our example further, if we would replace the image of Figure 2 with a picture showing a supermarket shelf with famous palm-oil-rich products, it should still be classified as non-literal. However, when regarding the caption as arbitrary text without the context of a picture, this does not have any iconic meaning. Likewise, image processing without considering text cannot predict the relationship to this abstract topic. Therefore, the classification into 'literal' or 'non-literal' (respectively 'media iconic') needs to integrate NLP and CV together. Our working assumption is that the iconic meaning reveals itself through the mismatches between objects mentioned in the caption and objects present in the image.

In this paper we set to find methods and measures to being able to classify these different image-text usage relationships. Consequently, we aim at answering the following research questions:

- What constitutes a literal class of image-caption pair?
- Which method or measure is required to classify a pair as being literal?
- Are we able to derive methods and measures to approach the detection of non-literal pairs?
- How to differentiate literal, non-literal, and not-related classes from each other?

As a first step towards answering these questions, we focus here on detecting literal text-image usages. Therefore, we focus on a dataset of images and captions with literal usages. Our hunch is that *the more links between entities from the caption and regions in the image we can create, the more literal the relationship becomes*. In order to verify this hypothesis, we need to create links between entities from the text and regions with an object in the image, a problem we next turn to.

2 Methods

We provide a first study of the problem of visual entity linking on the basis of a machine learning approach. To the best of our knowledge, Weegar et al. (2014) is the only previous work to address the problem of automatically creating links between image segments and entities from the corresponding caption text. For their work, they use the segmented and annotated extension of the IAPR-TC12 dataset (Grubinger et al., 2006), which consists of segmented and textual annotated images and corresponding captions – we refer to this dataset as SAIAPR-TC12 (Escalante et al., 2010) in the following. In contrast to their work we aim at exploring the benefits of a supervised learning approach for the task at hand: this is because, in line with many other tasks in NLP and CV, we expect a learning framework such as the one provided by a Ranking SVM to effectively leverage labeled data, while coping with ambiguity within the images and associated text captions.

2.1 Ranking SVM

Given a tuple (Q, S, M), with Q as a query, S the ranked segments of an image, and M defined based on the different methods to generate and extract features. Then the score $H_\theta(Q, S)$ between a query Q and a segment S, can be obtained by maximizing over M (Lan et al., 2012; Joachims, 2002): $H_\theta(Q, S) = \arg\max_M F_\theta(Q, S, M)$, where θ is the feature vector consisting of at least one feature or a combination of features. We now proceed to describe such features in details.

2.2 Ranking SVM with Textual Features

GloVe-based cosine similarity: We use the distributional vectors from Pennington et al. (2014) to provide us with a semantic representation of the captions. For each noun of the caption, the GloVe vector calculated on a pre-trained model (Wikipedia 2014, 300d) is used to calculate semantic similarity as:

$$\sum_{q_i \in q \setminus q_{color} \cap l} \alpha(f(q), f(l))$$

where $q \setminus q_{color}$ refers to queries without color entities. l is defined with $l \in I_j$, where l denotes the label of the segment of the current image (I_j). $f(q)$ and $f(l)$ is defined as the feature vector from GloVe and α is defined as the cosine similarity function between those vectors.

GloVe-based cosine similarity with color entities: Besides nouns, GloVe is also able to implicitly associate colors to words, allowing us to determine that, e.g., the color name 'green' and the noun 'meadow' have a high similarity. The SAIAPR-TC12 dataset has more descriptive captions, where a lot of color names are used to describe how the objects and scenes look like. Besides, the text-based label catalog uses color names to further specify a subcategory of a diverse hypernym, e.g., 'sky' can be 'blue', 'light', 'night' and, 'red-sunset-desk'. We accordingly extend the GloVe feature as:

$$\sum_{q_i \in q \cap l} \alpha(f(q), f(l))$$

where q consists of all possible queries, including the color entities.

In the text-only setting the ranking SVM uses only the textual description of the labels and no visual features. The ranking SVM features thus consist of cosine similarities between segment labels and a query consisting of entities and color names. The result thus consists of a ranking of potential segment labels.

2.3 Ranking SVM with Visual Features

HOG: Since images usually do not come with manual segmented and textual annotated regions, we include visual features to systematically substitute textual and manually set information in the images. Thus, we make use of image features as an alternative to the text-based label catalog.

Histogram of Oriented Gradients (HOG): In this stage we still leverage from the image segments, but instead of using the textual label, we apply a classification to every segment. Based on the label statistics from our dataset, models are trained using a binary SVM. For each label, we collect data from ImageNet (Deng et al., 2009), where bounding box information for some objects are provided. With the images from ImageNet, SVM classifiers based on Histogram of Oriented Gradients (HOG) (Dalal and Triggs, 2005) are trained[1]. After training, bounding boxes around every segment are defined. From the normalized version of bounding boxes, HOG features are extracted. These features are then used to classify the test data within every of the trained models. The resulting predictions are stored and serve as features for the Ranking SVM. Thus, our HOG-based features are defined as:

$$\sum_{q_i \in q \setminus q_{color} \cap s} \beta_i^T f(S)$$

Where β_i is the prediction of a linear SVM of detecting object i and $f(S)$ denotes the HOG feature vector of segment S.

HOG and Color Names: Based on Ionescu et al. (2014), we use eleven different color names, which are extracted from the captions of the texts from our dataset. For every normalized bounding box of the segments from the training dataset, color histograms are calculated. The bins of the color histograms serves as a feature vector for the color Ranking SVM. The colors of the bounding boxes are ranked with respect to the context of the color in the caption:

$$\sum_{q_i \in q \setminus q_{entities} \cap s} \gamma_i^T f(S)$$

The queries are now color names without object entities, $f(S)$ defines the distribution of a color defined in γ. We assume entities, which are further described with a color name in the caption, as multi-word queries. The predictions from both rankings are summed to build the final ranking.

3 Evaluation

3.1 Dataset

We conduct experiments on the SAIAPR-TC12 dataset (Escalante et al., 2010). Whilst the Flickr30k dataset (Plummer et al., 2015) is 1.5 the size of the SAIAPR-TC12, it lacks accurate segmentations, which might be relevant for image processing. The IAPR-TC12 consists of 20,000 images with a caption each. The images are covering topics of interesting places, landscapes, animals, sports, and similar topics, which can typically be found in image collections taken from tourists on their holidays. A caption consists of one to four sentences (23.06 words per caption on average (Grubinger et al., 2006)). In addition, the extension delivers segmentation masks of each image, where an image can have multiple segmentation (4.97 segments per image on average (Es-

[1] Note that for our purposes we cannot use existing models, like Pascal VOC (Everingham et al., 2010), for instance, because it has only a small overlap in the set of objects in our data.

Figure 3: Figure 1 with segmentation masks. The segments are labeled with: mammal-other, mountain, woman, sand-desert

calante et al., 2010)). Each segmentation has exactly one label from a predefined catalog of 276 annotations created by a concept hierarchy. Furthermore, spatial relations (adjacent, disjoint, beside, X-aligned, above, below and Y-aligned) of the segmentation masks are defined and image features are given, with respect to the segments (area, boundary/area, width and height of the region, average and standard deviation in x and y, convexity, average, standard deviation and skewness in both color spaces RGB and CIE-Lab).

An example image of the SAIPR-TC12 with segmentation masks and the affiliated caption is given in Figure 1 and 3. The example also shows that due to the limited amount of labels objects are not inevitably represented by the same word in images and captions. Links between entities of the captions and corresponding image segments are not given by default. Due to the topics, covered by the dataset, which are similar to other datasets, the SAIAPR-TC12 can be used as training data. Whereas other, non segmented datasets can be used as testing data, e.g., MediaEval Benchmarking (Ionescu et al., 2014).

3.2 Baseline

We build upon previous work from Weegar et al. (2014) and develop a text-based baseline for our task. To this end, we selected 39 images with 240 segments (from 69 different objects) and corresponding captions with 283 entities (133 different entities), with an average of 6.15 and 7.26, respectively. An overview of object representations in the amount of labels and entities, and their distribution within the test data is given by Table 1.

Entity	Amount	Label	Amount
Sky	12	Leaf	16
Mountain	9	Rock	14
Rock	8	Sky (Blue)	13
Tree	7	Plant	13
House	7	Man	11
Wall	6	Woman	11
People	6	Mountain	10
Building	5	Ground	9
Woman	4	Grass	8
Water	4	Vegetation	8

Table 1: Most common 10 labels and entities of test data selection.

From each of the 39 images we use the textual image segment labels (in the latter referred to as label) and the captions. With Stanford CoreNLP (Manning et al., 2014) we extract the nouns (NN/NNS) from the captions (in the latter referred to as 'entity'). If a noun is mentioned in plural form (NNS), we use the lemma instead (e.g., horses is stored as horse). The extracted entities and labels are stored and further processed image-wise, so that only links between an image segment and an entity from the corresponding caption can be created.

With WordNet and the similarity measure according to WUP (Wu and Palmer, 1994), we calculated the similarity between every label and every entity. A link is stored between the most similar label and entity. Whereas we allow to link multiple segments to one entity. This is done to be able to link multiple instances of one object in an image to the lemmatized entity. To simplify the method with respect to any ambiguity, we used the most frequent sense in WordNet. Overall, the method results in precision of 0.538 and F1 measure of 0.493, thus providing us with a baseline approach with results comparable to the original ones from Weegar et al..

3.3 Experimental Settings and Results

We manually created links between the 240 segments and 231 entities of the originally 281 extracted ones. Since some entities are abstract words, describing images, e.g. 'background',

Different Ranking SVM	Precision	Recall	F1-Measure
Baseline	0.5375	0.45583	0.4933
Cosine Similarity of GloVe	0.7853	0.9392	0.7473
Cosine Similarity of GloVe (Color Entities included)	0.6848	0.9003	0.6551
HOG	0.5459	0.5322	0.3512
HOG and CN	0.6379	0.5796	0.4059

Table 2: Results of the baseline and the different ranking SVM with the two metrics for relevance (Precision), diversity (Recall), and mean of relevance and diversity (F1-Measure).

those entities are filtered in advance (already in the baseline). Overall, 98 color names, that are further describing entities, can be extracted. All links are rated with respect to the query. Within a leave-one-out approach we cross validated every method. As color features are low level features, and rather supposed to enrich the HOG model, it is not separately evaluated. All Ranking SVM results are evaluated for Precision (P), Recall (R) and F1-Measure (F1).

The text-based Baseline achieves precision and F1 with around 50% (cf Table 2). The also text-based Cosine Similarity of GloVe achieves around one and a half better results than the baseline, but these results are reduced for around 10% after integrating the cosine similarities of color names and labels. Vice versa, the two visual feature approaches show better results when integrating both feature types – HOG and color (P: 63.79% vs. 54.59%, F1:40.59% vs. 35.12%).

The results indicate, that visual feature selection and extraction needs further improvement, but they also show, that a post-processing, e.g., re-ranking with aggregation can have positive impacts.

4 Related Work

Recent years have seen a growing interest for interdisciplinary work which aims at bringing together processing of visual data such as video and images with NLP and text mining techniques. However, while most of the research efforts so far concentrated on the problem of image-to-text and video-to-text generation – namely, the automatic generation of natural language descriptions of images (Kulkarni et al., 2011; Yang et al., 2011; Gupta et al., 2012), and videos (Das et al., 2013b; Krishnamoorthy et al., 2013) – few researchers focused on the complementary, yet more challenging, task of associating images or videos to arbitrary texts – Feng and Lapata (2010) and Das et al. (2013a) being notable exceptions. However, even these latter contributions address the easier task of generating visual descriptions for standard, news text. But while processing newswire text is of great importance, this completely disregards other commonly used, yet extremely challenging, dimensions of natural language like metaphorical and figurative language usages in general, which are the kinds of contexts we are primarily interested in. The ubiquity of metaphors and iconic images, in particular, did not inspire much work in Computer Science yet: researchers in NLP, in fact, only recently started to look at the problem of automatically detecting metaphors (Shutova et al., 2013), whereas research in computer vision and multimedia processing did not tackle the problem of iconic images at all.

To the best of our knowledge there is only one related work about the link creation between image segments and entities from the corresponding caption text, namely the study from Weegar et al. (2014), who use the segmented and annotated extension (Escalante et al., 2010) of the IAPR-TC12 dataset (Grubinger et al., 2006), which consists of segmented and textual annotated images and corresponding captions. Due to the textual annotated images, Weegar et al. are able to follow a text-only approach for the linking problem. They propose a method which is based on word similarity using WordNet, between extracted nouns (entities) from the caption and the textual annotation labels of the image segments. For evaluation purposes, they manually created links in 40 images from the dataset with 301 segments and 389 entities. The method results in a precision of 55.48% and serves as an inspiration for the baseline used to compare our own method.

In Plummer et al. (2015) annotators were asked to annotate only objects with bounding boxes that were mentioned in the caption. Not every object in images is asked for a bounding box and an annotation, but those which are mentioned in the captions. Within experiments (bidirectional image-sentence retrieval and text-to-image co reference), they showed the usefulness of links between images and captions, but they also pointed out the issue we are addressing here: Leveraging the links is dependent on a high accuracy between the regions of an image and the textual phrases.

Hodosh at al. (2015) formulates the image description task as ranking problem. Within their method five different captions for one image are ranked. Their results show that metrics using ranked lists, and not only one query result, are more robust.

Dodge et al. (2012) developed methods to classify noun phrases into visual or non-visual text. Visual means things that can be seen on an image. Their results indicate, that using visual features improves the classification. Overall, the classification of visual and non-visual text is especially interesting for the classification of literal and non-literal pairings.

5 Conclusions and Future work

In this work we developed a supervised ranking approach to visual linking. Ranking links between entities and segments is inspired by several aspects of creating the links between caption entities and segments. First, there might be several segments which perfectly fit to one mention in the caption. Second, as object detection approaches are far from being robust and perfect, it might be helpful to limit ourselves not to one decision (binary) but rather to use a ranking, where correct object class might be on lower rank but still to considered. Third, if an object is not covered within a pre-trained model, these objects either will not be considered in the detection and evaluation or wrongly classified.

Visual linking provides us with a first attempt in the direction of solving the question of whether caption is the literal description of the image it is associated with. That is, our goal is not to find an object detector with the highest precision (e.g., answering the question “Is there an orangutan or a chimpanzee on the image?”), but rather if and how much related the images and the captions are to each other. If the caption is talking about palm-oil harvesting and the image shows an orangutan to depict the endangered species, we are interested in receiving detector results with a high probability for an animal as such, and being able to create the non-literal link between these two topics.

In the short term, a necessary step is to develop a model that does not rely on manually defined enrichments of the dataset (e.g., textual labels or segmentation masks). We will accordingly look at ways to perform predictions about regions of interest from the linear SVM and work without the bounding boxes from the dataset. To this end, our dataset needs to be extended, so that we can apply our improved methods also on non-literal image-caption pairings.

In the long term, we need to directly investigate the hypothesis of whether the more links between entities from the caption and regions in the image can be created, the more literally the relationship becomes. That is, a hypothesis for non-literal relationships needs to be computationally formulated and also investigated. Besides this, it would be interesting to discover interesting discriminative characteristics between literal and non-literal images. Finally, future work will concentrate on the differentiation of cultural influences in the interpretation of non-literal image-caption pairs, for instance by taking the background of coders into account (e.g., on the basis of a crowdsourced-generated dataset).

Acknowledgments

The authors would like to thank Vier Pfoten (`www.vier-pfoten.de`) for the permission to use the orangutan photograph in this publication. This work is funded by the Research Seed Capital (RiSC) programme of the Ministry of Science, Research and the Arts Baden-Württemberg, and used computational resources offered from the bwUni-Cluster within the framework program bwHPC.

References

Navneet Dalal and Bill Triggs. 2005. Histograms of oriented gradients for human detection. In *CVPR*, pages 886–893.

Pradipto Das, Rohini K. Srihari, and Jason J. Corso. 2013a. Translating related words to videos and back through latent topics. In *Proc. of WSDM-13*, pages 485–494.

Pradipto Das, Chenliang Xu, Richard F. Doell, and Jason J. Corso. 2013b. A thousand frames in just a few words: Lingual description of videos through latent topics and sparse object stitching. In *Proc. of CVPR-13*, pages 2634–2641.

Jia Deng, Wei Dong, Richard Socher, Li-Jia Li, Kai Li, and Li Fei-Fei. 2009. Imagenet: A large-scale hierarchical image database. In *CVPR09*.

Jesse Dodge, Amit Goyal, Xufeng Han, Alyssa Mensch, Margaret Mitchell, Karl Stratos, Kota Yamaguchi, Yejin Choi, Hal Daumé, III, Alexander C. Berg, and Tamara L. Berg. 2012. Detecting visual text. In *Proceedings of the 2012 Conference of the North American Chapter of the Association for Computational Linguistics: Human Language Technologies*, pages 762–772.

Benjamin Drechsel. 2010. The berlin wall from a visual perspective: comments on the construction of a political media icon. *Visual Communication*, 9(1):3–24.

Hugo Jair Escalante, Carlos A. Hernández, Jess A. González, Aurelio López-López, Manuel Montes y Gómez, Eduardo F. Morales, Luis Enrique Sucar, Luis Villaseñor Pineda, and Michael Grubinger. 2010. The segmented and annotated IAPR TC-12 benchmark. *Computer Vision and Image Understanding*, 114(4):419–428.

Mark Everingham, Luc Gool, Christopher K. Williams, John Winn, and Andrew Zisserman. 2010. The pascal visual object classes (VOC) challenge. *Int. J. Comput. Vision*, 88(2):303–338.

Yansong Feng and Mirella Lapata. 2010. Topic models for image annotation and text illustration. In *Proc. of NAACL-HLT-10*, pages 831–839.

Michael Grubinger, Paul Clough, Henning Müller, and Thomas Deselaers. 2006. The IAPR TC-12 benchmark – a new evaluation resource for visual information systems.

Ankush Gupta, Yashaswi Verma, and C. V. Jawahar. 2012. Choosing linguistics over vision to describe images. In *Proc. of AAAI-12*, pages 606–612.

Micah Hodosh, Peter Young, and Julia Hockenmaier. 2015. Framing image description as a ranking task: Data, models and evaluation metrics (extended abstract). In *Proceedings of the Twenty-Fourth International Joint Conference on Artificial Intelligence, IJCAI 2015, Buenos Aires, Argentina, July 25-31, 2015*, pages 4188–4192.

Bogdan Ionescu, Anca-Livia Radu, María Menéndez, Henning Müller, Adrian Popescu, and Babak Loni. 2014. Div400: A social image retrieval result diversification dataset. In *MMSys '14*, pages 29–34.

Thorsten Joachims. 2002. Optimizing search engines using clickthrough data. In *KDD '02*, pages 133–142.

Niveda Krishnamoorthy, Girish Malkarnenkar, Raymond Mooney, Kate Saenko, and Sergio Guadarrama. 2013. Generating natural-language video descriptions using text-mined knowledge. In *Proc. of AAAI-13*.

Girish Kulkarni, Visruth Premraj, Sagnik Dhar, Siming Li, Yejin Choi, Alexander C. Berg, and Tamara L. Berg. 2011. Baby talk: Understanding and generating image descriptions. In *In Proc. of CVPR-11*, pages 1601–1608.

Tian Lan, Weilong Yang, Yang Wang, and Greg Mori. 2012. Image retrieval with structured object queries using latent ranking svm. In *Proc. of ECCV'12*, pages 129–142.

Christopher D. Manning, Mihai Surdeanu, John Bauer, Jenny Finkel, Steven J. Bethard, and David McClosky. 2014. The Stanford CoreNLP natural language processing toolkit. In *Proc. of ACL-14*, pages 55–60.

Vicente Ordonez, Girish Kulkarni, and Tamara L. Berg. 2011. Im2text: Describing images using 1 million captioned photographs. In *Neural Information Processing Systems (NIPS)*.

Alexander Panchenko, Pavel Romanov, Olga Morozova, Hubert Naets, Andrey Philippovich, Alexey Romanov, and Cédrick Fairon. 2013. Serelex: Search and visualization of semantically related words. In *Proc. of ECIR-13*, pages 837–840.

Jeffrey Pennington, Richard Socher, and Christopher D. Manning. 2014. Glove: Global vectors for word representation. In *Proc. of EMNLP-14*, pages 1532–1543.

David D. Perlmutter and Gretchen L. Wagner. 2004. The anatomy of a photojournalistic icon: Marginalization of dissent in the selection and framing of 'a death in genoa'. *Visual Communication*, 3(1), February.

Bryan Plummer, Liwei Wang, Chris Cervantes, Juan Caicedo, Julia Hockenmaier, and Svetlana Lazebnik. 2015. Flickr30k entities: Collecting region-to-phrase correspondences for richer image-to-sentence models. *CoRR*.

Ekaterina Shutova, Simone Teufel, and Anna Korhonen. 2013. Statistical metaphor processing. *Computational Linguistics*, 39(2):301–353.

Rebecka Weegar, Linus Hammarlund, Agnes Tegen, Magnus Oskarsson, Kalle Åström, and Pierre Nugues. 2014. Visual entity linking: A preliminary study. In *Proc. of the AAAI-14 Workshop on Computing for Augmented Human Intelligence*.

Zhibiao Wu and Martha Stone Palmer. 1994. Verb semantics and lexical selection. In *Proc. of ACL-94*, pages 133–138.

Yezhou Yang, Ching Lik Teo, Hal Daumé, III, and Yiannis Aloimonos. 2011. Corpus-guided sentence generation of natural images. In *Proc. of EMNLP-11*, pages 444–454.

Visual Classifier Prediction by Distributional Semantic Embedding of Text Descriptions

Mohamed Elhoseiny and Ahmed Elgammal
Department of Computer Science, Rutgers University
m.elhoseiny@cs.rutgers.edu, elgammal@cs.rutgers.edu

Extended Abstract

One of the main challenges for scaling up object recognition systems is the lack of annotated images for real-world categories. It is estimated that humans can recognize and discriminate among about 30,000 categories (Biederman and others, 1987). Typically there are few images available for training classifiers form most of these categories. This is reflected in the number of images per category available for training in most object categorization datasets, which, as pointed out in (Salakhutdinov et al., 2011), shows a Zipf distribution.

The problem of lack of training images becomes even more sever when we target recognition problems within a general category, i.e., subordinate categorization, for example building classifiers for different bird species or flower types (estimated over 10000 living bird species, similar for flowers).

In contrast to the lack of reasonable size training sets for large number of real world categories, there are abundant of textual descriptions of these categories. This comes in the form of dictionary entries, encyclopedia entries, and various online resources. For example, it is possible to find several good descriptions of "Bobolink" in encyclopedias of birds, while there are only few images available for it online.

The main question we address in this paper is how to use purely textual description of categories with no training images to learn a visual classifiers for these categories. In other words, we aim at zero-shot learning of object categories where the description of unseen categories comes in the form of typical text such as an encyclopedia entry; see Fig 1. This is a domain adaptation problem between heterogeneous domain (textual and visual). We explicitly address the question of how to automatically decide which information to transfer between classes without the need of any human intervention. In contrast to most related work, we go beyond simple use of tags and image captions, and apply standard Natural Language Processing techniques to typical text to learn visual classifiers.

Similar to the setting of zero-shot learning, we use classes with training data ("seen classes") to predict classifiers for classes with no training data ("unseen classes"). Recent works on zero-shot learning of object categories focused on leveraging knowledge about common attributes and shared parts (Lampert et al., 2009; Farhadi et al., 2009). Typically, attributes are manually defined by humans and are used to transfer knowledge between seen and unseen classes. In contrast, in our work, we do not use any explicit attributes. The description of a new category is purely textual, and the process is totally automatic without human annotation beyond the category labels.

In general, knowledge transfer aims at enhancing recognition by exploiting shared knowledge between classes. This can come in different ways. Sharing knowledge can by achieved by enforcing a hierarchical structure on the classes, general to specific. Such hierarchy is used to impose constraints on the classifier parameters. Such hierarchies can be exported from text domain, e.g., WordNet, or learned from visual features. Our work can be seen in this context, where, we use learned visual classifiers and textual information to learn across-domain

Proceedings of the 2015 Workshop on Vision and Language (VL'15), pages 48–50,
Lisbon, Portugal, 18 September 2015.

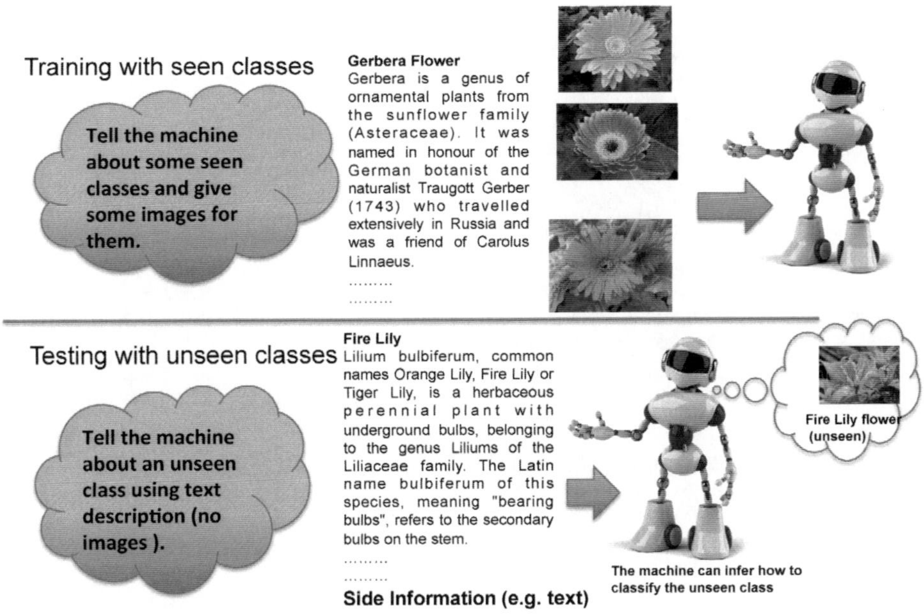

Figure 1: Zero Shot Learning from Side Information (e.g., text)

correlation that facilitates the prediction of visual classifiers for unseen classes.

Scope of the presentation

In this talk, we will present an on-going research on the task of learning visual classifiers from purely textual description with zero or very few visual examples. In an ICCV13 (Elhoseiny et al., 2013), we investigated this new problem, we proposed two baseline formulations based on regression and domain adaptation. Then, we proposed a new constrained optimization formulation that combines a regression function and a knowledge transfer function with additional constraints to solve the problem. In this talk/presentation, we will present our new zero-shot learning framework for predicting kernelized classifiers in the visual domain for categories with no training images where the knowledge comes from textual description about these categories. Through our new optimization framework, the proposed approach is capable of embedding the class-level knowledge from the text domain as kernel classifiers in the visual domain. We also proposed a distributional semantic kernel between text descriptions which is shown to be effective in our setting. The proposed framework is not restricted to textual descriptions, and can also be applied to other forms knowledge representations. Our approach was applied for the challenging task of zero-shot learning of fine-grained categories from text descriptions of these categories. The results surpasses the results in (Elhoseiny et al., 2013) under the same setting, and also other baselines including (Norouzi et al., 2014). We also show the value of our proposed distributional semantic kernel under this setting. We also show that our framework is applicable to other form of side information including weak attributes in addition to text.

References

Irving Biederman et al. 1987. Recognition-by-components: A theory of human image understanding. *Psychological review*.

Mohamed Elhoseiny, Babak Saleh, and Ahmed Elgammal. 2013. Write a classifier: Zero shot learning using purely textual descriptions. In *ICCV*.

Ali Farhadi, Ian Endres, Derek Hoiem, and David A. Forsyth. 2009. Describing objects by their attributes. In *CVPR*.

Christoph H. Lampert, Hannes Nickisch, and Stefan Harmeling. 2009. Learning to detect unseen object classes by betweenclass attribute transfer. In *CVPR*.

Mohammad Norouzi, Tomas Mikolov, Samy Bengio, Yoram Singer, Jonathon Shlens, Andrea Frome, Greg S Corrado, and Jeffrey Dean. 2014. Zero-shot learning by convex combination of semantic embeddings. *ICLR*.

Ruslan Salakhutdinov, Antonio Torralba, and Joshua B. Tenenbaum. 2011. Learning to share visual appearance for multiclass object detection. In *CVPR*.

Understanding Urban Land Use through the Visualization of Points of Interest

Evgheni Polisciuc
CISUC
Departement of
Informatics Engineering
University of Coimbra
Coimbra, Portugal
evgheni@dei.uc.pt

Ana Alves
CISUC, DEI
University of Coimbra
& Polytechnic Institute
of Coimbra
Coimbra, Portugal
ana@dei.uc.pt

Penousal Machado
CISUC
Departement of
Informatics Engineering
University of Coimbra
Coimbra, Portugal
machado@dei.uc.pt

Abstract

Semantic data regarding points of interest in urban areas are hard to visualize. Due to the high number of points and categories they belong, as well as the associated textual information, maps become heavily cluttered and hard to read. Using traditional visualization techniques (e.g. dot distribution maps, typographic maps) partially solve this problem. Although, these techniques address different issues of the problem, their combination is hard and typically results in an efficient visualization. In our approach, we present a method to represent clusters of points of interest as shapes, which is based on vacuum package metaphor. The calculated shapes characterize sets of points and allow their use as containers for textual information. Additionally, we present a strategy for placing text onto polygons. The suggested method can be used in interactive visual exploration of semantic data distributed in space, and for creating maps with similar characteristics of dot distribution maps, but using shapes instead of points.

1 Introduction

Understanding the urban land use is one of the central pillars of urban planning and management. Traditionally this analysis relies on census surveys having limitations in terms of spatial and temporal scale. However, with the advent, and wide deployment of pervasive computing devices (e.g. cell phones, GPS devices, smart cards and digital cameras) some of these limitations may be overcome. For instance, collecting and analyzing information of how people use urban space may be done dynamically and in more precise way.

By using services of modern web platforms (e.g. Facebook, Foursquare, etc.), a user leaves "digital footprints". These are precise data in terms of temporal (when) and spatial locations (where), and in general, can be captured without human intervention. The information about human activity (what) if not explicitly introduced by humans may be inferred by other ways. One of which is about to retrieve the information about visited place. This place, denominated *Point of Interest* (POI), offers a range of services and has special utility. Such information is not always available. Hence, it is necessary to *enrich semantically* the information about the visited places, in order to understand what was done there. Collecting information of how people use urban space has become a very important task on creating the city image from the perspective of its inhabitants, since places are often associated by meaning, i.e. relationship between people and places.

Most smart devices integrate contextual processing. However, it is difficult to enable context-awareness without semantic information. Although, semantic information has been available for years, the Internet, in most cases, abandons such information. In a recent work Alves (2012) presented various perspectives on semantic enrichment of places and extraction of such information from the Internet.

That said, there is a necessity of proper visualization that depicts large amounts of point-based data along with textual information. Geovisualization field provides techniques to visualize georeferenced data, known as thematic maps. One of the well known techniques to represent point-based data is a dot distribution map. However, this kind of maps is limited to representation of points on the map, additionally using color to distinguish points that belong to different groups. On the other hand, typographic maps are used to represent textual information on the map regarding natural and artificial features of urban space (e.g. street names, rivers, places, etc.). But, in order to visu-

Proceedings of the 2015 Workshop on Vision and Language (VL'15), pages 51–59,
Lisbon, Portugal, 18 September 2015.

alize both textual and point-based information one cannot simply overlay two maps. In this case the visualization becomes highly cluttered and illegible. Moreover, it would be difficult to reveal spatial patterns in such hard-overlapped maps. Therefore, from these observations we propose a method to represent this kind of information in a visualization with low degree of visual clutter retaining the possibility to both reveal high-level information and detailed exploration of the map.

Our approach consists in creating visual elements that convey spatial distribution of POIs of same type (a *cluster*), as well as the distribution of clusters in urban area. More precisely, our algorithm generates a shape for each group of POIs revealing its unique visual form in regard to their geographic distribution. Additionally, textual information – clusters tags and POI names – are drawn using different typeface weights and scaled according to the relevance of each cluster.

With that said, in this paper we present a method for visualizing clusters of POIs and the associated semantic information. The dataset is detailed in section 3. The shape of each cluster is calculated using a vacuum package metaphor (see details in section 4). Additionally, this paper presents an interactive web-based application that allows exploring the data with varying degree of details (see section 5).

2 Background and Related Work

Our approach touches on diverse methods and techniques of visualization of spatial information. In this work we consider dot distribution maps. This type of maps are especially efficient in visualization of distribution and densities of point-based data. Regarding the visualization of textual information our approach relies on typographic maps. This particular type of subjective maps efficiently communicates textual information prioritizing typographic hierarchy depending on the relevance of information.

Dot distribution maps, often referred to as density map, they represent spatial distribution of geo-referenced data using basic graphical element – a point (Slocum, 2009). Each point on the map is used to represent either one datum with known geo-location, or aggregation of values. Additionally, dot distribution maps are used to depict densities in corresponding geographic areas, rather than specific locations.

A historical example of the use of a dot distribution map is the disease map produced by John Snow (Tufte and Graves-Morris, 1983). This map depicts the distribution of cholera in London. Deaths are represented by dots and eleven water pumps are represented by crosses. The observation led Snow to discover that cholera occurred in the areas near the Broad Street water pump. This map helped understand the issue of the cholera by revealing disease patterns in spatial context.

One of a more recent example of density map is the *Racial Dot Map* by Cable (2013). This visualization depicts geographical distribution, population density and racial diversity of people living in USA. Each dot represents one individual person at smaller zoom levels and aggregation of dots at national or regional levels. The color encodes race and ethnicity of inhabitants.

Typographic maps may be seen as an "artistic" representation of textual information, rather than an accurate mapping of spatial data. Often, the information being represented by these maps is a description of the relationship of the place and its meaning, which depends of many human, cultural, political, social or historical factors. Therefore, these kind of maps are considered subjective maps (Chen, 2011).

In typographic maps, as the name indicates, textual information is represented using typography. For instance, the maps drawn by Paula Scher are mainly typographical, representing the world, its continents, countries, islands, etc. through typography (Scher, 1990 2010). Likewise, the maps produced by Axis Maps, depict the information about locations and space using text (Axis Maps, nd). Moreover, the geometry of each word is curved along a path, mimicking the shape of the object being represented (e.g. streets, parks, rivers, etc.). This typographic maps were composed with auxiliary of software-based tools (e.g. Adobe Illustrator) and represent information using digital typography. Finally, the graphical elements are placed over OpenStreetMap. These works, the maps by Scher and axisMaps, are good examples of intelligent usage of typographical hierarchy, which makes these maps efficient in the communication of subjective and imprecise information, even with high degree of visual overload.

A more recent research presents a method for automatic construction of typographic maps by merging textual information with spatial data

(Afzal et al., 2012). Given a vector map the algorithm places textual labels in space along the polylines and polygons in accordance with defined visual attributes and constrains. Additionally, the authors describe a method to represent regions as text by filling its interior and repeating the text as necessary. Likewise, our approach uses principles of this technique to align textual labels to a path.

Finally, the work of Cranshaw et al. (2012) is tightly related to our approach, especially in what concerns portraying a city using methods to visualize point-based data and their clusters. The authors introduce a method that consists of a clustering model for mapping a city regarding collective behaviors of its inhabitants and further visualization on the map. This map depicts dynamics, structure and portrayal of a city using clusters, so called *Livehoods*, of geospatial data from Foursquare check-ins. Given geospatial social data generated by hundreds of thousands of people the visualization represents distinct areas of the city regarding activity patterns. The resulting aggregated clusters of check-ins represent so called mental map of the city, the vision of urban space from the perspective of its inhabitants. This enables the study of the structure and composition of a city based on social media its residents generate.

3 Data Description and Design Requirements

Our dataset consists of points of interest (POIs) from the greater metropolitan area of Boston, Massachusetts, USA. POIs contain associated semantic information and are aggregated in meaningful groups (e.g. restaurants, colleges, industry, etc.). More precisely, POIs were tagged with semantic information retrieved from diverse web sources (e.g. Foursquare, Upcoming Yahoo, etc.) (Oliveirinha et al., 2010), and aggregated in clusters using methods proposed by Alves et al. (2011). The dataset comprises 751 clusters of POIs with the following attributes: tag and id of each cluster, geographic coordinates of their centroids, and relevance of a cluster. Additionally, each POI in the dataset is characterized by geographic location (latitude and longitude), name and id. Ultimately, the data types are categorical – POI names and cluster tags – and quantitative – relative relevance of each cluster.

In order to guide the design of our visualization, we established the following design requirements, that define the boundaries for the project:

- The visualization should create a digital layer of urban space.
- It should use a simple and clear visual language, establishing a strong relationship between urban space and POIs.
- In order to reflect geographic nature of data the information should be visualized on a map.
- It should be interactive and run in real-time, supporting the process of data exploration and high-level information acquisition.
- The interactive application should follow the so called *Visual Information-Seeking Mantra*, introduced by Shneiderman (1996), which consists of overview first, zoom and filter, then details-on-demand.
- Finally, the visualization should be easy-to-understand by a general user with no analytic background, therefore presenting a good balance between aesthetics and functionality, without visual overload of display.

4 Representation of POI Clusters

This section covers the process for determining the shapes that describe POI clusters. More precisely, first the concept of vacuum package metaphor is introduced. Then we proceed with the description of an algorithm for polygon calculation given a set of points. Then, we present a method for smoothing the corners of generated polygons. Finally, we discuss the strategy for using typeface weight as visual variable and text placing.

4.1 Concept

In order to understand the distribution of POIs in space and within the corresponding clusters we plotted them using a dot distribution map (see Figure 1). In this visualization each POI is depicted by a point; The category it belongs to is represented with a color. The observation of this visualization led us to the conclusion that each cluster has its unique and recognizable shape. For instance, the same happens with the shapes for countries and continents of the world, to which diverse meanings and symbolisms are associated.

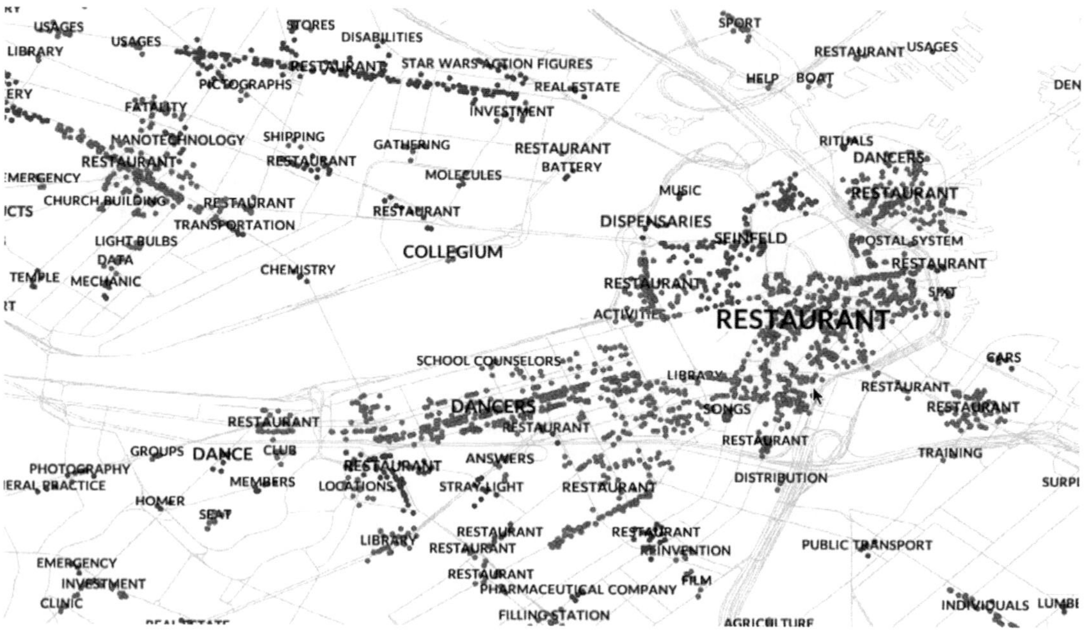

Figure 1: Direct representation of data – names of categories and POIs represented as colored points. Points of equal color belong to the same cluster.

We found this idea particularly interesting and implemented a method that allows us to characterize sets of POIs through their shapes. This approach allows us to eliminate color from representation reducing visual overload. Ultimately, due to amount and diversity of categorical data the use of color is inefficient.

The shape that characterizes a given set of points is known as *convex hull*, i.e. the polygon that encompasses a set of points. This is, the minimal convex set of points containing the entire set. One of the many algorithms to compute convex hull was proposed by Andrew (1979), which is based on the rubber band metaphor. The convex hull can be visualized as a rubber band that is stretched so that it surrounds all the points and then released enclosing all the points.

For certain applications the convex hull does not represent well the boundaries of a set of points. For instance, a convex hull for a set of points that form a C letter would have a shape close to ellipse. In other words, the region that is defined by convex hull does not represent the region that is formed by the points.

This problem has already been addressed by many researches, and is know as computation of non-convex or concave hull (see e.g. Moreira and Santos (2007) and Duckham et al. (2008)). One of the methods to compute shape of a set of points was introduced by Edelsbrunner et al. (1983), and is know as two-dimensional alpha-shapes. As mentioned by Edelsbrunner, an alpha shape can be imagined as a huge mass of ice-cream containing pieces of chocolate; then using a sphere-formed ice-cream spoon we carve all the parts of ice-cream without bumping into chocolate pieces; if we now straighten all the "round" faces we will get an intuitive description of what is called the alpha-shape. Although, the alpha-shape is a standardized formal description of a set of points this method assumes multi-polygon reconstruction of the geometry, and often produces polygons that contain holes, which is not desirable in our visualization.

We address this problem by combining the principles of alpha-shape and vacuum packing metaphor. This metaphor can approximately be seen as following: imagine a plastic bag containing a set of points; then the oxygen is removed creating vacuum inside the bag; when the bag is completely shrunk it become tightly fitted to its content. This metaphor is intuitive description of our approach. The following section gives a formal description of the algorithm to compute a shape of a set of points heterogeneously distributed in geographic space.

4.2 Algorithm

This section describes an algorithm for the calculation of a concave hull based on the vacuum package metaphor. The calculation of a polygon is an iterative process with the maximum number of iterations defined by an user. The process passes through the calculation of convex hull, which defines an initial set of edges. Each edge is characterized by starting and ending points in ordered array, and by stretchiness, which models a behavior of an elastic band. Finally, the shape of each set of points is calculated independently.

Considering the set of points S to be our input, the algorithm proceeds as follows:

1. Let L be an initially empty list that will contain the points that define the polygon.

2. Calculate the convex hull, and store the set of points in L in clock-wise order.

3. For each iteration and for each edge – i.e., for each pair of consecutive points in L, which we designate by A and B:

    - If the length of the edge is bigger than predefined minimum length, then continue to the next step. Otherwise, skip.
    - The edge AB is divided by half at the center, defining an isosceles triangle $\triangle ABC$, where A and B are the starting and ending points in L, respectively, and C is the central point.
    - C is pushed inside the polygon by a force vector $\vec{f}$, which is perpendicular to the edge AB.
    - The magnitude of the force $\vec{f}$ varies proportionally to the stretchiness of AB edge, which is a function of its length, and the distance of C from its original location, say M. i.e. shorter edges have smaller $\vec{f}$.
    - If one of the points, say P, in the set S is inside the triangle, then the P is appended to the L in the order AP and PB, consequently, creating two new edges.
    - The process is repeated until the maximum number of iterations is reached or all the edges have their lengths smaller than defined minimum length.

Determining if a point P is inside the triangle $\triangle ABC$ is done by calculating cross products of vectors $\vec{AP}\times\vec{AB}$, $\vec{BP}\times\vec{BC}$, and $\vec{CP}\times\vec{CA}$. If all the values are negative, then the point is inside the triangle. Otherwise, the point is outside. Finally, at a simulation instance there might be two points inside the triangle. In this case considered only the one that is closest to the M point – middle point that divides AB by half.

Figure 2 displays two shapes of clusters that were calculated by the algorithm given two sets of points from our dataset. Also, this figure schematically illustrates the described algorithm at a simulation instance – the points that compose a polygon are marked with circles, the edges are represented with black line, and the lines that makeup the triangles are painted in red. As can be observed in Figure 2, image on the right, even complex shapes are well defined.

Figure 2: Calculated shape of clusters for "Trading", image on the left, and "Seinfeld" categories, image on the right. Circles represent points that compose a hull, with the arrows inside that indicate the order of points.

4.3 Visual Refinement and Label Placing

Having calculated all the polygons we proceed to smooth their corners, which gives an organic representation of a shape. Also, this facilitates the process of placing textual labels onto polygons.

The problem of corner smoothing can be divided in two parts – round the corners that make interior angles smaller and greater than 180° (for the purpose of simplicity we label them as S and G corners, respectively). In order to create a smooth polygon there should be enough free space allocated to append additional points that compose a new polygon. This is done by translating perpendicularly each edge to a certain distance, say d, placing them outside the original polygon. Then we proceed by calculating the S corners, simply connecting two consecutive translated segments with an arc that is centered at the corner point and with the radius equal to d. The arc is then fragmented with small segments, the number of which is dictated by defined minimum length. The G corners, on the other hand, are computed using Bezier equation (Farin et al., 2002). The two control points have the same location, which is the point of intersection of the two edges that makeup the corner. The end points are the middle point of each of two translated edges. Finally, the curve is partitioned with small segments. The Figure 3 is a schematic representation of the smoothing of polygons.

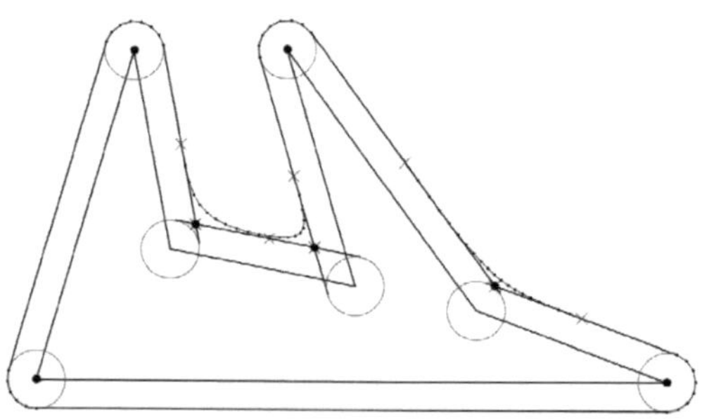

Figure 3: Schematic construction of round corners.

The second part of visual refinement consists of placing textual information onto polygons. As was mentioned earlier, our data consist of two types of text data – most relevant tag for each cluster, and names of each individual POI. In order to represent this data two different strategies were used. In the first case, the cluster tags were positioned on center of the polygon being represented using typeface weights to represent their weights. In the second case, the names of POIs were placed onto the polygon and curved along the contour of the shape.

As mentioned above, we used typographic weight as a visual variable to represent relevance of each category of POIs. According to Lupton (2014), in typography, all typefaces are organized into families . Within a family typefaces are divided and ordered according their weights (e.g. regular, bold, etc.). In modern typography there are families that contain up to nine weights classified as fallowing – thin, extra light, light, regular, medium, semi-bold, bold, black and heavy. So, we used these to encode the relevance of each category, by dividing all values in eight ranges and assigning each range to a typographic weight. Due to ordered nature of data the typographic weights were assigned starting with thin up to heavy typefaces (see Figure 4).

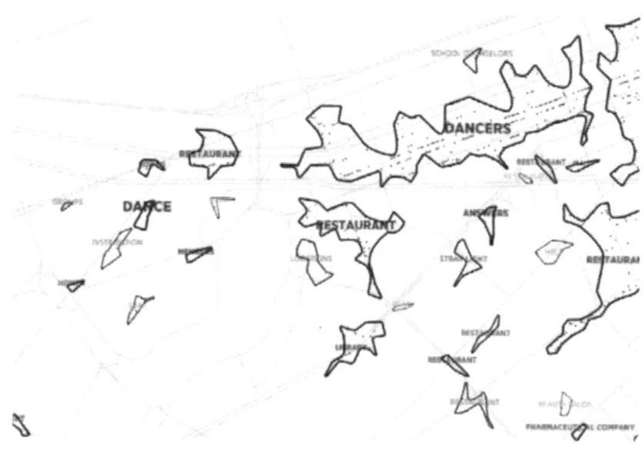

Figure 4: Close-up of an area with categories that have different relevance encoded with typographic weight and font size.

For the second type of textual information we used an approach inspired in typographic maps. The name of POIs are placed onto polygon and the words are curved along with the shape. One of the problems of curved words is the fact that they visually distort the word when placed on the path junctions. This is, the words are visually breaking apart creating discontinuous reading. One of the solutions to address this problem is to distort the characters, like in maps by Paula Scher. However, in digital typography these manipulations are undesirable and are considered a bad practice (Lupton, 2014). So, our solution consisted in: drawing the letters perpendicularly to the path they are placed onto; when a letter appears on a junction of two segments we use a weighted angle depending on the percentage of occupied space on each of segments. In other words, the imaginable rectangle that holds a character always keeps its base corners on top of each segment (see Figure 5). Finally, the tracking – space between characters – is increased, when the letters are placed on G corners, and decreased, when the letters are placed on S corners. This diminishes the visual discontinuities in reading.

Finally, all the methods were combined and the result is displayed on Figure 6. As can be observed

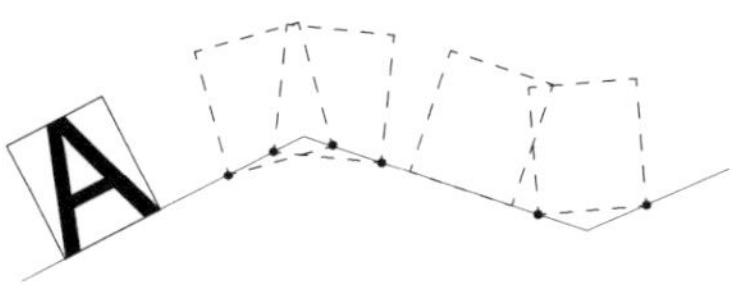

Figure 5: Placing characters onto segment and segment joint.

the visualization become less cluttered in comparison with dot map representation. The clusters of POIs are characterized by an organic shape, which facilitates the placement and continuous reading of textual information. Text labels, on the other hand, try to mimic the contour without substantial visual distortion. Also, it is easy to understand that this approach is less efficient when small clusters are considered, due to limited space to display all the textual information.

5 Application and Limitations

This section presents an application of the described techniques combined into one visualization model. First, an interactive web-based application, which uses the described methods applied on another dataset with a similar nature of information, is discussed. Then, we enumerate the limitations of presented approach.

The interactive web-based application follows the principles of Visual Seeking Mantra – overview first, zoom and filter, then details-on-demand. In the first screen the user can find a general view of the map. In this view the visualization depicts only the shapes of clusters, which gives a first impression about the data and its distribution in space. It is important to note that in the second dataset POIs have multiple associated tags, i.e. a POI may belong to different categories. Consequently, POI clusters may overlap, which means that overlapping areas provide multiple services. For instance the area of restaurants might coincide with the area of shopping. That said, the user can easily identify these cases in general view (see Figure 7, image on the left).

Filtering and zoom-and-pan are also important functionalities of the application. Using the panel on the left the user can select individual categories to display and filter the visualization by average weight of the relevance, by the number of POIs in cluster, among others. Selecting the categories also reveals their names and places them as described in previous sections, although using only one typographic weight. To navigate on the map the user can use zoom-and-pan. The visualization dynamically updates details of the shapes and presents different levels of cluster aggregation according to zoom level (see Figure 7, image in the middle).

Finally, the application provides additional details on demand. This is done by directly selecting clusters on the map. In this case the panel on the left updates and displays more detailed information about the selected cluster (e.g. a list of POIs in the group, impact of each category the cluster belongs to, number of POIs). Additionally, the clusters that share the same category are also highlighted on the map, such that the distribution of clusters within similar category is revealed (see Figure 7, image on the right).

As can be observed in the web-application the labels are not shown, due to high amount of textual information, which makes the visualization run slow in a web browser. Nevertheless, this functionality is implemented in offline visualization. As it can be observed, there are overlapping areas. As such, the shapes are painted with transparent color, in order to highlight highly overlapped areas on the map. Allowing the user to perceive urban areas that provide multiple services can be easily found on the map. Thus, providing higher-level information that would be difficult to visualize by other means.

6 Conclusion

In this article, we presented a method to represent clusters of POIs along with their semantic information. This method integrates visual characterization of a set of points and the methods to represent textual information. Given clusters of POIs the presented method creates a visual layer that characterizes urban space in accordance with the meanings of places, which derives from the digital footprints that the inhabitants leave. For this reason, we presented a novel approach that calculates a concave hull of a set of points. This method enables the creation of a unique integral polygon, which is calculated using vacuum package metaphor. Ultimately, each polygon characterizes a set of points with a unique organic looking shape.

Additional textual information is added by placing names of POIs on a path defined by a poly-

Figure 6: A zoom-in of downtown area of Boston. The final visualization combines all the presented methods: shapes of clusters; rounded corners; label placing.

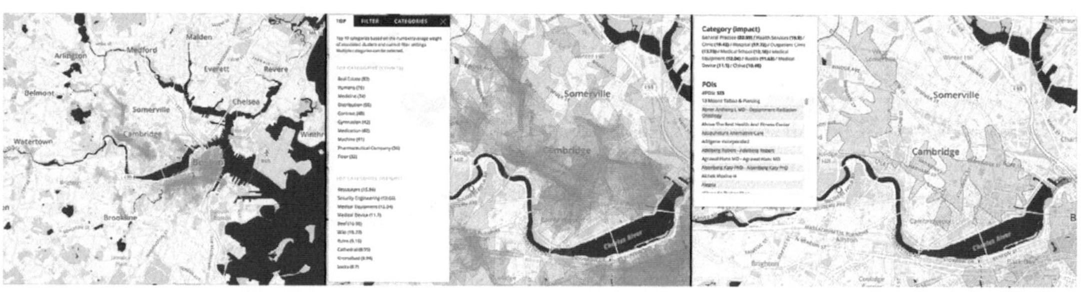

Figure 7: Screenshots of interactive application. General view, image on the left; filter and zoom, middle; and details-on-demand, image on the right.

gon. In the proposed strategy the characters were placed perpendicularly to the segment they belong, and using a weighted angle when placed on the corners. Additionally, we introduced a visual variable to encode the relevance of a category – the typographic weight. The data variable's values are divided in equal ranges, and then each bin is associated with a typographic weight in the order from thin to heavy.

Finally, this visualization was implemented as web-based application and applied on another dataset. The interactive web application gives an overview of data at general zoom level. Then the user can zoom-in and obtain a detailed view of the visualization. Additionally, using the filter panel the user can choose individual category and filter the visualization by different parameters. Finally, more details, such as cluster impact or the list of POIs in cluster, are given on demand.

Acknowledgements

This work was supported by the InfoCrowds project - FCT-PTDC/ECM-TRA/1898/2012FCT.

References

Shehzad Afzal, Ross Maciejewski, Yun Jang, Niklas Elmqvist, and David S Ebert. 2012. Spatial text visualization using automatic typographic maps. *IEEE Transactions on Visualization & Computer Graphics*, (12):2556–2564.

Ana O Alves, Filipe Rodrigues, and Francisco C Pereira. 2011. Tagging space from information extraction and popularity of points of interest. In *Ambient Intelligence*, pages 115–125. Springer.

Ana Cristina da Costa Oliveira Alves. 2012. Semantic enrichment of places. understanding the meaning of public places from natural language texts.

Alex M Andrew. 1979. Another efficient algorithm for convex hulls in two dimensions. *Information Processing Letters*, 9(5):216–219.

Axis Maps. n.d. Typographic maps. `http://store.axismaps.co.uk/`. Accessed: 2015-06-10.

Dustin Cable. 2013. Racial dot map. *Weldon Cooper Center for Public Service, University of Virginia.*

Xiaoji Chen. 2011. *Seeing differently: cartography for subjective maps based on dynamic urban data.* Ph.D. thesis, Massachusetts Institute of Technology.

Justin Cranshaw, Raz Schwartz, Jason I Hong, and Norman M Sadeh. 2012. The livehoods project: Utilizing social media to understand the dynamics of a city. In *ICWSM*.

Matt Duckham, Lars Kulik, Mike Worboys, and Antony Galton. 2008. Efficient generation of simple polygons for characterizing the shape of a set of points in the plane. *Pattern Recognition*, 41(10):3224–3236.

Herbert Edelsbrunner, David G Kirkpatrick, and Raimund Seidel. 1983. On the shape of a set of points in the plane. *Information Theory, IEEE Transactions on*, 29(4):551–559.

Gerald E Farin, Josef Hoschek, and Myung-Soo Kim. 2002. *Handbook of computer aided geometric design*. Elsevier.

Ellen Lupton. 2014. *Thinking with type*. Chronicle Books.

Adriano Moreira and Maribel Yasmina Santos. 2007. Concave hull: A k-nearest neighbours approach for the computation of the region occupied by a set of points.

João Oliveirinha, Francisco Pereira, and Ana Alves. 2010. Acquiring semantic context for events from online resources. In *Proceedings of the 3rd International Workshop on Location and the Web*, page 8. ACM.

Paula Scher. 1990–2010. Typographic maps. `http://paulaschermaps.com/`. Accessed: 2015-06-18.

Ben Shneiderman. 1996. The eyes have it: A task by data type taxonomy for information visualizations. In *Visual Languages, 1996. Proceedings., IEEE Symposium on*, pages 336–343. IEEE.

Terry A Slocum. 2009. *Thematic cartography and geovisualization*. Prentice hall.

Edward R Tufte and PR Graves-Morris. 1983. *The visual display of quantitative information*, volume 2. Graphics press Cheshire, CT.

Comparing attribute classifiers for interactive language grounding

Yanchao Yu
Interaction Lab
Heriot-Watt University
y.yu@hw.ac.uk

Arash Eshghi
Interaction Lab
Heriot-Watt University
a.eshghi@hw.ac.uk

Oliver Lemon
Interaction Lab
Heriot-Watt University
o.lemon@hw.ac.uk

Abstract

We address the problem of interactively learning perceptually grounded word meanings in a multimodal dialogue system. We design a semantic and visual processing system to support this and illustrate how they can be integrated. We then focus on comparing the performance (Precision, Recall, F1, AUC) of three state-of-the-art attribute classifiers for the purpose of interactive language grounding (MLKNN, DAP, and SVMs), on the aPascal-aYahoo datasets. In prior work, results were presented for *object* classification using these methods for attribute labelling, whereas we focus on their performance for attribute labelling itself. We find that while these methods can perform well for some of the attributes (e.g. *head, ears, furry*) none of these models has good performance over the whole attribute set, and none supports incremental learning. This leads us to suggest directions for future work.

1 Introduction

Identifying, classifying and talking about objects or events in the surrounding environment are key capabilities for intelligent, goal-driven systems that interact with other agents and the external world (e.g. smart phones, robots, and other automated systems), as well as for image search/retrieval systems. To this end, there has recently been a surge of interest and significant progress made on a variety of related tasks, including generation of Natural Language (NL) descriptions of images, or identifying images based on NL descriptions (Karpathy and Fei-Fei, 2014; Bruni et al., 2014; Socher et al., 2014). Another strand of work has focused on learning to generate object descriptions and object classification based on low level concepts/features (such as colour, shape and material), enabling systems to identify and describe novel, unseen images (Farhadi et al., 2009; Silberer and Lapata, 2014; Sun et al., 2013).

Our goal is to build *interactive* systems that can learn grounded word meanings relating to their perceptions of real-world objects – rather than abstract coloured shapes as in some previous work e.g. (Roy, 2002). For example, we aim to build multimodal interfaces for Human-Robot Interaction which can learn object descriptions and references in interaction with humans. In contrast to recent work on image description using 'deep learning' methods, this setting means that the system must be *trainable from little data, compositional, able to handle dialogue, and adaptive* – for instance so that it can learn visual concepts suitable for specific tasks/domains, and even new idiosyncratic language usage for particular users.

However, most of the existing systems for image description rely on training data of both high quantity and high quality with no possibility of online error correction. Furthermore, they are unsuitable for robots and multimodal systems that need to continuously, and incrementally learn from the environment, and may encounter objects they haven't seen in training data. These limitations are likely to be alleviated if systems can learn concepts, as and when needed, from situated dialogue with humans. Interaction with a human tutor enables systems to take initiative and seek the particular information they need or lack by e.g. asking questions with the highest information gain (see e.g. (Skocaj et al., 2011), and Fig. 1).

For example, a robot could ask questions to learn the color of a "mug" or to request to be presented with more "red" things to improve its performance on the concept (see e.g. Figure 1). Furthermore, such systems could allow for meaning negotiation in the form of clarification interactions

Proceedings of the 2015 Workshop on Vision and Language (VL'15), pages 60–69,
Lisbon, Portugal, 18 September 2015.

Dialogue	Image	Final semantics
S: Is this a green mug? T: No it's red S: Thanks.		$\left[\begin{array}{lll} x_{=o1} & : & e \\ p2 & : & red(x) \\ p3 & : & mug(x) \end{array}\right]$
T: What can you see? S: something red. What is it? T: A book. S: Thanks.		$\left[\begin{array}{lll} x1_{=o2} & : & e \\ p & : & book(x1) \\ p1 & : & red(x1) \\ p2 & : & see(sys, x1) \end{array}\right]$

Figure 1: Example dialogues & resulting semantic representations

with the tutor.

This paper presents initial work in a larger programme of research with the aim of developing dialogue systems that learn (visual) concepts – word meanings – through situated dialogue with a human tutor. Specifically, we compare several existing state-of-the-art classifiers with regard to their suitability for interactive language grounding tasks. We compare the performance of MLKNN (Zhang and Zhou, 2007), DAP (zero-shot learning (Lampert et al., 2014)), and SVMs (Farhadi et al., 2010) on the image datasets aPascal (for training) and aYahoo (testing) – see section 4. To our knowledge, this paper is the first to compare these attribute classifiers in terms of their suitability for interactive language grounding.

Our other contribution is to integrate an incremental semantic grammar suited to dialogue processing – DS-TTR[1] (Purver et al., 2011; Eshghi et al., 2012), see section 3 – with visual classification algorithms that provide perceptual grounding for the basic semantic atoms in the representations produced by the parser through the course of a dialogue (see Fig. 1). In effect, the dialogue with the tutor continuously provides semantic information about objects in the scene which is then fed to an online classifier in the form of training instances. Conversely, the system can utilise the grammar and its existing knowledge about the world, encoded in its classifiers, to make reference to and formulate questions about the different attributes of an object identified in the scene.

2 Related work

There has recently been a lot of research into learning to classify and describe images/objects. Some approaches attempt to ground meaning of words/phrases/sentences in images/objects by mapping these modalities into the same vector space (Karpathy and Fei-Fei, 2014; Silberer and Lapata, 2014; Kiros et al., 2014), or using distributional semantic models that build distributional representations with the conjunction of textual and visual information (Bruni et al., 2014). Other approaches, such as (Socher et al., 2014), propose Neural Network models based on Dependency Trees (DT), which project all words in a sentence into a DT structured representation to explore parents of each node and correlations between nodes.

In contrast to these approaches, which do not support NL dialogues, some approaches are designed based on logical semantic representations and some of them are incorporated with spoken dialogue systems (Skocaj et al., 2011; Matuszek et al., 2012; Kollar et al., 2013). A well-known logical semantic parser is the Combinatory Categorial Grammar (CCG) parser, which represents natural language sentences from human tutors in the logical forms. The "Logical Semantics with Perception" (LSP) framework by Kollar et al. (Krishnamurthy and Kollar, 2013) and the joint language/perception model by Matuszek et al. (Matuszek et al., 2012) are based on a CCG parser or using a CCG lexicon respectively. Although a CCG parser could generate similar logical representations to the DS-TTR parser/generator we use here, we believe that DS-TTR would show better performance than CCG in terms of handling the inherent incremental, fragmentary and highly context-dependent nature of dialogue.

The "Describer" system (Roy, 2002) learns to generate image descriptions, but it works at the level of word sequences rather than logical seman-

[1]Downloadable from http://dylan.sourceforge.net

tics, and uses only synthetically generated scenes rather than real images and image processing. Our approach extends (Dobnik et al., 2012) in integrating vision and language within a single formal system: Type Theory with Records (TTR). This combination will allow complex multi-turn dialogues for language grounding with deep NL semantics, including natural correction and clarification subdialogues (e.g. "No this isn't red, it's green.").

2.1 Attribute classification

Regarding attribute-based classification or description, Farhadi et al. (Farhadi et al., 2009) have successfully described objects with attributes by sharing appearance attributes across object categories. Silberer and Lapata (Silberer and Lapata, 2014) extend Farhadi et al.'s work to predict attributes using L2-loss linear SVMs and to learn the associations between visual attributes and particular words using Auto-encoders. Sun et al. (Sun et al., 2013) also build an attribute-based identification model based on hierarchical sparse coding with a K-SVD algorithm, which recognizes each attribute type using multinomial logistic regression. However, as these models require a large mass of training data, an increasing amount of research attempts to learn novel objects using 'one-shot' (Li et al., 2006; Krause et al., 2014) or 'zero-shot' learning algorithms (Li et al., 2007; Lampert et al., 2014). They enable a system to classify unseen objects with fewer or no examples by sharing *attributes* between known and unknown objects. Note that these methods ultimately focus on object class labels, using attributes as intermediate representations.

On the other hand, to learn attribute-based objects through NL interaction, some approaches learn unknown objects or attributes with online incremental learning algorithms (Li et al., 2007; Kankuekul et al., 2012). The "George" system (Skocaj et al., 2011), which is similar in spirit to our work, learns object attributes from a human tutor and creates specific questions to request information to fill detected knowledge gaps. However, the George system only learns about 2 shapes and 8 colours. Our goal is to couple attribute classifiers with much wider coverage to the formal semantics of a full Natural Language dialogue system.

3 System Architecture

We are developing a system to support an attribute-based object learning process through natural, incremental spoken dialogue interaction. The architecture of the system is shown in Fig. 2. The system has two main modules: a vision module for visual feature extraction and classification; and a dialogue system module using DS-TTR (see below). Visual feature representations are built based on base features akin to (Farhadi et al., 2009). We do not yet have a fully integrated dialogue system, so for our experiments presented below, we assume access to logical semantic representations, that will be output by the DS-TTR parser/generator as a result of processing dialogues with a human tutor (more on this below) – and interface these representations with attribute-based image classifiers. Below we describe these components individually and then explain how they interact.

3.1 Attribute-based Classifiers used

In this research, in order to explore the best solution for attribute classification for an interactive system, we compare several methods which have previously shown good performance on image-labelling tasks – a multi-label classification model, a zero-shot learning model, and a linear SVM:

(a) MLkNN (Zhang and Zhou, 2007) is a supervised multi-label learning model based on the k-Nearest Neighbour algorithm, which predicts a label set for unknown instances. It has previously been used for scene labelling with 5 labels (sunset, desert, mountains, sea, trees) and reached a Precision of 0.8;

(b) L2-loss Linear SVM as used by (Farhadi et al., 2009). We used the published feature extraction and attribute training code[2], though we appear to have achieved slightly worse AUC results than achieved in (Farhadi et al., 2009) (see section 4);

(c) Direct Attribute Prediction (DAP) (Lampert et al., 2014), is a kind of zero-shot learning model, which implements a multi-layer classifier - the layer of attributes and the layer of labels - which apply the attribute variables in the attribute layer to decompose the object images in the label layer. This model allows the use of any supervised classification models for learning per-attribute coefficients. Once the image-attribute parameters are predicted, DAP can explore the class-

[2]From http://vision.cs.uiuc.edu/attributes/

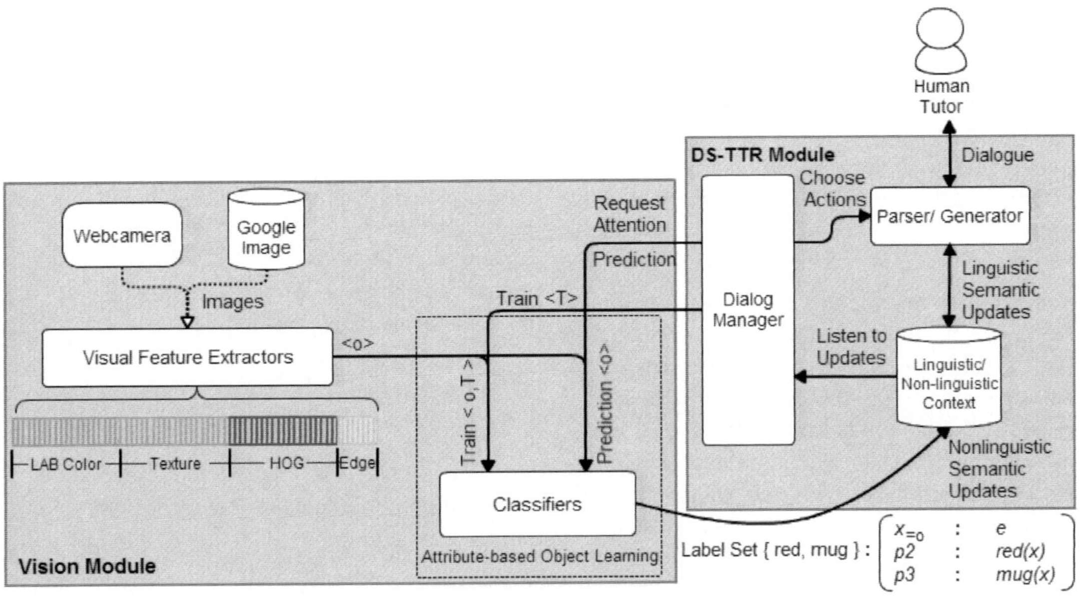

Figure 2: Architecture of the simulated teachable system

attribute relations and infer the corresponding object classes using a probabilistic model. In this paper, we reimplement the DAP zero-shot learning model based on Lampert's work; but since we are here concerned only with attribute classification we only test the first tier of their algorithm for attribute classification. (Note that although both (Farhadi et al., 2009) and (Lampert et al., 2014) implement a SVM classifier for each attribute, DAP learns the supervised model with the linearly combined χ^2-kernels rather than the original visual representations.) Note that the implementation of the DAP model is not identical to that of (Lampert et al., 2014), so our results are not directly comparable to that paper. We used the Libsvm 3.0 library (Chang and Lin, 2011), differing from the Shogun library in the original implementation for learning visual classifiers. To more directly compare the DAP model with other methods, we moreover generated the visual representation using the feature extraction algorithms by (Farhadi et al., 2009) instead of the original methods.

All models will output attribute-based label sets for novel unseen images by predicting binary label vectors. We build visual representations and binary label vectors as inputs to train new classifiers for learning attributes, as explained in the following subsections.

3.1.1 Visual Feature Representation

Following the feature extraction methods proposed by (Farhadi et al., 2009), we extract a feature representation consisting of the base features for learning to classify and describe novel objects, i.e. the colour space for colour attributes, texture for materials, visual words for object components, as well as edges for shapes.

Colour descriptors, consisting of L*A*B colour space values, are extracted for each pixel and then are quantized to the nearest 128 k-means centres. These descriptors inside the bounding box are binned into individual histograms. Edges and their orientations are detected using a MATLAB canny edge detector, which contributes to finding both edges and boundaries of objects within an image. Detected edges are quantized into 8 unsigned bins. A texture descriptor is computed for each pixel and then quantized to the nearest 256 k-means centres. Finally, object visual words are built in HOG descriptors using 8x8 blocks, a 4-pixel step size, and quantized into 512 k-means centres.

The feature extractor in the vision module presents a feature matrix with dimensions $w \times 9751$, where w is the number of training instances, and each training instance has a 9751-dimensional vector generated by stacking all quantized features, as shown in Figure 2.

3.1.2 Binary Label Vectors

For learning multi-attribute objects, the multi-label models require a label vector for each training instance. In the interactive system, an instance χ and its related label set $\eta \subseteq Y$ are given by the feature extractor and DS-TTR parser individually, where Y is a total collection of attribute-based labels. We suppose $\overrightarrow{l}$ is the binary label vector for χ, where its i-th component $\overrightarrow{l}(i)(i \in \eta)$ will take the value 1 if $i \in Y$ and -1 otherwise. Eventually, the system builds a binary label matrix with dimensions $w \times n$, where w is the number of instances and n is the total number of labels for all training instances. Each instance contains a full binary label vector. The label vectors and feature representations are used to learn new classifiers once novel object instances are learned incrementally from interaction.

3.2 Dynamic Syntax (DS)

The DS module is a word-by-word incremental semantic parser/generator, based around the Dynamic Syntax (DS) grammar framework (Cann et al., 2005) especially suited to the fragmentary and highly contextual nature of dialogue. In DS, dialogue is modelled as the interactive and incremental construction of contextual and semantic representations (Purver et al., 2011). The contextual representations afforded by DS are of the fine-grained semantic content that is jointly negotiated/agreed upon by the interlocutors, as a result of processing questions and answers, clarification requests, corrections, acceptances, etc (see Eshghi et al (2015) for an account of how this can be achieved grammar-internally as a low-level semantic update process). Recent versions of DS incorporate Type Theory with Records (TTR) as the logical formalism in which meaning representations are couched (Purver et al., 2011; Eshghi et al., 2012), due to its useful properties. Here we do not introduce DS due to space limitations but proceed to introducing TTR.

3.3 Type Theory with Records

Type Theory with Records (TTR) is an extension of standard type theory shown to be useful in semantics and dialogue modelling (Cooper, 2005; Ginzburg, 2012). TTR is particularly well-suited to our problem here as it allows information from various modalities, including vision and language, to be represented within a single semantic framework (see e.g. Larsson (2013); Dobnik et al. (2012) who use it to model the semantics of spatial language and perceptual classification).

In TTR, logical forms are specified as *record types* (RTs), which are sequences of *fields* of the form $[\, l : T \,]$ containing a label l and a type T. RTs can be witnessed (i.e. judged true) by *records* of that type, where a record is a sequence of label-value pairs $[\, l = v \,]$. We say that $[\, l = v \,]$ is of type $[\, l : T \,]$ just in case v is of type T.

$$R_1 : \begin{bmatrix} l_1 & : T_1 \\ l_{2=a} & : T_2 \\ l_{3=p(l_2)} & : T_3 \end{bmatrix} \quad R_2 : \begin{bmatrix} l_1 & : T_1 \\ l_2 & : T_{2'} \end{bmatrix} \quad R_3 : []$$

Figure 3: Example TTR record types

Fields can be *manifest*, i.e. given a singleton type e.g. $[\, l : T_a \,]$ where T_a is the type of which only a is a member; here, we write this using the syntactic sugar $[\, l_{=a} : T \,]$. Fields can also be *dependent* on fields preceding them (i.e. higher) in the record type (see Fig. 3).

The standard subtype relation $\sqsubseteq$ can be defined for record types: $R_1 \sqsubseteq R_2$ if for all fields $[\, l : T_2 \,]$ in R_2, R_1 contains $[\, l : T_1 \,]$ where $T_1 \sqsubseteq T_2$. In Figure 3, $R_1 \sqsubseteq R_2$ if $T_2 \sqsubseteq T_{2'}$, and both R_1 and R_2 are subtypes of R_3. This subtyping relation allows semantic information to be incrementally specified, i.e. record types can be indefinitely extended with more information/constraints. For us here, this is a key feature since it allows the system to encode *partial* knowledge about objects, and for this knowledge (e.g. object attributes) to be extended in a principled way, as and when this information becomes available.

3.4 Integration

Fig. 2 shows how the various parts of the system interact. At any point in time, the system has access to an ontology of (object) types and attributes encoded as a set of TTR Record Types, whose individual atomic symbols, such as 'red' or 'mug' are grounded in the set of classifiers trained so far.

Given a set of individuated objects in a scene, encoded as a TTR Record (see above), the system can utilise its existing ontology to output some maximal set of Record Types characterising these objects (see e.g. Fig. 1). Since these representations are shared by the DS-TTR module, they provide a direct interface between perceptual classification and semantic processing in dialogue: they can be used directly at any point to generate utterances, or ask questions about the objects.

On the other hand, the DS-TTR parser incrementally produces Record Types (RT), representing the meaning jointly established by the tutor and the system so far. In this domain, this is ultimately one or more type judgements, i.e. that some scene/image/object is judged to be of a particular type, e.g. in Fig. 1 that the individuated object, $o1$ is a red mug. These jointly negotiated type judgements then go on to provide training instances for the classifiers. In general, the training instances are of the form, $\langle O, T \rangle$, where O is an image/scene segment (an object), and T, a record type. T is then converted automatically to an input format suitable for specific classifiers; e.g. the dialogues in Fig. 1 provide the following instances to our classifiers: $\langle o1, \{red, mug\} \rangle$ and $\langle o2, \{red, book\} \rangle$.

What sets our approach apart from other work is that these types are constructed/negotiated interactively, and so both the system and the tutor can contribute to a single representation (see e.g. second row of Fig. 1).

4 Experiments and Results

4.1 Datasets for Attribute-based classification

In order to compare the different classifiers with previous work (Farhadi et al., 2009), we perform our experiments on a benchmark dataset of natural object-based images with attribute annotations – the aPascal-aYahoo data set[3] – which is introduced by Farhadi et al. The aPascal-aYahoo data set has two subsets: the Pascal VOC 2008 dataset and the aYahoo dataset. The Pascal VOC 2008 dataset is created for visual object classifications and detections. The aPascal data set covers 20 attribute-labelled classes and each class contains a number of samples, ranging from 150 to 1000. The aYahoo dataset, as a supplement of the aPascal dataset, contains objects similar to aPascal, but with different correlations between attributes. The aYahoo dataset only contains 12 objects classes. Images in both aPascal and aYahoo sets are annotated with 64 binary attributes, covering shape and material as well as object components (see table 1). We use the 6340 images selected by (Farhadi et al., 2009) from the aPascal dataset for training and use the whole aYahoo dataset with 2644 images as the test set. As both aPascal and aYahoo data sets are imbalanced in the number of positive instances for each attribute, as shown in table 1, this might affect the performance of the models on attribute classification.

[3]http://vision.cs.uiuc.edu/attributes/

4.2 Experiment Setup

We test how well the different classifiers work on learning object attributes. We implemented several classification models – MLkNN, DAP, and SVMs as described in Section 3.1. Most work on attribute classification reports the Precision and Recall only for *object classes* – which are computed using the attribute labels – but we are directly interested in the performance of the attribute classifiers themselves. Thus we report Precision, Recall, and F1-Score for the attribute labels for each model. We also show the average scores across all attributes in table 2.

4.3 Results

We first plot the Precision and Recall for each attribute for the different models, as shown in figures 4 and 5. We take Precision to be 1 where the number of True Positives and False Negatives are both 0 for an attribute (otherwise it would be undefined).

Figures 4 - 7 compare the different methods for each attribute in terms for Precision, Recall, F1, and AUC (Area Under ROC Curve). The AUC scores are computed using an open library for computer vision algorithms – Vlfeat (Vedaldi and Fulkerson, 2010).

Table 2 shows the average scores for each method, computed across all of the attributes. The results show that DAP generally has better performance across all of the attributes, although each method has specific strengths and weaknesses.

5 Discussion

The results presented above show that while the models sometimes perform quite well on specific attributes, the performance over all attributes in general is rather poor. But we note that the shapes of the plots in the Precision and the Macro-F1 Figures, 4 and 6, are very similar, showing that the performance of the algorithms are correlated with external factors, certainly including the number of positive training instances, but also how distinctive (easy to detect) an attribute generally is. For example, the attribute 'Furry' with 250 training instances is performing relatively well using all three algorithms while other attributes with sim-

Attribute Label	aPascal	aYahoo	Attribute Label	aPascal	aYahoo	Attribute Label	aPascal	aYahoo
2D Boxy	207	146	3D Boxy	393	752	Round	39	179
Vert Cyl	195	334	Horiz Cyl	94	286	Occluded	1913	778
Tail	184	529	Head	1737	1157	Ear	1097	1048
Snout	237	708	Nose	995	345	Mouth	930	332
Hair	1095	216	Face	1022	392	Eye	1183	1061
Torso	1538	1024	Hand	811	364	Arm	1080	383
Leg	994	922	Foot/Shoe	604	719	Wing	114	11
Window	304	167	Row Wind	86	224	Wheel	336	64
Door	192	13	Headlight	162	36	Taillight	104	5
Side mirror	150	71	Exhaust	50	41	Handlebars	92	37
Engine	35	71	Text	84	388	Horn	4	145
Rein	32	284	Saddle	20	121	Skin	1396	161
Metal	581	739	Plastic	260	459	Wood	195	167
Cloth	1591	123	Furry	250	996	Glass	180	34
Feather	99	1	Wool	12	15	Clear	32	42
Shiny	432	527	Leather	6	85			

Table 1: The Number of Positive instances on each attribute in aPascal-aYahoo Datasets (aPascal for training set, aYahoo for testing Set, attributes with no testing instances removed)

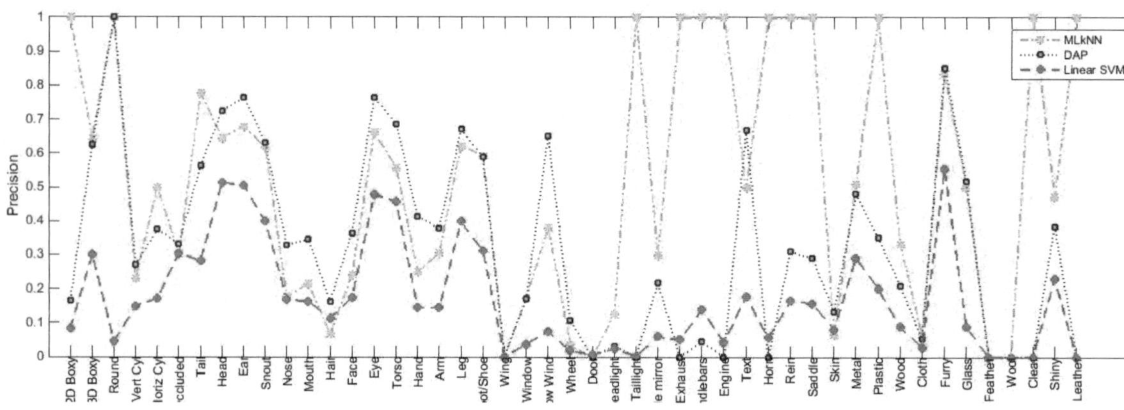

Figure 4: Precisions on each attribute for each method: MLkNN, DAP and Linear SVM (note that Precision is defined as 1 when there are in fact no True positives or False positives returned)

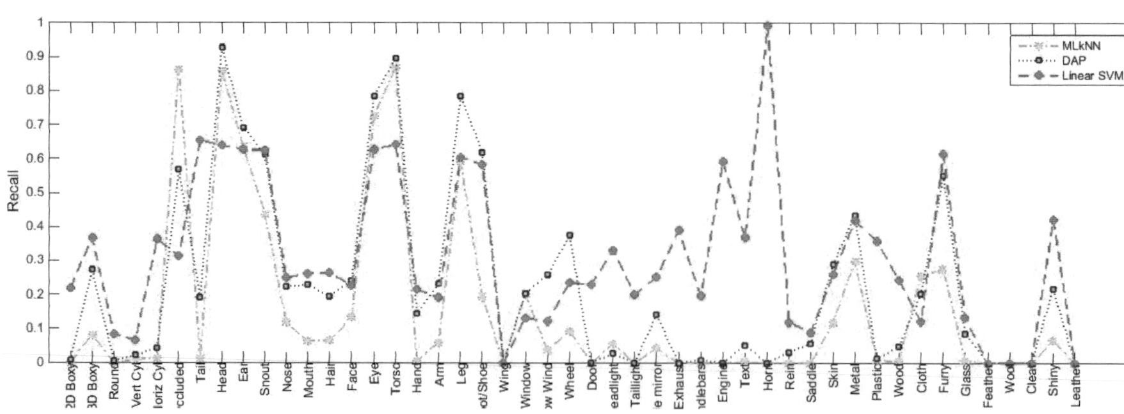

Figure 5: Recalls on each attribute for each method (MLkNN, DAP and Linear SVM)

ilar numbers of training instances are performing far worse.

Since our ultimate goal here is to create a full dialogue system that can learn concepts (word

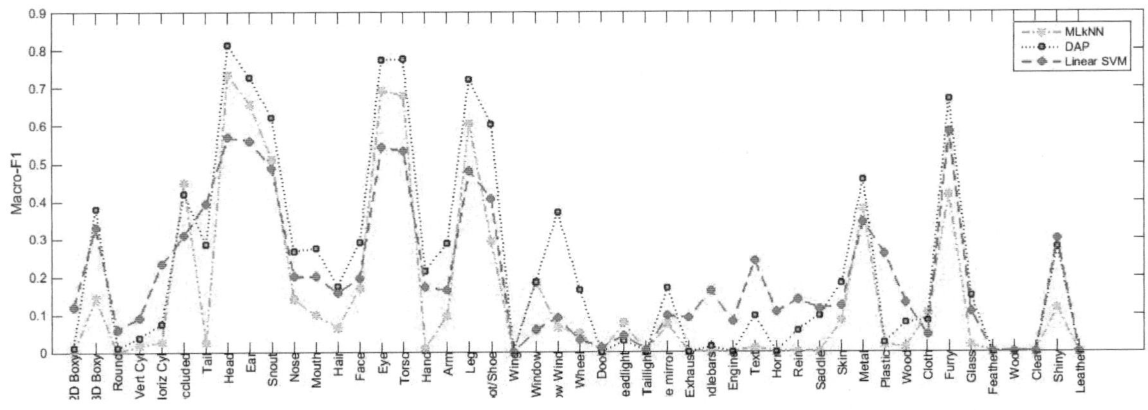

Figure 6: Macro-F1 on each attribute for each method (MLkNN, DAP and Linear SVM)

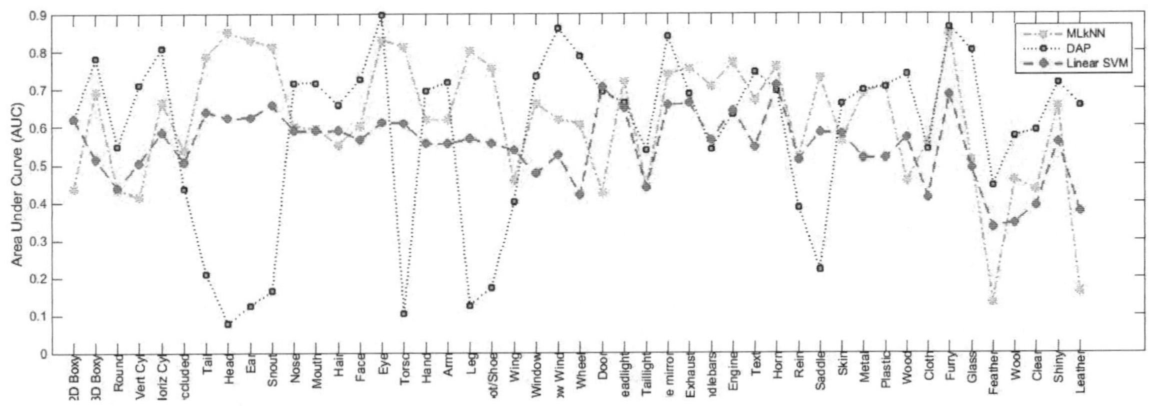

Figure 7: Area Under ROC curve for each attribute for each method (MLkNN, DAP and Linear SVM)

meanings) from human tutors, these results would lead us to pick, at least in an initial proof-of-concept system, attributes that show rapid learning rates. Presumably this is why prior work on this problem has often used 'toy' images where real image processing is not required (e.g. (Roy, 2002; Kennington et al., 2015)).

What we would need ultimately are attribute classifier learning methods which can operate effectively on small numbers of examples, and which can improve performance robustly when new examples are presented, without "unlearning" previous examples and without needing long retraining times. The dialogue abilities of the overall system will allow correction and clarification interactions to correct false positives (e.g "it's not red it's green") and other errors, and the attribute classification model must allow for such rapid retraining.

Finally we note that none of these algorithms are *incremental*. Incremental learning methods (Kankuekul et al., 2012; Tsai et al., 2014; Furao et al., 2007; Zheng et al., 2013) have been developed to train object classification networks without abandoning previously learned knowledge or destroying the old trained prototypes. These methods (such as (Kankuekul et al., 2012)) could enable systems to label known/unknown attributes gradually through NL interaction with human tutors. Incremental learning approaches can also speed up the object learning/prediction process and the system responses, rather than taking a long computational time.

We will explore these approaches in future work, to learn objects and their perceptual attributes gradually from conversational Human-Robot interaction.

Model	average Precision	average Recall	average Macro-F1
MLkNN	0.5186	0.1537	0.2372
DAP	0.3326	0.2276	0.2703
SVMs	0.1676	0.3118	0.2180

Table 2: Average scores across attribute labels for each method, trained on aPascal and tested on aYahoo

6 Conclusion

We are developing a multimodal interface to explore the effectiveness of situated dialogue with a human tutor for learning perceptually-grounded word meanings. The system integrates the semantic/contextual representations from an incremental semantic parser/generator, DS-TTR, with attribute classification models to evaluate their performance.

We compared the performance (Precision, Recall, F1, AUC) of several state-of-the-art attribute classifiers for the purpose of interactive language grounding (MLKNN, DAP, and SVMs), on the aPascal-aYahoo datasets. The results show that the models can sometimes perform quite well on specific attributes (e.g. *head, ears, torso*), but the performance over all attributes in general is rather poor. This leads us to either restrict the attributes actually used in a real system, or to explore other methods, such as incremental learning.

The immediate future direction our research will take is in developing and evaluating a fully implemented system involving classifiers incorporated with incremental learning algorithms for each visual attribute, DS-TTR, and a pro-active dialogue manager that formulates the right questions to gain information and increase accuracy.

We envisage the use of such technology in multimodal systems interacting with humans, such as robots and smart spaces.

Acknowledgements

This research is partially supported by the EPSRC, under grant number EP/M01553X/1 (BABBLE project[4]).

References

Elia Bruni, Nam-Khanh Tran, and Marco Baroni. 2014. Multimodal distributional semantics. *J. Artif. Intell. Res.(JAIR)*, 49(1–47).

Ronnie Cann, Ruth Kempson, and Lutz Marten. 2005. *The Dynamics of Language*. Elsevier, Oxford.

Chih-Chung Chang and Chih-Jen Lin. 2011. LIBSVM: A library for support vector machines. *ACM TIST*, 2(3):27.

Robin Cooper. 2005. Records and record types in semantic theory. *Journal of Logic and Computation*, 15(2):99–112.

Simon Dobnik, Robin Cooper, and Staffan Larsson. 2012. Modelling language, action, and perception in type theory with records. In *Proceedings of the 7th International Workshop on Constraint Solving and Language Processing (CSLPÄô12)*, pages 51–63.

Arash Eshghi, Julian Hough, Matthew Purver, Ruth Kempson, and Eleni Gregoromichelaki. 2012. Conversational interactions: Capturing dialogue dynamics. In S. Larsson and L. Borin, editors, *From Quantification to Conversation: Festschrift for Robin Cooper on the occasion of his 65th birthday*, volume 19 of *Tributes*, pages 325–349. College Publications, London.

A. Eshghi, C. Howes, E. Gregoromichelaki, J. Hough, and M. Purver. 2015. Feedback in conversation as incremental semantic update. In *Proceedings of the 11th International Conference on Computational Semantics (IWCS 2015)*, London, UK. Association for Computational Linguisitics.

Ali Farhadi, Ian Endres, Derek Hoiem, and David Forsyth. 2009. Describing objects by their attributes. In *Proceedings of the IEEE Computer Society Conference on Computer Vision and Pattern Recognition (CVPR*.

Ali Farhadi, Ian Endres, and Derek Hoiem. 2010. Attribute-centric recognition for cross-category generalization. In *Computer Vision and Pattern Recognition (CVPR), 2010 IEEE Conference on*, pages 2352–2359. IEEE.

Shen Furao, Tomotaka Ogura, and Osamu Hasegawa. 2007. An enhanced self-organizing incremental neural network for online unsupervised learning. *Neural Networks*, 20(8):893–903.

Jonathan Ginzburg. 2012. *The Interactive Stance: Meaning for Conversation*. Oxford University Press.

Pichai Kankuekul, Aram Kawewong, Sirinart Tangruamsub, and Osamu Hasegawa. 2012. Online incremental attribute-based zero-shot learning. In

[4]https://sites.google.com/site/hwinteractionlab/babble

2012 IEEE Conference on Computer Vision and Pattern Recognition, Providence, RI, USA, June 16-21, 2012, pages 3657–3664.

Andrej Karpathy and Li Fei-Fei. 2014. Deep visual-semantic alignments for generating image descriptions. *CoRR*, abs/1412.2306.

Casey Kennington, Livia Dia, and David Schlangen. 2015. A discriminative model for perceptually-grounded incremental reference resolution. In *Proceedings of the 11th International Conference on Computational Semantics*, pages 195–205.

Ryan Kiros, Ruslan Salakhutdinov, and Rich Zemel. 2014. Multimodal neural language models. In *Proceedings of the 31st International Conference on Machine Learning (ICML-14)*, pages 595–603.

Thomas Kollar, Jayant Krishnamurthy, and Grant Strimel. 2013. Toward interactive grounded language acqusition. In *Robotics: Science and Systems*.

Evan A. Krause, Michael Zillich, Thomas Emrys Williams, and Matthias Scheutz. 2014. Learning to recognize novel objects in one shot through human-robot interactions in natural language dialogues. In *Proceedings of the Twenty-Eighth AAAI Conference on Artificial Intelligence, July 27 -31, 2014, Québec City, Québec, Canada.*, pages 2796–2802.

Jayant Krishnamurthy and Thomas Kollar. 2013. Jointly learning to parse and perceive: Connecting natural language to the physical world. *TACL*, 1:193–206.

Christoph H. Lampert, Hannes Nickisch, and Stefan Harmeling. 2014. Attribute-based classification for zero-shot visual object categorization. *IEEE Trans. Pattern Anal. Mach. Intell.*, 36(3):453–465.

Staffan Larsson. 2013. Formal semantics for perceptual classification. *Journal of logic and computation*.

Fei-Fei Li, Robert Fergus, and Pietro Perona. 2006. One-shot learning of object categories. *IEEE Trans. Pattern Anal. Mach. Intell.*, 28(4):594–611.

Fei-Fei Li, Robert Fergus, and Pietro Perona. 2007. Learning generative visual models from few training examples: An incremental bayesian approach tested on 101 object categories. *Computer Vision and Image Understanding*, 106(1):59–70.

Cynthia Matuszek, Nicholas FitzGerald, Luke Zettlemoyer, Liefeng Bo, and Dieter Fox. 2012. A joint model of language and perception for grounded attribute learning. In *Proc. of the 2012 International Conference on Machine Learning*, Edinburgh, Scotland, June.

Matthew Purver, Arash Eshghi, and Julian Hough. 2011. Incremental semantic construction in a dialogue system. In J. Bos and S. Pulman, editors, *Proceedings of the 9th International Conference on Computational Semantics*, pages 365–369, Oxford, UK, January.

Deb Roy. 2002. A trainable visually-grounded spoken language generation system. In *Proceedings of the International Conference of Spoken Language Processing*.

Carina Silberer and Mirella Lapata. 2014. Learning grounded meaning representations with autoencoders. In *Proceedings of the 52nd Annual Meeting of the Association for Computational Linguistics (Volume 1: Long Papers)*, volume 1, pages 721–732, Baltimore, Maryland, June. Association for Computational Linguistics.

Danijel Skocaj, Matej Kristan, Alen Vrecko, Marko Mahnic, Miroslav Janícek, Geert-Jan M. Kruijff, Marc Hanheide, Nick Hawes, Thomas Keller, Michael Zillich, and Kai Zhou. 2011. A system for interactive learning in dialogue with a tutor. In *2011 IEEE/RSJ International Conference on Intelligent Robots and Systems, IROS 2011, San Francisco, CA, USA, September 25-30, 2011*, pages 3387–3394.

Richard Socher, Andrej Karpathy, Quoc V Le, Christopher D Manning, and Andrew Y Ng. 2014. Grounded compositional semantics for finding and describing images with sentences. *Transactions of the Association for Computational Linguistics*, 2:207–218.

Yuyin Sun, Liefeng Bo, and Dieter Fox. 2013. Attribute based object identification. In *Robotics and Automation (ICRA), 2013 IEEE International Conference on*, pages 2096–2103. IEEE.

Cheng-Hao Tsai, Chieh-Yen Lin, and Chih-Jen Lin. 2014. Incremental and decremental training for linear classification. In *The 20th ACM SIGKDD International Conference on Knowledge Discovery and Data Mining, KDD '14, New York, NY, USA - August 24 - 27, 2014*, pages 343–352.

Andrea Vedaldi and Brian Fulkerson. 2010. Vlfeat: an open and portable library of computer vision algorithms. In *Proceedings of the 18th International Conference on Multimedia 2010, Firenze, Italy, October 25-29, 2010*, pages 1469–1472.

Min-Ling Zhang and Zhi-Hua Zhou. 2007. ML-KNN: A lazy learning approach to multi-label learning. *Pattern Recognition*, 40(7):2038–2048.

Jun Zheng, Furao Shen, Hongjun Fan, and Jinxi Zhao. 2013. An online incremental learning support vector machine for large-scale data. *Neural Computing and Applications*, 22(5):1023–1035.

Generating Semantically Precise Scene Graphs from Textual Descriptions for Improved Image Retrieval

Sebastian Schuster, Ranjay Krishna, Angel Chang,
Li Fei-Fei, and **Christopher D. Manning**

Stanford University, Stanford, CA 94305
{sebschu,rak248,angelx,feifeili,manning}@stanford.edu

Abstract

Semantically complex queries which include attributes of objects and relations between objects still pose a major challenge to image retrieval systems. Recent work in computer vision has shown that a graph-based semantic representation called a *scene graph* is an effective representation for very detailed image descriptions and for complex queries for retrieval. In this paper, we show that scene graphs can be effectively created automatically from a natural language scene description. We present a rule-based and a classifier-based scene graph parser whose output can be used for image retrieval. We show that including relations and attributes in the query graph outperforms a model that only considers objects and that using the output of our parsers is almost as effective as using human-constructed scene graphs (Recall@10 of 27.1% vs. 33.4%). Additionally, we demonstrate the general usefulness of parsing to scene graphs by showing that the output can also be used to generate 3D scenes.

1 Introduction

One of the big remaining challenges in image retrieval is to be able to search for very specific images. The continuously growing number of images that are available on the web gives users access to almost any picture they can imagine, but in order to find these images users have to be able to express what they are looking for in a detailed and efficient way. For example, if a user wants to find an image of *a boy wearing a t-shirt with a plane on it*, an image retrieval system has to understand that the image should contain a boy who is wearing a shirt and that on that shirt is a picture of a plane.

Figure 1: Actual results using a popular image search engine (top row) and ideal results (bottom row) for the query *a boy wearing a t-shirt with a plane on it.*

Keyword-based image retrieval systems are clearly unable to deal with the rich semantics of such a query (Liu et al., 2007). They might be able to retrieve images that contain a boy, a t-shirt and a plane but they are unable to interpret the relationships and attributes of these objects which is crucial for retrieving the correct images. As shown in Figure 1, a possible but incorrect combination of these objects is that a boy is wearing a t-shirt and playing with a toy plane.

One proposed solution to these issues is the mapping of image descriptions to multi-modal embeddings of sentences and images and using these embeddings to retrieve images (Plummer et al., 2015; Karpathy et al., 2014; Kiros et al., 2015; Mao et al., 2015; Chrupala et al., 2015). However, one problem of these models is that they are trained on single-sentence captions which are typically unable to capture the rich content of visual scenes in their entirety. Further, the coverage of the description highly depends on the subjectivity of human perception (Rui et al., 1999). Certain details such as whether there is a plane on the boy's shirt or not might seem irrelevant to the per-

Proceedings of the 2015 Workshop on Vision and Language (VL'15), pages 70–80,
Lisbon, Portugal, 18 September 2015.

son who writes the caption, but for another user this difference might determine whether a result is useful or not.

Johnson et al. (2015) try to solve these problems by annotating images with a graph-based semantic representation called a *scene graph* which explicitly captures the objects in an image, their attributes and the relations between objects. They plausibly argue that paragraph-long image descriptions written in natural language are currently too complex to be mapped automatically to images and instead they show that very detailed image descriptions in the form of scene graphs can be obtained via crowdsourcing. They also show that they can perform semantic image retrieval on unannotated images using partial scene graphs.

However, one big shortcoming of their model is that it requires the user to enter a query in the form of a scene graph instead of an image description in natural language which is unlikely to find widespread adoption among potential users. To address this problem, we propose a new task of parsing image descriptions to scene graphs which can then be used as a query for image retrieval.

While our main goal is to show the effectiveness of parsing image descriptions for image retrieval, we believe that scene graphs can be a useful intermediate representation for many applications that involve text and images. One great advantage of such an intermediate representation is the resulting modularity which allows independent development, improvement and reuse of NLP, vision and graphics subsystems. For example, we can reuse a scene graph parser for systems that generate 2D-scenes (Zitnick et al., 2013) or 3D-scenes (Chang et al., 2014) which require input in the form of similar graph-based representations to which a scene graph can be easily converted.

In this paper, we introduce the task of parsing image descriptions to scene graphs. We build and evaluate a rule-based and a classifier-based scene graph parser which map from dependency syntax representations to scene graphs. We use these parsers in a pipeline which first parses an image description to a scene graph and then uses this scene graph as input to a retrieval system. We show that such a pipeline outperforms a system which only considers objects in the description and we show that the output of both of our parsers is almost as effective as human-constructed scene graphs in retrieving images. Lastly, we demonstrate the more general applicability of our parsers by generating 3D scenes from their output.

We make our parsers and models available at http://nlp.stanford.edu/software/scenegraph-parser.shtml.

2 Task Description

Our overall task is retrieving images from image descriptions which we split into two sub-tasks: Parsing the description to scene graphs and retrieving images with scene graphs. In this paper, we focus exclusively on the first task. For the latter, we use a reimplementation of the system by Johnson et al. (2015) which we briefly describe in the next section.

2.1 Image Retrieval System

The image retrieval system by Johnson et al. (2015) is based on a conditional random field (CRF) (Lafferty et al., 2001) model which – unlike the typical CRFs in NLP – is not a chain model but instead capturing image region proximity. This model ranks images based on how likely it is that a given scene graph is grounded to them. The model first identifies potential object regions in the image and then computes the most likely assignment of objects to regions considering the classes of the objects, their attributes and their relations. The likelihood of a scene graph being grounded to an image is then approximated as the likelihood of the most likely assignment of objects to regions.

2.2 Parsing to Scene Graphs

The task of parsing image descriptions to scene graphs is defined as following. Given a set of object classes C, a set of relation types R, a set of attribute types A, and a sentence S we want to parse S to a scene graph $G = (O, E)$. $O = \{o_1, ..., o_n\}$ is a set of objects mentioned in S and each o_i is a pair (c_i, A_i) where $c_i \in C$ is the class of o_i and $A_i \subseteq A$ are the attributes of o_i. $E \subseteq O \times R \times O$ is the set of relations between two objects in the graph. For example, given the sentence S = *"A man is looking at his black watch"* we want to extract the two objects $o_1 = (man, \emptyset)$ and $o_2 = (watch, \{black\})$, and the relations $e_1 = (o_1, look\ at, o_2)$ and $e_2 = (o_1, have, o_2)$. The sets C, R and A consist of all the classes and types which are present in the training data.

2.3 Data

We reuse a dataset which we collected for a different task using Amazon Mechanical Turk (AMT) in a similar manner as Johnson et al. (2015) and Plummer et al. (2015). We originally annotated 4,999 images from the intersection of the YFCC100m (Thomee et al., 2015) and Microsoft COCO (Lin et al., 2014b) datasets. However, unlike previous work, we split the process into two separate passes with the goal of increasing the number of objects and relations per image.

In the first pass, AMT workers were shown an image and asked to write a one sentence description of the entire image or any part of it. To get diverse descriptions, workers were shown the previous descriptions written by other workers for the same image and were asked to describe something about the image which had not been described by anyone else. We ensured diversity in sentence descriptions by a real-time BLEU score (Papineni et al., 2002) threshold between a new sentence and all the previous ones.

In the second pass, workers were presented again with an image and with one of its sentences. They were asked to draw bounding boxes around all the objects in the image which were mentioned in the sentence and to describe their attributes and the relations between them. This step was repeated for each sentence of an image and finally the partial scene graphs are combined to one large scene graph for each image. While the main purpose of the two-pass data collection was to increase the number of objects and relations per image, it also provides as a byproduct a mapping between sentences and partial scene graphs which gives us a corpus of sentence-scene graph pairs that we can use to train a parser.

2.3.1 Preprocessing

The AMT workers were allowed to use any label for objects, relations and attributes and consequently there is a lot of variation in the data. We perform several preprocessing steps to canonicalize the data. First, we remove leading and trailing articles from all labels. Then we replace all the words in the labels with their lemmata and finally we split all attributes with a conjunction such as *red and green* into two individual attributes.

We also follow Johnson et al. (2015) and discard all objects, relations and attributes whose class or type appears less than 30 times in the entire dataset for the following two reasons. First and foremost, computer vision systems require multiple training examples for each class and type to be able to learn useful generalizations, and second, rare classes and types are often a result of AMT workers making mistakes or not understanding the task properly. As we make the assumption that the scene graph of one sentence is complete, i.e., that it captures all the information of the sentence, we have to apply a more aggressive filtering which discards the entire scene graph of a sentence in case one of its objects, attributes or relations is discarded due to the threshold. In case we discard all sentences of an image, we discard the entire image from our data. Despite the aggressive filtering, the average number of objects, relations and attributes per image only drops by 30-45% and we only discard around 9% of the images (see Table 1).

	Raw	Processed	Filtered
Images	4,999	4,999	4,524
Sentences	88,188	88,188	50,448
Sentences per image	17.6	17.6	11.2
Object classes	18,515	15,734	798
Attribute types	7,348	6,442	277
Relation types	9,274	7,507	131
Objects per image	21.2	21.2	14.6
Attributes per image	16.2	16.4	10.7
Relations per image	18.6	18.6	10.3
Attributes per sent.	0.92	0.93	0.93
Relations per sent.	1.06	1.06	0.96

Table 1: Aggregate statistics of the raw, canonicalized (processed) and filtered datasets.

3 Scene Graph Parsers

We implement two parsers: a rule-based parser and a classifier-based parser. Both of our parsers operate on a linguistic representation which we refer to as a *semantic graph*. We obtain semantic graphs by parsing the image descriptions to dependency trees followed by several tree transformations. In this section, we first describe these tree transformations and then explain how our two parsers translate the semantic graph to a scene graph.

3.1 Semantic Graphs

A Universal Dependencies (de Marneffe et al., 2014) parse is in many ways close to a shallow semantic representation and therefore a good starting point for parsing image descriptions to scene

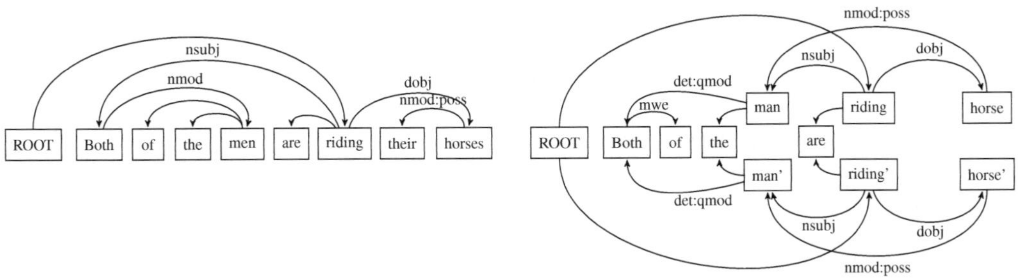

Figure 2: Dependency tree and final semantic graph of a sentence. *men* is promoted to be the subject; *men*, *riding*, and *horses* are duplicated; and *their* is deleted following coreference resolution.

graphs. Basic dependency trees, however, tend to follow the linguistic structure of sentences too closely which requires some post-processing of the parses to make them more useful for a semantic task. We start with the *enhanced* dependency representation output by the Stanford Parser v3.5.2 (Klein and Manning, 2003)[1] and then perform three additional processing steps to deal with complex quantificational modifiers, to resolve pronouns and to handle plural nouns.

3.1.1 Quantificational modifiers

Several common expressions with light nouns such as *a lot of* or *a dozen of* semantically act like quantificational determiners (Simone and Masini, 2014). From a syntactic point of view, however, these expressions are the head of the following noun phrase. While one of the principles of the Universal Dependencies representation is the primacy of content words (de Marneffe et al., 2014), light nouns are treated like any other noun. To make our dependency trees better suited for semantic tasks, we change the structure of all light noun expressions from a manually compiled list. We make the first word the head of all the other words in the expression and then make this new multi-word expression a dependent of the following noun phrase. This step guarantees that the semantic graph for *both cars* and for *both of the cars* have similar structures in which the semantically salient word *cars* is the head.

3.1.2 Pronoun resolution

Some image descriptions such as *"a bed with a pillow on it"* contain personal pronouns. To recover all the relations between objects in this sentence it is crucial to know that *it* refers to the object *a bed* and therefore we try to resolve all pronouns. We found in practice that document-level coreference systems (e.g. Lee et al. (2013)) were too conservative in resolving pronouns and hence we implement an intrasential pronoun resolver inspired by the first three rules of the Hobbs algorithm (Hobbs, 1978) which we modified to operate on dependency trees instead of constituency trees. We evaluate this method using 200 randomly selected image descriptions containing pronouns. Our pronoun resolver has an accuracy of 88.5% which is significantly higher than the accuracy of 52.8% achieved by the coreference system of Lee et al. (2013).

3.1.3 Plural nouns

Plural nouns are known to be a major challenge in semantics in general (Nouwen, 2015), and also in our task. One particular theoretical issue is the collective-distributive ambiguity of sentences with multiple plural nouns. For example, to obtain the intended distributive reading of *"three men are wearing jeans"* we have to extract three *man* objects and three *jeans* objects and we have to connect each *man* object to a different *jeans* object. On the other hand, to get the correct parse of *"three men are carrying a piano"* we probably want to consider the collective reading and extract only one *piano* object. A perfect model thus requires a lot of world knowledge. In practice, however, the distributive reading seems to be far more common so we only consider this case.

To make the dependency graph more similar to scene graphs, we copy individual nodes of the graph according to the value of their numeric modifier. We limit the number of copies per node to 20

[1] We augment the parser's training data with the Brown corpus (Marcus et al., 1993) to improve its performance on image descriptions which are often very different from sentences found in newswire corpora.

as our data only contains scene graphs with less than 20 objects of the same class. In case a plural noun lacks such a modifier we make exactly one copy of the node.

Figure 2 shows the original dependency tree and the final semantic graph for the sentence "*Both of the men are riding their horses*".

3.2 Rule-Based Parser

Our rule-based parser extracts objects, relations and attributes directly from the semantic graph. We define in total nine dependency patterns using Semgrex[2] expressions. These patterns capture the following constructions and phenomena:

- Adjectival modifiers
- Subject-predicate-object constructions and subject-predicate constructions without an object
- Copular constructions
- Prepositional phrases
- Possessive constructions
- Passive constructions
- Clausal modifiers of nouns

With the exception of possessives for which we manually add a *have* relation, all objects, relations and attributes are words from the semantic graph. For example, for the semantic graph in Figure 2, the *subject-predicate-object* pattern matches $man \xleftarrow{nsubj} riding \xrightarrow{dobj} horse$ and $man' \xleftarrow{nsubj} riding' \xrightarrow{dobj} horse'$. From these matches we extract two *man* and two *horse* objects and add *ride* relations to the two *man-horse* pairs. Further, the *possessive* pattern matches $man \xleftarrow{nmod:poss} horse$ and $man' \xleftarrow{nmod:poss} horse'$ and we add *have* relations to the two *man-horse* pairs.

3.3 Classifier-Based Parser

Our classifier-based parser consists of two components. First, we extract all candidate objects and attributes, and second we predict relations between objects and the attributes of all objects.

[2] http://nlp.stanford.edu/software/tregex.shtml

3.3.1 Object and Attribute Extraction

We use the semantic graph to extract all object and attribute candidates. In a first step we extract all nouns, all adjectives and all intransitive verbs from the semantic graph. As this does not guarantee that the extracted objects and attributes belong to known object classes or attribute types and as our image retrieval model can only make use of known classes and types, we predict for each noun the most likely object class and for each adjective and intransitive verb the most likely attribute type. To predict classes and types, we use an L_2-regularized maximum entropy classifier which uses the original word, the lemma and the 100-dimensional GloVe word vector (Pennington et al., 2014) as features.

3.3.2 Relation Prediction

The last step of the parsing pipeline is to determine the attributes of each object and the relations between objects. We consider both of these tasks as a pairwise classification task. For each pair (x_1, x_2) where x_1 is an object and x_2 is an object or an attribute we predict the relation y which can be any relation seen in the training data, or one of the two special relations *IS* and *NONE* which indicate that x_2 is an attribute of x_1 or no relation exists, respectively. We noticed that for most pairs for which a relation exists, x_1 and x_2 are in the same constituent, i.e. their lowest common ancestor is either one of the two objects or a word in between them. We therefore consider only pairs which satisfy this constraint to improve precision and to limit the number of predictions.

For the predictions, we use again an L_2-regularized maximum entropy classifier with the following features:

Object features The original word and lemma, and the predicted class or type of x_1 and x_2.

Lexicalized features The word and lemma of each token between x_1 and x_2. If x_1 or x_2 appear more than once in the sentence because they replace a pronoun, we only consider the words in between the closest mentions of x_1 and x_2.

Syntactic features The concatenated labels (i.e., syntactic relation names) of the edges in the shortest path from x_1 to x_2 in the semantic graph.

We only include objects in the scene graph which have at least one attribute or which are involved in at least one relation. The idea behind that is to prevent very abstract nouns such as *setting* or *right* to be part of the scene graph which are typically not part of relations. However, we observed for around 30% of the sentences in the development set that the parser did not extract any relations or attributes from a sentence which resulted in an empty scene graph. In these cases, we include all candidate objects in the scene graph.

3.3.3 Training

As the scene graph's objects and attributes are not aligned to the sentence, we have to align them in an unsupervised manner. For each sentence, we extract object and attribute candidates from the semantic graph. For each object-relation-object triple or object-attribute pair in the scene graph we try to align all objects and attributes to a candidate by first checking for exact string match of the word or the lemma, then by looking for candidates within an edit distance of two, and finally by mapping the object or attribute and all the candidates to 100-dimensional GloVe word vectors and picking the candidate with the smallest euclidean distance. To limit the number of false alignments caused by annotators including objects in the scene graph that are not present in the corresponding sentence, we also compute the euclidean distances to all the other words in the sentence and if the closest match is not in the candidate set we discard the training example.

We use this data to train both of our classifiers. For the object and attribute classifier, we only consider the alignments between words in the description and objects or attributes in the graph.

For the relation predictor, we consider the complete object-relation-object and object-*is*-attribute triples. All the aligned triples constitute our positive training examples for a sentence. For all the object-object and object-attribute pairs without a relation in a sentence, we generate negative examples by assigning them a special $NONE$ relation. We sample from the set of $NONE$ triples to have the same number of positive and negative training examples.

4 Experiments

For our experiments, we split the data into training, development and held-out test sets of size 3,614, 454, and 456 images, respectively. Table 2 shows the aggregated statistics of our training and test sets. We compare our two parsers against the following two baselines.

	Train	Dev	Test
Images	3,614	454	456
Sentences	40,315	4,953	5,180
Relation instances	38,617	4,826	4,963
Attribute instances	37,580	4,644	4,588

Table 2: Aggregate statistics of the training, development (dev) and test sets.

Nearest neighbor Our first baseline computes a term-frequency vector for an input sentence and returns the scene graph of the nearest neighbor in the training data.

Object only Our second baseline is a parser that only outputs objects but no attributes or relationships. It uses the first two components of the classifier-based parser, namely the semantic graph processor and the object extractor, and then simply outputs all candidate objects.

We use the downstream performance on the image retrieval task as our main evaluation metric. We train our reimplementation of the model by Johnson et al. (2015) on our training set with human-constructed scene graphs. For each sentence we use the parser's output as a query and rank all images in the test set. For evaluation, we consider the human-constructed scene graph G_h of the sentence and construct a set of images $I = i_1, ..., i_n$ such that G_h is a subgraph of the image's complete scene graph. We compute the rank of each image in I and compute recall at 5 and 10 based on these ranks[3]. We also compute the median rank of the first correct result. We compare these numbers against an oracle system which uses the human-constructed scene graphs as queries instead of the scene graphs generated by the parser.

One drawback of evaluating on a downstream task is that evaluation is typically slower compared to using an intrinsic metric. We therefore also compare the parsed scene graphs to the human-constructed scene graphs. As scene graphs consist of object instances, attributes, and relations and are therefore similar to Abstract Meaning Representation (AMR) (Banarescu et al., 2013) graphs, we use Smatch F1 (Cai and Knight, 2013) as an additional intrinsic metric.

[3]As in Johnson et al. (2015), we observed that the results for recall at 1 were very unstable so we only report recall at 5 and 10 which are typically also more relevant for real-world systems that return multiple results.

	Development set				Test set			
	Smatch	R@5	R@10	Med. rank	Smatch	R@5	R@10	Med. rank
Nearest neighbor	32%	1.2%	2.3%	206	32%	1.1%	2.3%	205
Object only	**48%**	15.0%	29.3%	20	**48%**	12.6%	24.8%	25
Rule	43%	16.4%	31.6%	17	44%	13.5%	**27.1%**	**20**
Classifier	47%	**16.7%**	**32.9%**	**16**	47%	**13.8%**	**27.1%**	**20**
Oracle	-	19.4%	39.8%	13	-	16.6%	33.4%	15

Table 3: Intrinsic (Smatch F1) and extrinsic (recall at 5 and 10, and median rank) performance of our two baselines, our rule-based and our classifier-based parser.

	R@5	R@10	Med. rank
Johnson et al. (2015)	30.3%	47.9%	11
Our implementation	27.6%	45.6%	12

Table 4: Comparison of the results of the original implementation by Johnson et al. (2015) and our implementation. Both systems were trained and tested on the data sets of the original authors.

5 Results and Discussion

Table 3 shows the performance of our baselines and our two final parsers on the development and held-out test set.

Oracle results Compared to the results of Johnson et al. (2015), the results of our oracle systems are significantly worse. To verify the correctness of our implementation, the original authors provided us with their training and test set. Table 4 shows that our reimplementation performs almost as well as their original implementation. We hypothesize that there are two main reasons for the drop in performance when we train and evaluate our system on our dataset. First, our dataset is a lot more diverse and contains many more object classes and relation and attribute types. Second, the original authors only use the most common queries for which there exist at least five results to retrieve images while we evaluate on all queries.

Effectiveness of Smatch F1 As mentioned in the previous section, having an intrinsic evaluation metric can reduce the length of development cycles compared to using only an extrinsic evaluation. We hoped that Smatch F1 would be an appropriate metric for our task but our results indicate that there is no strong correlation between Smatch F1 and the performance of the downstream task.

Comparison of rule-based and classifier-based system In terms of image retrieval performance, there does not seem to be a significant difference between our rule-based system and our classifier-based system. On the development set the classifier-based system slightly outperforms the rule-based system but on the test set both seem to work equally well. Nevertheless, their results differ in some cases. One strength of the classifier-based system is that it learns that some adjectival modifiers like *several* should not be attributes. It is also able to learn some basic implications such as *the shirt looks dirty* implies in the context of an image that the shirt is dirty. On the other hand, the rule-based system tends to be more stable in terms of extracting relations while the classifier-based system more often only extracts objects from a sentence.

Comparison to baselines As shown in Table 3, both of our parsers outperform all our baselines in terms of recall at 5 and 10, and the median rank. This difference is particularly significant compared to the *nearest neighbor* baseline which confirms the complexity of our dataset and shows that it is not sufficient to simply memorize the training data.

The *object only* baseline is a lot stronger but still performs consistently worse than our two parsers. To understand in what ways our parsers are superior to the *object only* baseline, we performed a qualitative analysis. A comparison of the results reveals that the image retrieval model is able to make use of the extracted relations and attributes. Figure 3 shows the top 5 results of our classifier-based parser and the *object only* baseline for the query *"The white plane has one blue stripe and one red stripe"*. While the *object only* model seems to be mainly concerned with finding good matches for the two *stripe* objects, the output of our parser successfully captures the relation between the plane and the stripes and correctly ranks the two planes with the blue and red stripes as the

Figure 3: Top 5 results of the object only baseline (top row) and our classifier-based parser (bottom row) for the query *"The white plane has one blue stripe and one red stripe"*. The *object only* system seems to be mainly concerned with finding images that contain two *stripe* objects at the expense of finding an actual plane. Our classifier-based parser also outputs the relation between the stripes and the plane and the colors of the stripes which helps the image retrieval system to return the correct results.

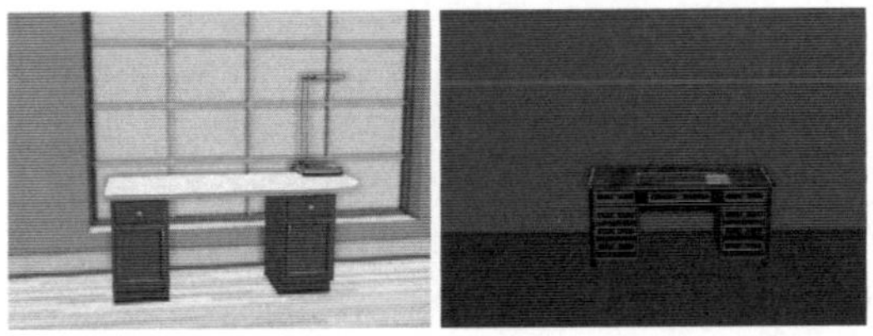

Figure 4: 3D scenes for the sentences *"There is a wooden desk with a red and green lamp on it"* and *"There is a desk with a notepad on it"*.

top results.

Error analysis The performance of both of our parsers comes close to the performance of the oracle system but nevertheless there still remains a consistent gap. One of the reasons for the lower performance is that some human-constructed scene graphs contain information which is not present in the description. The human annotators saw both the description and the image and could therefore generate scene graphs with additional information.

Apart from that, we find that many errors occur with sentences which require some external knowledge. For example, our parser is not able to infer that *"a woman in black"* means that a woman is wearing black clothes. Likewise it is not able to infer that *"a jockey is wearing a green shirt and matching helmet"* implies that he is wearing a green helmet.

Other errors occur in some sentences which talk about textures. For example, our parsers assume that "a dress with polka dots" implies that there is a relation between one *dress* object and multiple *polka dot* objects instead of inferring that there is one *dress* object with the attribute *polka-dotted*.

One further source of errors are wrong dependency parses. Both of our parsers heavily rely on correct dependency parses and while making the parser's training data more diverse did improve results, we still observe some cases where sentences are parsed incorrectly leading to incorrect scene graphs.

6 Other Tasks

As mentioned before, one appeal of parsing sentences to an intermediate representation is that we can also use our parser for other tasks that make use of similar representations. One of these tasks is generating 3D scenes from textual descriptions (Chang et al., 2014). Without performing any further modifications, we replaced their parser with our classifier-based parser and used the resulting system to generate 3D scenes from several indoor scene descriptions. Two of these generated scenes are shown in Figure 4. Our impression is that the system performs roughly equally well using this parser compared to the one used in the original work.

7 Related Work

Image retrieval Image retrieval is one of the most active areas in computer vision research. Very early work mainly focused on retrieving images based on textual descriptions, while later work focused more on content-based image retrieval systems which perform retrieval directly based on image features. Rui et al. (1999), Liu et al. (2007), and Siddiquie et al. (2011) provide overviews of the developments of this field over the last twenty years. Most of this work focused on retrieving images from keywords which are not able to capture many semantic phenomena as well as natural language or our scene graph representation can.

Multi-modal embeddings Recently, multi-modal embeddings of natural language and images got a lot of attention (Socher et al., 2014; Karpathy et al., 2014; Plummer et al., 2015; Kiros et al., 2015; Mao et al., 2015; Chrupala et al., 2015). These embeddings can be used to retrieve images from captions and generating captions from images. As mentioned in the introduction, these models are trained on single-sentence image descriptions which typically cannot capture all the details of a visual scene. Further, unlike our modular system, they cannot be used for other tasks that require an interpretable semantic representation.

Parsing to graph-based representations Representing semantic information with graphs has recently experienced a resurgence caused by the development of the Abstract Meaning Representation (AMR) (Banarescu et al., 2013) which was followed by several works on parsing natural language sentences to AMR (Flanigan et al., 2014; Wang et al., 2015; Werling et al., 2015). Considering that AMR graphs are, like dependency trees, very similar to scene graphs, we could have also used this representation and transformed it to scene graphs. However, the performance of AMR parsers is still not competitive with the performance of dependency parsers which makes dependency trees are more stable starting point.

There also exists some prior work on parsing scene descriptions to semantic representations. As mentioned above, Chang et al. (2014) present a rule-based system to parse natural language descriptions to *scene templates*, a similar graph-based semantic representation. Elliott et al. (2014) parse image descriptions to a dependency grammar representation which they also use for image retrieval. Lin et al. (2014a) also use rules to transform dependency trees into semantic graphs which they use for video search. All of this work, however, only consider a limited set of relations while our approach can learn an arbitrary number of relations. Further, they all exclusively use very specific rule-based systems whereas we also introduced a more general purposed classifier-based parser.

8 Conclusion

We presented two parsers which can translate image descriptions to scene graphs. We showed that their output is almost as effective for retrieving images as human-generated scene graphs and that including relations and attributes in queries outperforms a model which only considers objects. We also demonstrated that our parser is well suited for other tasks which require a semantic representation of a visual scene.

Acknowledgments

We thank the anonymous reviewers for their thoughtful feedback. This work was supported in part by a gift from IPSoft, Inc. and in part by the Defense Advanced Research Projects Agency (DARPA) Broad Operational Language Translation (BOLT) program through IBM. The second author is also supported by a Magic Grant from The Brown Institute for Media Innovation. Any opinions, findings, and conclusions or recommendations expressed are those of the author(s) and do not necessarily reflect the view of either DARPA or the US government.

References

Laura Banarescu, Claire Bonial, Shu Cai, Madalina Georgescu, Kira Griffitt, Ulf Hermjakob, Kevin Knight, Philipp Koehn, Martha Palmer, and Nathan Schneider. 2013. Abstract meaning representation for sembanking. In *Proceedings of the 7th Linguistic Annotation Workshop and Interoperability with Discourse*.

Shu Cai and Kevin Knight. 2013. Smatch: An evaluation metric for semantic feature structures. In *Proceedings of the 51st Annual Meeting of the Association offor Computational Linguistics*.

Angel X Chang, Manolis Savva, and Christopher D Manning. 2014. Learning spatial knowledge for text to 3D scene generation. In *Proceedings of the 2014 Conference on Empirical Methods in Natural Language Processing*.

Grzegorz Chrupala, Akos Kadar, and Afra Alishahi. 2015. Learning language through pictures. In *Proceedings of the 53rd Annual Meeting of the Association for Computational Linguistics*.

Marie-Catherine de Marneffe, Timothy Dozat, Natalia Silveira, Katri Haverinen, Filip Ginter, Joakim Nivre, and Christopher D. Manning. 2014. Universal Stanford dependencies: A cross-linguistic typology. In *Proceedings of the Ninth International Conference on Language Resources and Evaluation (LREC-2014)*.

Desmond Elliott, Victor Lavrenko, and Frank Keller. 2014. Query-by-example image retrieval using visual dependency representations. In *Proceedings of COLING 2014, the 25th International Conference on Computational Linguistics: Technical Papers*.

Jeffrey Flanigan, Sam Thomson, Jaime Carbonell, Chris Dyer, and Noah A. Smith. 2014. A discriminative graph-based parser for the abstract meaning representation. In *Proceedings of the 52nd Annual Meeting of the Association for Computational Linguistics*.

Jerry R Hobbs. 1978. Resolving pronoun references. *Lingua*, 44(4):311–338.

Justin Johnson, Ranjay Krishna, Michael Stark, Li-Jia Li, David A Shamma, Michael Bernstein, and Li Fei-Fei. 2015. Image retrieval using scene graphs. In *Proceedings of the 2015 IEEE Conference on Computer Vision and Pattern Recognition (CVPR)*.

Andrej Karpathy, Armand Joulin, and Fei Fei F Li. 2014. Deep fragment embeddings for bidirectional image sentence mapping. In *Advances in neural information processing systems*.

Ryan Kiros, Ruslan Salakhutdinov, and Richard Zemel. 2015. Unifying visual-semantic embeddings with multimodal neural language models. *Transactions of the Association for Computational Linguistics*.

Dan Klein and Christopher D Manning. 2003. Accurate unlexicalized parsing. In *Proceedings of the 41st Annual Meeting of the Association for Computational Linguistics*.

John Lafferty, Andrew McCallum, and Fernando CN Pereira. 2001. Conditional random fields: Probabilistic models for segmenting and labeling sequence data. In *Proceedings of the 18th International Conference on Machine Learning (ICML)*.

Heeyoung Lee, Angel Chang, Yves Peirsman, Nathanael Chambers, Mihai Surdeanu, and Dan Jurafsky. 2013. Deterministic coreference resolution based on entity-centric, precision-ranked rules. *Computational Linguistics*, 39(4):885–916.

Dahua Lin, Sanja Fidler, Chen Kong, and Raquel Urtasun. 2014a. Visual semantic search: Retrieving videos via complex textual queries. In *Proceedings of the 2014 IEEE Conference on Computer Vision and Pattern Recognition (CVPR)*. IEEE.

Tsung-Yi Lin, Michael Maire, Serge Belongie, James Hays, Pietro Perona, Deva Ramanan, Piotr Dollár, and C Lawrence Zitnick. 2014b. Microsoft COCO: Common objects in context. In *Computer Vision–ECCV 2014*. Springer.

Ying Liu, Dengsheng Zhang, Guojun Lu, and Wei-Ying Ma. 2007. A survey of content-based image retrieval with high-level semantics. *Pattern Recognition*, 40(1):262–282.

Junhua Mao, Wei Xu, Yi Yang, Jiang Wang, Heng Huangzhi, and Alan Yuille. 2015. Deep captioning with multimodal recurrent neural networks (m-RNN). In *Proceedings of the International Conference on Learning Representations (ICLR) 2015*.

Mitchell P Marcus, Mary Ann Marcinkiewicz, and Beatrice Santorini. 1993. Building a large annotated corpus of english: The Penn treebank. *Computational linguistics*, 19(2):313–330.

Rick Nouwen. 2015. Plurality. In Paul Dekker and Maria Aloni, editors, *Cambridge Handbook of Semantics*. Cambridge University Press, Cambridge.

Kishore Papineni, Salim Roukos, Todd Ward, and Wei-Jing Zhu. 2002. BLEU: a method for automatic evaluation of machine translation. In *Proceedings of the 40th Annual Meeting of the Association for Computational Linguistics*, pages 311–318. Association for Computational Linguistics.

Jeffrey Pennington, Richard Socher, and Christopher D. Manning. 2014. GloVe: Global vectors for word representation. In *Proceedings of the 2014 Conference on Empirical Methods in Natural Language Processing*.

Bryan Plummer, Liwei Wang, Chris Cervantes, Juan Caicedo, Julia Hockenmaier, and Svetlana Lazebnik. 2015. Flickr30k Entities: Collecting region-to-phrase correspondences for richer image-to-sentence models. *arXiv preprint arXiv:1505.04870*.

Yong Rui, Thomas S Huang, and Shih-Fu Chang. 1999. Image retrieval: Current techniques, promising directions, and open issues. *Journal of visual communication and image representation*, 10(1):39–62.

Behjat Siddiquie, Rogerio S Feris, and Larry S Davis. 2011. Image ranking and retrieval based on multi-attribute queries. In *Proceedings of the 2011 IEEE Conference on Computer Vision and Pattern Recognition (CVPR)*.

Raffaele Simone and Francesca Masini. 2014. On light nouns. *Word Classes: Nature, typology and representations*, 332:51.

Richard Socher, Andrej Karpathy, Quoc V Le, Christopher D Manning, and Andrew Y Ng. 2014. Grounded compositional semantics for finding and describing images with sentences. *Transactions of the Association for Computational Linguistics*, 2.

Bart Thomee, David A Shamma, Gerald Friedland, Benjamin Elizalde, Karl Ni, Douglas Poland, Damian Borth, and Li-Jia Li. 2015. The new data and new challenges in multimedia research. *arXiv preprint arXiv:1503.01817*.

Chuan Wang, Nianwen Xue, Sameer Pradhan, and Sameer Pradhan. 2015. A transition-based algorithm for amr parsing. In *Proceedings of the 2015 Conference of the North American Chapter of the Association for Computational Linguistics Human Language Technologies (NAACL HLT 2015)*.

Keenon Werling, Gabor Angeli, and Christopher D. Manning. 2015. Robust subgraph generation improves abstract meaning representation parsing. In *Proceedings of the 53rd Annual Meeting of the Association for Computational Linguistics*.

C Lawrence Zitnick, Devi Parikh, and Lucy Vanderwende. 2013. Learning the visual interpretation of sentences. In *2013 IEEE International Conference on Computer Vision (ICCV)*, pages 1681–1688. IEEE.

Do Distributed Semantic Models Dream of Electric Sheep? Visualizing Word Representations through Image Synthesis

Angeliki Lazaridou and **Dat Tien Nguyen** and **Marco Baroni**
Center for Mind/Brain Sciences
University of Trento
`{angeliki.lazaridou|tiendat.nguyen|marco.baroni}@unitn.it`

Abstract

We introduce the task of visualizing distributed semantic representations by generating images from word vectors. Given the corpus-based vector encoding the word *broccoli*, we convert it to a visual representation by means of a cross-modal mapping function, and then use the mapped representation to generate an image of broccoli as "dreamed" by the distributed model. We propose a baseline dream synthesis method based on averaging pictures whose visual representations are topologically close to the mapped vector. Two experiments show that we generate dreams that generally belong to the the right semantic category, and are sometimes accurate enough for subjects to distinguish the intended concept from a related one.

1 Introduction

When researchers "visualize" distributed/distributional semantic models, they typically present 2D scatterplots illustrating the distances between a set of word representations (Van der Maaten and Hinton, 2008). We propose a much more direct approach to visualization. Given a vector representing a word in a corpus-derived distributed space, we generate a picture depicting how the denotatum of the word looks like, according to the model. Given, say, the word2vec vector of *broccoli*, we want to know how broccoli looks like to word2vec (see Figure 1 for the answer).

Besides the inherent coolness of the task, it has many potential applications. Current qualitative analysis of distributed semantic models is limited to assessing the *relation* between words, e.g., by looking at, or plotting, nearest neighbour sets, but it lacks methods to inspect the properties of a specific word directly. Our image synthesis approach will allow researchers to "see", in a very literal sense, how a model represents a single word. Moreover, in the spirit of the "*A picture is worth a thousand words*" adage, the generated images will allow researchers to quickly eyeball the results, getting the gist of what a model is capturing much faster than from textual neighbour lists. For example, a more "topical" model might produce pictures depicting the wider scenes in which objects occur (a ball being dribbled by soccer players), whereas a model capturing strictly conceptual aspects might produce narrow views of the denoted objects (a close-up of the ball). Image synthesis could also be used to explore the effect of different input corpora on representations: e.g., given a historical corpus, generate images for the *car* word representations induced from early 20th-century vs. 21st-century texts. As a last example, Aletras and Stevenson (2013) proposed to examine the topics of Topic Models by associating them with images retrieved from the Web. Given that topics are represented by vectors, we could directly *generate* images representing these topics.

In cognitive science, there is a lively debate on whether abstract words have embodied representations, (Barsalou and Wiemer-Hastings, 2005; Lakoff and Johnson, 1999), an issue that has recently attracted the attention of the distributed semantics community (Hill and Korhonen, 2014; Kiela et al., 2014; Lazaridou et al., 2015). An intriguing application of image synthesis would be to produce and assess imagery for abstract concepts. Recent work in neuroscience attempts to generate images of "what people think", as encoded in vector-based representations of fMRI patterns (Naselaris et al., 2009; Nishimoto et al., 2011). With our method, we could then directly compare images produced from corpus-based representations to what humans visualize when thinking of the same words.

Proceedings of the 2015 Workshop on Vision and Language (VL'15), pages 81–86,
Lisbon, Portugal, 18 September 2015.

In the long term, we would like to move beyond words, towards generating images depicting the meaning of phrases (e.g., an angry cat vs. a cute cat vs. a white cat) and sentences. This would nicely complement current work on generating verbal descriptions of images (Karpathy and Fei-Fei, 2015; Kiros et al., 2014) with the inverse task of generating images from verbal descriptions.

Generating images from vectorial word representations is of course extremely challenging. However, various relevant strands of research have reached a level of maturity that makes it a realistic goal to pursue. First, tools such as word2vec (Mikolov et al., 2013a) and Glove (Pennington et al., 2014) produce high-quality word representations, making us confident that we are not trying to generate visual signals from semantic noise. Second, there is very promising recent work on learning to map between word representations and an (abstract) image space, for applications such as image retrieval and annotation (Frome et al., 2013; Karpathy and Fei-Fei, 2015; Kiros et al., 2014; Lazaridou et al., 2014; Socher et al., 2014). Finally, the computer vision community is starting to explore the task of image generation (Gregor et al., 2015), typically in an attempt to understand the inner workings of visual feature extraction algorithms (Zeiler and Fergus, 2014).

The main aim of this paper is to present proof-of-concept evidence that the task is feasible. To this end, we rely on state-of-the-art word representation and cross-modality mapping methods, but we adopt an image synthesis strategy that could be seen as an interesting baseline to compare other approaches against. Briefly, our pipeline works as follows. Our input is given by pre-computed word representations (word2vec) and a set of labeled images together with their pre-compiled representations in a high-level visual feature space (specifically, we use activations on one of the top layers (fc7) of a convolutional neural network as high-level image representations). Given an input word vector, we use a linear *cross-modal function* to map it into visual space, and we retrieve the n nearest image representations. Finally, we overlay the actual images corresponding to these nearest neighbours in order to derive a visualization of the mapped word, a method we refer to as *averaging*. For example, the first image in Figure 1 below is our visualization of broccoli, obtained by projecting the *broccoli* word vector onto visual space, retrieving the 20 nearest images and averaging them.

Importantly, we apply this synthesis method to words that are not used to train the cross-modal mapping function, and that do not match the label of any picture in the image data set. So, for example, our system had to map *broccoli* onto visual space without having ever been exposed to labeled broccoli images (*zero-shot* setting), and it generated the *broccoli* image by averaging pictures that do not depict broccoli.

2 General setup

We refer to the words we generate images for as *dreamed* words, and to the corresponding images as *dreams*. We refer to the set of words that are associated to real pictures as *seen* words. The real picture set contains approximately 500K images extracted from ImageNet (Deng et al., 2009) representing 5.1K distinct seen words. The dreamed word set includes 510 concrete, base-level concepts from the semantic norms of McRae et al. (2005) (we excluded 31 McRae concepts because they were marked as ambiguous there, or for technical reasons).

Linguistic and Visual Representations For all seen and dreamed concepts, we build 300-dimensional word vectors with the word2vec toolkit,[1] choosing the CBOW method.[2] CBOW, which learns to predict a target word from the ones surrounding it, produces state-of-the-art results in many linguistic tasks (Baroni et al., 2014). Word vectors are induced from a corpus of 2.8 billion words.[3] The 500K images are represented by 4096-dimensional visual vectors, extracted with the pre-trained convolutional neural network model of Krizhevsky et al. (2012) through the Caffe toolkit (Jia et al., 2014).

Cross-modal mapping We use 5.1K training pairs $(\mathbf{w}_c, \mathbf{v}_c) = \{\mathbf{w}_c \in \mathbb{R}^{300}, \mathbf{v}_c \in \mathbb{R}^{4096}\}$, where $\mathbf{w}_c$ is the word vector and $\mathbf{v}_c$ the visual vector for (seen) concept c, the latter obtained by averaging all visual representations labeled with the concept (no dreamed concept is included in the training

[1] `https://code.google.com/p/word2vec/`

[2] Other hyperparameters, adopted without tuning, include a context window size of 5 words to either side of the target, setting the sub-sampling option to 1e-05 and estimating the probability of target words by negative sampling, drawing 10 samples from the noise distribution (Mikolov et al., 2013b).

[3] Corpus sources: `http://wacky.sslmit.unibo.it`, `http://www.natcorp.ox.ac.uk`

set, given the zero-shot setup). Following previous work on cross-modal mapping (Frome et al., 2013; Lazaridou et al., 2014), we assume a linear mapping function. To estimate its parameters $\mathbf{M} \in \mathbb{R}^{300\times 4096}$, given word vectors $\mathbf{W}$ paired with visual vectors $\mathbf{V}$, we use L1-penalized least squares (Lasso) regression:[4]

$$\hat{\mathbf{M}} = \underset{\mathbf{M}\in\mathbb{R}^{300\times 4096}}{\operatorname{argmin}} \|\mathbf{WM} - \mathbf{V}\|_F + \lambda\|\mathbf{M}\|_1$$

Image synthesis Suppose you have never seen cougars, but you know they are big cats. You might reasonably visualize a cougar as resembling a combination of lions, cheetahs and other felines. One simple way to simulate this process is through *image averaging*. Specifically, given the word representation $\mathbf{w}_c$ of a dreamed concept c, we apply cross-modal mapping $\mathbf{M}$ to obtain an estimate of its visual vector $\hat{\mathbf{v}}_c$. Following that, we search for the top $k = 20$ nearest images in 4096-dimensional visual space. Finally, the dream of concept c is obtained by averaging the colors in each pixel position (x, y) across the 20 images. These images do *not* contain the dreamed concept, and they will typically depict *several* distinct concepts (e.g., with a fairly accurate mapping $\mathbf{M}$, we might get the dream of cougar by averaging images of 5 cheetahs and 15 lions).[5]

3 Experiment 1: Naming the dream

Task definition and data collection In this experiment we presented a dream, and asked subjects if they thought it was more likely to denote the correct dreamed word or a confounder randomly picked from the seen word set (we did not use the "dream" terminology to explain the task to subjects). Since the confounder is a randomly picked term, the task is relatively easy. At the same time, since the confounders are picked from a set of concrete concepts, just like the dreamed words, it sometimes happens that the two concepts are quite related, as illustrated in Figure 1. Moreover, all confounders were used to train the mapping function, and their pictures are present in the averaging pool. These factors could introduce a bias in favour of them. We tested all 510 McRae words, collecting 20 ratings for each. We randomized word order both across and within trials. We used the CrowdFlower[6] platform to collect the judgments, limiting participation to subjects from English-speaking countries who self-declared English as their native language.

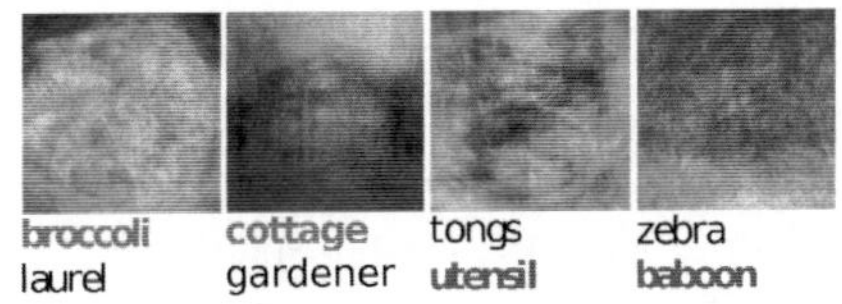

Figure 1: **Experiment 1:** Example dreams with correct dreamed word and confounder. Subjects showed a significant preference for the colored word (green if right, red if wrong).

Results Subjects show a consistent preference for the correct (dreamed) word (median proportion of votes in favor of it: 90%). Preference for the correct word is significantly different from chance in 419/510 cases (two-sided exact binomial tests, corrected for multiple comparisons with the false discovery rate method, $\alpha = .05$). Subjects expressed a significant preference for the confounder in only 5 cases (*budgie/parakeet*, *cake/pie*, *camel/ox*, *shotgun/revolver*, *squid/octopus*).

For the first two dreams in Figure 1, subjects showed a significant preference for the dreamed word, despite the fact that the confounder is a related term. Still, when the two words are closely related, it is more likely that subjects will be at random. The figure also shows two interesting examples in which dreamed word and confounder are related, and subjects significantly preferred the latter. The *tongs/utensil* case is very challenging, because any tongs picture would also be an utensil picture (and the dreamed object does not look like tongs to start with). For *zebra/baboon*, we conjecture that subjects could make up an animal in the dream, but one lacking the salient black-and-white pattern of zebras.

4 Experiment 2: Picking the right dream

Task definition and data collection In this experiment, we matched each dreamed word with its own dream and a confounder dream generated from the *most similar* dreamed term (see Figure 2 for examples). Word similarity was

[4] λ is 10-fold cross-validated on the training data.

[5] The idea of generating a more abstract depiction of something by averaging a number of real pictures is popular in contemporary art (Salavon, 2004) and it has recently been adopted in computer vision, as a way to visualize large sets of images of the same concept, e.g., averaging across different cat breeds (Zhu et al., 2014).

[6] `http://www.crowdflower.com`

measured in a space defined by subject-generated properties describing the concepts of interest (this method is known to produce high-quality similarity estimates, better than those obtained with text-based distributional models, see, e.g., Baroni et al. (2010)). Subjects were asked which of the two images is more likely to contain the thing denoted by the word. This is a very challenging task, as in most cases target and confounder are closely related concepts, and thus their dreams must have considerable granularity to allow subjects to make the correct choice. Again, we used CrowdFlower to collect 20 votes per item, with the same modalities of Experiment 1.

Results We expected the simple averaging method to fail completely at the level of accuracy required by this task. The results, however, suggest at least a trend in the right direction. This time, the median proportion of votes for the correct dream is at 60%. In 165/510 cases, there is a significant preference for the correct dream (same statistical testing setup as above), and in 57 cases for the confounder. A manual annotation of higher-level categories of dreamed word and confounder (e.g., *garment*, *mammal*, etc.) revealed that the proportion of votes for the correct dream was much higher in the 100 cases in which the two items belonged to different categories (80% vs. 55% for same-category pairs). The top row of Figure 2 illustrates cases where the pairs belong to the same category, and yet subjects still showed a strong preference for the correct dream. In the *tractor/truck* case, both dreams represent vehicles, but the correct one is evoking the rural environment a tractor. For *swan/dove*, we can make out birds in both dreams, but the *swan* dream is clearly of a larger, aquatic bird. Still, the more common case is the one where, if the two concepts are closely related, subjects assign random preferences, as they did for the examples in the second row.

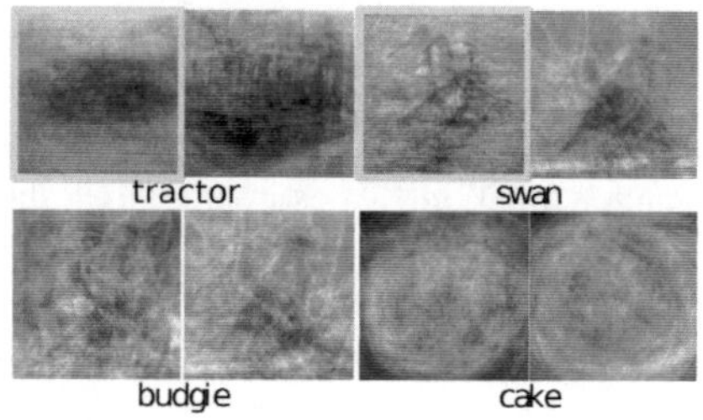

Figure 2: **Experiment 2:** Example dream pairs: the one on the left was generated from the word below the pair, the other from a confounder (clockwise from top left: *truck, dove, pie, parakeet*). Subjects showed significant preference for the green-framed correct dreams, and were at chance level in the other cases.

5 Discussion

Averaging lets common visual properties in the source images emerge, as discussed in the next paragraphs in relation to the examples of Figure 3.

Shape The typical position and orientation of objects in images is an important factor determining dream quality. For example, weapons often appear in opposite orientations, which gives the averaged *bayonet* dream an improbable X-like shape. Other concepts, like *umbrella*, whose dream averages circular objects, are not so strongly affected by the orientation problem.

Context Even when bad object alignment leads to blurry dreams with unrecognizable concepts, averaging might highlight a shared context, sufficient to reveal the general category the dreamed concept belongs to. While both dreams in the 2nd column of Figure 3 are blurry, we can guess that the first one is related to water or to the sea, while the second is related to forest nature (dreams of a *mackerel* and *bison*, respectively).[7]

Color Visual averaging can differentiate concepts by capturing characteristics that are not typically verbalized. In black and white, the *skirt* and *trousers* dreams look almost identical (and they wrongly depict an upper-body garment). What differentiates the two images is color, red for *skirt* black for *trousers*. Indeed, a Google image search reveals that skirts tend to be colorful and trousers dark. The McRae norms list `is_colorful` as a property of *skirts*, but not trousers. We thus conjecture that image synthesis could provide fine-grained perceptual information complementing linguistic properties encoded in classic nearest neighbour lists.

6 Conclusion

We presented a proof-of-concept study taking the first steps toward generation of novel images from text-based word vectors. Obviously, the next step is to use genuine image generation methods in-

[7]Interestingly, Torralba (2003) used same-object image averaging to illustrate contextual priming during object detection.

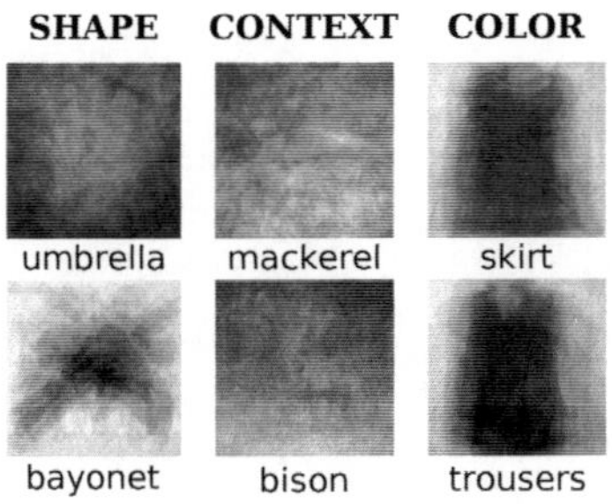

Figure 3: Examples illustrating properties of dream synthesis by image averaging.

stead of averaging (Gregor et al., 2015; Mahendran and Vedaldi, 2015; Vondrick et al., 2014; Zeiler and Fergus, 2014).

We would also like to consider alternative evaluation methods: for example, as suggested by a reviewer, asking subjects to label the generated dreams, and then measuring distance between the volunteered labels and the ground truth.

In a relatively short-term application perspective, given the intriguing results on context and other visual properties we reported, a natural first step would be to see how such properties change when different embeddings are used as input.

References

Nikolaos Aletras and Mark Stevenson. 2013. Representing topics using images. In *In Proceedings of NAACL-HLT*, pages 158–167.

Marco Baroni, Eduard Barbu, Brian Murphy, and Massimo Poesio. 2010. Strudel: A distributional semantic model based on properties and types. *Cognitive Science*, 34(2):222–254.

Marco Baroni, Georgiana Dinu, and Germán Kruszewski. 2014. Don't count, predict! a systematic comparison of context-counting vs. context-predicting semantic vectors. In *Proceedings of ACL*.

Lawrence Barsalou and Katja Wiemer-Hastings. 2005. Situating abstract concepts. In D. Pecher and R. Zwaan, editors, *Grounding Cognition: The Role of Perception and Action in Memory, Language, and Thought*, pages 129–163. Cambridge University Press, Cambridge, UK.

Jia Deng, Wei Dong, Richard Socher, Lia-Ji Li, and Li Fei-Fei. 2009. Imagenet: A large-scale hierarchical image database. In *Proceedings of CVPR*, pages 248–255, Miami Beach, FL.

Andrea Frome, Greg Corrado, Jon Shlens, Samy Bengio, Jeff Dean, Marc'Aurelio Ranzato, and Tomas Mikolov. 2013. DeViSE: A deep visual-semantic embedding model. In *Proceedings of NIPS*, pages 2121–2129, Lake Tahoe, NV.

Karol Gregor, Ivo Danihelka, Alex Graves, and Daan Wierstra. 2015. Draw: A recurrent neural network for image generation. *arXiv preprint arXiv:1502.04623*.

Felix Hill and Anna Korhonen. 2014. Learning abstract concept embeddings from multi-modal data: Since you probably can't see what I mean. In *Proceedings of EMNLP*, pages 255–265, Doha, Qatar.

Yangqing Jia, Evan Shelhamer, Jeff Donahue, Sergey Karayev, Jonathan Long, Ross Girshick, Sergio Guadarrama, and Trevor Darrell. 2014. Caffe: Convolutional architecture for fast feature embedding. *arXiv preprint arXiv:1408.5093*.

Andrej Karpathy and Li Fei-Fei. 2015. Deep visual-semantic alignments for generating image descriptions. In *Proceedings of CVPR*, Boston, MA. In press.

Douwe Kiela, Felix Hill, Anna Korhonen, and Stephen Clark. 2014. Improving multi-modal representations using image dispersion: Why less is sometimes more. In *Proceedings of ACL*, pages 835–841, Baltimore, MD.

Ryan Kiros, Ruslan Salakhutdinov, and Richard Zemel. 2014. Unifying visual-semantic embeddings with multimodal neural language models. In *Proceedings of the NIPS Deep Learning and Representation Learning Workshop*.

Alex Krizhevsky, Ilya Sutskever, and Geoffrey Hinton. 2012. ImageNet classification with deep convolutional neural networks. In *Proceedings of NIPS*, pages 1097–1105, Lake Tahoe, Nevada.

George Lakoff and Mark Johnson. 1999. *Philosophy in the Flesh: The Embodied Mind and Its Challenge to Western Thought*. Basic Books, New York.

Angeliki Lazaridou, Elia Bruni, and Marco Baroni. 2014. Is this a wampimuk? cross-modal mapping between distributional semantics and the visual world. In *Proceedings of ACL*, pages 1403–1414, Baltimore, MD.

Angeliki Lazaridou, Nghia The Pham, and Marco Baroni. 2015. Combining language and vision with a multimodal skip-gram model. In *Proceedings of NAACL*, pages 153–163, Denver, CO.

Aravindh Mahendran and Andrea Vedaldi. 2015. Understanding deep image representations by inverting them. In *Proceedings of CVPR*.

Ken McRae, George Cree, Mark Seidenberg, and Chris McNorgan. 2005. Semantic feature production norms for a large set of living and nonliving things. *Behavior Research Methods*, 37(4):547–559.

Tomas Mikolov, Kai Chen, Greg Corrado, and Jeffrey Dean. 2013a. Efficient estimation of word representations in vector space. http://arxiv.org/abs/1301.3781/.

Tomas Mikolov, Wen-tau Yih, and Geoffrey Zweig. 2013b. Linguistic regularities in continuous space word representations. In *Proceedings of NAACL*, pages 746–751, Atlanta, Georgia.

Thomas Naselaris, Ryan J Prenger, Kendrick N Kay, Michael Oliver, and Jack L Gallant. 2009. Bayesian reconstruction of natural images from human brain activity. *Neuron*, 63(6):902–915.

Shinji Nishimoto, An T Vu, Thomas Naselaris, Yuval Benjamini, Bin Yu, and Jack L Gallant. 2011. Reconstructing visual experiences from brain activity evoked by natural movies. *Current Biology*, 21(19):1641–1646.

Jeffrey Pennington, Richard Socher, and Christopher Manning. 2014. Glove: Global vectors for word representation. In *Proceedings of EMNLP*, pages 1532–1543, Doha, Qatar.

Jason Salavon. 2004. http://cabinetmagazine.org/issues/15/salavon.php.

Richard Socher, Quoc Le, Christopher Manning, and Andrew Ng. 2014. Grounded compositional semantics for finding and describing images with sentences. *Transactions of the Association for Computational Linguistics*, 2:207–218.

Antonio Torralba. 2003. Contextual priming for object detection. *International journal of computer vision*, 53:169–191.

Laurens Van der Maaten and Geoffrey Hinton. 2008. Visualizing data using t-SNE. *Journal of Machine Learning Research*, 9(2579-2605).

Carl Vondrick, Hamed Pirsiavash, Aude Oliva, and Antonio Torralba. 2014. Acquiring visual classifiers from human imagination. *arXiv preprint arXiv:1410.4627.*

Matthew Zeiler and Rob Fergus. 2014. Visualizing and understanding convolutional networks. In *Proceedings of ECCV (Part 1)*, pages 818–833, Zurich, Switzerland.

Jun-Yan Zhu, Yong Jae Lee, and Alexei A Efros. 2014. Averageexplorer: Interactive exploration and alignment of visual data collections. *ACM Transactions on Graphics (TOG)*, 33:160.

A Weighted Combination of Text and Image Classifiers for User Gender Inference

Tomoki Taniguchi, Shigeyuki Sakaki, Ryosuke Shigenaka,
Yukihiro Tsuboshita and Tomoko Ohkuma
Fuji Xerox Co., Ltd. , 6-1, Minatomirai, Nishiku, Yokohama-shi, Kanagawa, Japan
{taniguchi.tomoki,sakaki.shigeyuki,shigenaka.ryosuke,
yukihiro.tsuboshita,ohkuma.tomoko}@fujixerox.co.jp

Abstract

Demographic attribute inference of social networking service (SNS) users is a valuable application for marketing and for targeting advertisements. Several studies have examined Twitter-user gender inference in natural language processing, image recognition, and other research domains. Reportedly, a combined approach using text data and image data outperforms an individual data approach. This paper presents a proposal of a novel hybrid approach. A salient benefit of our system is that features provided from a text classifier and from an image classifier are combined appropriately to infer male or female gender using logistic regression. The experimentally obtained results demonstrate that our approach markedly improves an existing combination-based method.

1 Introduction

Concomitantly with rapid growth in SNS, consumers increasingly use SNS to exchange and share their opinions related to products, services, politics, and other matters. Many companies are motivated to use SNS data for marketing or advertisement to satisfy needs for improvements of their products or services in real time with low cost. However, in many cases, SNS user information such as gender, age or residence is not openly available, although such information is extremely important for marketing. To meet that objective, several studies have been conducted to infer demographic information of anonymous users using text or image data posted on Twitter, and community membership (Rao and Yarowsky, 2010; Ikeda et al., 2013; Ma et al., 2014; Sakaki et al., 2014). Sakaki et al. (2014) demonstrated that a hybrid-based method outperformed other approaches using individual sources. However we observed an important issue: each probability score output from the image classifiers and the text classifier was simply summed, although the degree of their respective contributions to the inference is presumably different.

As described herein, considering that issue, we propose a novel method with a hybrid approach using logistic regression. In addition, from examination of experimentally obtained results, we show which image contents contribute strongly to the inference of a Twitter user being male or female.

2 Related Work

Earlier studies investigated demographic attribute inference for SNS users based on machine learning. Text and images posted on SNS, membership in virtual communities, and combined information have been used as training data.

Burger et al. (2011) and Liu et al. (2012) applied text to infer user demographic attributes. Burger et al. (2011) realized a classifier that discerns SNS user gender. Liu et al. (2012) estimated the gender makeup of commuting populations using text.

Ma et al. (2014) and Ulges et al. (2012) used images and videos posted on SNS. Ma et al. (2014) defined 30 sub-categories, which were combinations of 10 image contents and 3 gender attributes (male, female, and unknown), and described a system that inferred a user's gender by classifying posted images into sub-categories. Ulges et al. (2012) detected TV viewers' gender and age via content-based concept detection.

Ikeda et al. (2013) and Sakaki et al. (2014) used methods that incorporate information. Ikeda et al. (2013) proposed a hybrid-based method using both text and community membership. Sakaki et al. (2014) proposed a hybrid-based method using a combination of text and images, which builds a meta-classifier using the probability score out-

Proceedings of the 2015 Workshop on Vision and Language (VL'15), pages 87–93,
Lisbon, Portugal, 18 September 2015.

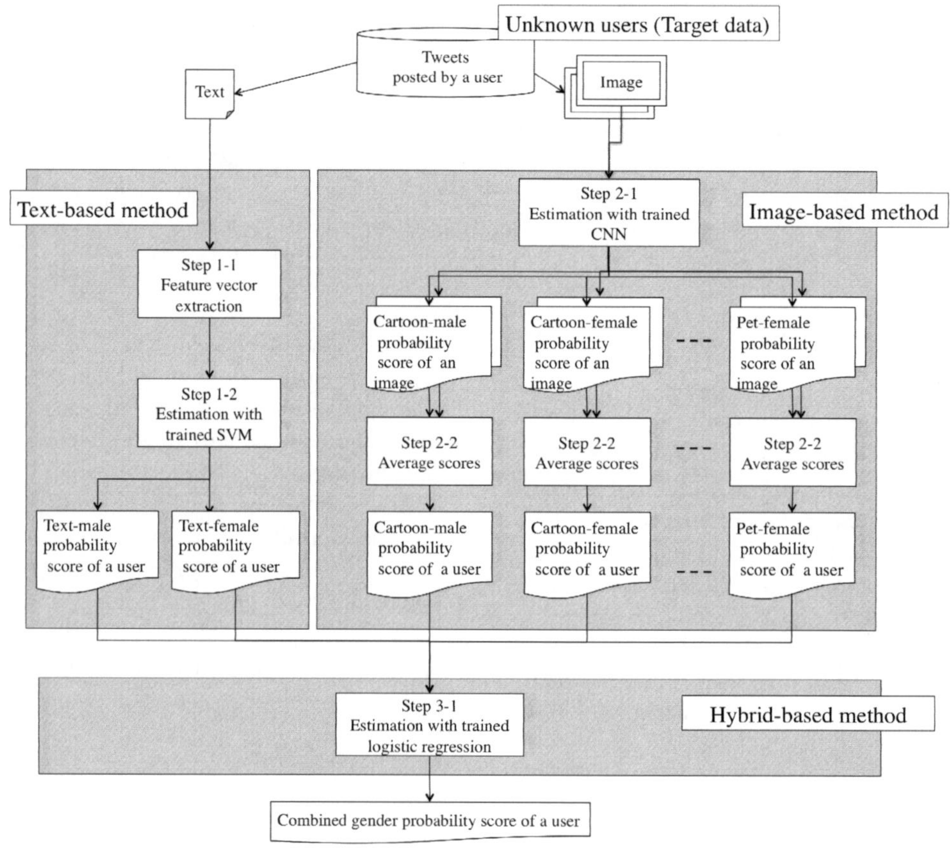

Figure 1: Overview of our proposed method.

put from text and image classifiers as input. This study demonstrated that a combination of text and images boosts the accuracy of a single source.

Since Krizhevsky et al. (2012) won first prize overwhelmingly at ILSVRC-2012, Convolutional Neural Networks (CNN) has gained great attention in the research field of image classifications. With the rise of efficient GPU computing, CNN has been used in practical applications. A few reports have described applications of CNN, which deals with inference of user attributes. Shigenaka et al. (2015) applied CNN for gender inference, demonstrating that CNN performs much better than a classifier based on SVM.

3 Proposed Method

Figure 1 presents an overview of our proposed method. Our method classifies some attributes (here, genders) of people who posted text and images. Our method includes three component methods that are: text-based, image-based, and hybrid-based.

3.1 Text-Based Method

The text-based method receives text as input and outputs the male and female probability scores. We used SVM to classify genders. To retrieve probability scores, we used logistic regression. The logistic function converts a distance from a hyper plane to probability scores of 0.0 - 1.0. As shown in Equation 1, the sum of the male and female probability scores is 1. The text-based method procedure is the following.

Step 1-1 Tokenization is done using Kuromoji (`http://www.atilika.org`), a Japanese morphological analyzer. Thereby, the unigram is obtained. Then, the bag-of-words feature is extracted from the unigram.

Step 1-2 The SVM receives the bag-of-words feature as input. The male probability score is obtained using SVM. Then, the female probability score is calculated using Equation 1.

$$score_{male} + score_{female} = 1 \quad (1)$$

3.2 Image-Based Method

The image-based method classifies the contents of posted images and estimates the gender of people who posted them. The image-based method receives an image as an input and outputs the probability score of each sub-category. Sub-categories are defined as combinations of image contents and user attributes: in this study, genders. Details of the sub-categories are presented later in section 4.1. We used a CNN model comprising 16 layers (Simonyan and Zisserman, 2014), which is pre-trained using the ILSVRC-2012 corpus. Neurons of the output layer of the pre-trained model are replaced with the same numbers of neurons as sub-categories. Weights of the new output layer are initialized to random values. Then, the weight of the pre-trained model is fine-tuned with the training dataset using backpropagation of error derivatives. Details of the dataset are presented later in section 4.1.

The image-based method procedures are the following.

Step 2-1 Probability score of images for sub-categories is obtained using the CNN model.

Step 2-2 The score of each user is obtained by averaging the probability score of images that the user posts since many users posted more than one image.

3.3 Hybrid-Based Method

The hybrid-based method classifies scores related to text-based and image-based method output and estimates the gender of people who posted text and images. We used logistic regression. In step 3-1, the male probability score is obtained using logistic regression. Then, the female probability score is calculated using Equation 1 in the same manner as that presented in step 1-2.

The training process for logistic regression involves two stages. In the first stage, the text-based and image-based method are trained to obtain training data for the hybrid-based method. In the second stage, the hybrid-based method is trained using them.

4 Experiment

We conducted a gender classification on Twitter.

4.1 Experimental Data

Experimental data are of two levels: a tweet level and an image level. We prepared a huge number of annotation data as a training corpus using Yahoo Crowd Sourcing (`http://crowdsourcing.yahoo.co.jp/Yahoo`).

Tweet level annotation: Tweet level annotation process refers to rules proposed by Sakaki et al. (2014), who defined the tweet level labels as male and female. Workers annotated the labels using many sources of potentially discriminative metadata, including user preferences, icons, text, and images.

Image level annotation: The image level annotation process refers to rules proposed by Ma et al. (2014), who defined image labels as the combination of the gender of users who had posted images and the contents that the images are likely to express. The image labels include two parts. The first is a gender category: female, male, and unknown. The former two are used to label images, for which people can infer the uploader gender. For images of which the uploader gender is unrecognizable, we use unknown. The second part defined in the image label is the category that expresses the classification of contents included in images. We designate the combination of these categories as sub-category. Table 1 shows typical contents of the sub-category.

Finally, we obtained 6000 tweet level annotations and 8162 image level annotations. As shown in Figure 2, the tweet level annotation data were split up into three subsets. Subset A was used for training the text-based method. Subset B was used for training the hybrid-based method. Subset C was used for evaluation. Image level annotation data were used for the training-image-based method.

4.2 Experimental Setup

LIBSVM (Chang and Lin, 2001) was used as the implementation of SVM. The linear kernel was selected. Then LIBLINEAR (Rong-En et al., 2008) was used as the implementation of logistic regression. Cost parameter C was set to 1.0.

(a) baseball stadium

(b) barbecue

(c) shaved ice

		Gender category		
		female	male	unknown
Contents category	cartoon	Romance cartoon	Hero cartoon	Unisex cartoon
	famous people	Famous male idol	Famous female idol	Comedian
	food contents	Shaved ice	Barbecue	Sandwich
	consumer goods	Jewelry	Electrical appliances	Cellular phone
	memo	Colorful memo	Black and white memo	Short memo
	outdoor	Amusement park	Baseball stadium	Landscape
	person	Girl,woman,baby	Boy,man	Crowd of people
	pet	Penguin,small dog	Frog,tiger	Cat
	screenshot	Pastel color screen	TV game screen	Weather news
	others	Beauty advertisement	Transportation	Black screen

Table 1: Sub-category composed with combinations of the gender and contents category. This table shows typical contents of the sub-category obtained using image-level annotation. For example, the combination of male and outdoor includes a baseball stadium image (a), the combination of male and food contents includes a barbecue image (b), and the combination of female and food contents includes the image of a shaved ice (c).

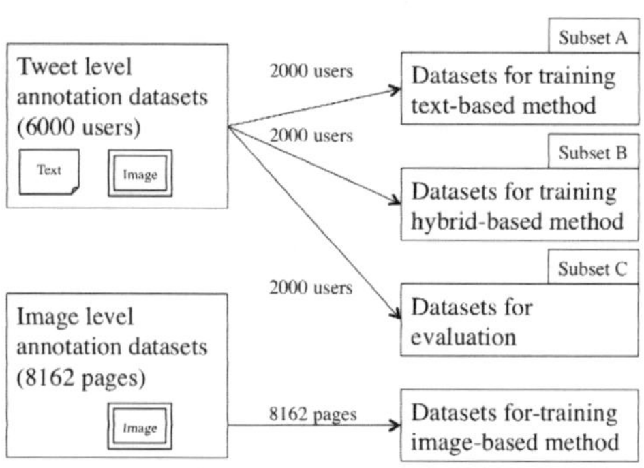

Figure 2: Datasets for training and evaluation.

As comparative methods, we selected the method presented by Sakaki et al. (2014) using the combination approach of text and image data and also the selected text-based and image-based method using the approach of a single source. In the experiment, classifiers of Sakaki et al. (2014) were replaced with the proposed classifiers to compare the performances of hybrid methods. The alpha value necessary for the method of Sakaki et al. (2014) to combine probability scores was set to 0.74 based on preliminary experiments.

5 Experimental Results

Table 2 shows the precision, recall, F-measure, and accuracy. The accuracy of our proposed method achieved 80.25 [%], which is 2.95 pt higher than that of the text-based method, 8.25 pt higher than that of the image-based method, and 1.35 pt higher than that of the method described by Sakaki et al. (2014). Especially, the female F-measure associated with our proposed method achieved 77.07 [%], which is 5.03 pt higher than that of the text based method, 13.69 pt higher than that of the image based method, and 2.0 pt higher than that of the method described by Sakaki et al. (2014).

We conducted a binomial test to assess our proposed method and the method described by Sakaki et al. (2014). Results confirmed that the p value is 0.0031, which indicates that the results obtained using our method are significantly better than those obtained using the existing combination-based method.

	Male			Female			
	Precision	Recall	F-measure	Precision	Recall	F-measure	Accuracy
Text-based method	76.20	86.12	80.88	79.16	66.10	72.04	77.30
Image-based method	70.41	85.97	77.41	75.58	54.58	63.38	72.00
Sakaki et al. (2014)	77.66	86.99	82.06	80.69	68.47	75.07	78.90
Proposed method	80.92	84.48	82.66	79.36	74.91	77.07	80.25

Table 2: Experimental results.

6 Discussion

This section presents a discussion of the effectiveness of the combination of the text-based and image-based methods. Then the discussion addresses the difference between the model proposed by Sakaki et al. (2014) and our proposed method. Finally, the applications of logistic regression weights of the combined sources are discussed.

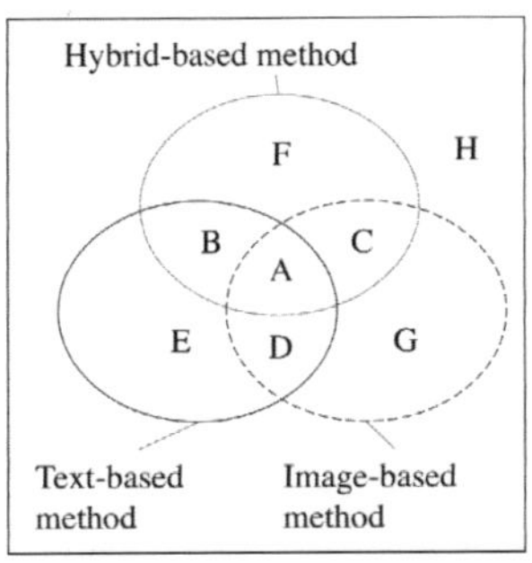

Set	T	I	P
A	⋆	⋆	⋆
B	⋆		⋆
C		⋆	⋆
D	⋆	⋆	
E	⋆		
F			⋆
G		⋆	
H			

Figure 3: Venn diagram: T denotes text-based method. I denotes image-based method. P denotes hybrid-based method. "⋆" denotes the set of users whose genders were inferred correctly using each method.

	Number of users		
Set	Conventional	Proposed	Difference
A	1105	1097	-8 ⇓
B	408	412	+4 ⇑
C	62	78	+16 ⇑
D	0	8	+8 ⇑
E	33	29	-4 ⇓
F	1	18	+17 ⇑
G	180	164	-16 ⇓
H	211	194	-17 ⇓

Table 3: Number of users included in each set. Conventional approach denotes the method of Sakaki et al. (2014).

6.1 Effectiveness of the Combination Approach

Figure 3 portrays the relation between the text-, image-, and hybrid-based methods. Each circle of the Venn diagram represents a set of users whose gender was inferred correctly using a method. The union of A, B, D, and E represents users whose gender was inferred correctly using the text-based method. B represents users whose gender was inferred correctly by the text-based and the hybrid-based method, but was misjudged using the image-based method.

Table 3 presents the number of users each set contains. We would like to examine C, D, E, and F specifically to assess the difference in the performance between the text-based and the hybrid-based method. C and F include users whose respective genders were inferred correctly using the hybrid-based method, but misjudged using the text-based method. D and E include users whose respective genders were inferred correctly using the text-based method, but misjudged using the hybrid-based method. Here we discuss the results obtained using the proposed method, which are shown at 3rd column. Regarding C, D, E, and F, C includes the maximum number of users, 78 (3.9 [%]), whose respective genders were inferred correctly using the proposed method. For C, a user's gender was inferred correctly using the image-based method. Therefore, it is apparent that our proposed method increased the number of correct answers considerably by taking in the correct region of the image-based method. It is particularly interesting that although the text-based and image-based methods both misjudged users (18 users : 0.9 [%]) in F, the proposed method can infer their genders correctly. However, D and E include only 37 users (8 + 29 users : 1.85 [%]) whose gender was misjudged using our proposed method. Therefore, our proposed method increased the number of correct inferences

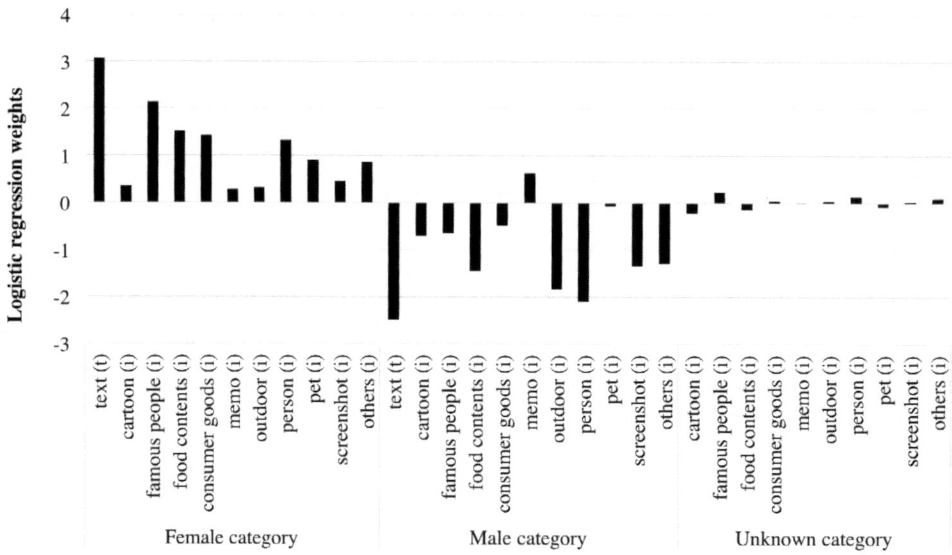

Figure 4: Logistic regression weights. Character (t) denotes weights with respect to the text-based method; (i) denotes weights with respect to the image-based method.

Rank	Male	Absolute weight	Female	Absolute weight
1_{st}	person	2.08	famous people	2.13
2_{nd}	outdoor	1.82	food contents	1.51
3_{rd}	food contents	1.45	consumer goods	1.42

Table 4: Top three absolute weights of the image content categories.

(59 users : 2.95 [%]) beyond the level of the individual text-based method.

6.2 Comparison of the Conventional Approach

The difference between the proposed method and that proposed by Sakaki et al. (2014) can be discussed with reference to Figure 3 and Table 3. Except for H, which includes users whose gender was misjudged by all methods, the difference between our method and the method presented by Sakaki et al. (2014) in F was the largest (+17 users). Actually, F includes users whose gender was newly inferred correctly by the hybrid-based method but whose gender was misjudged using individual methods. Therefore, our method more correctly infers a new user's gender by combining sources of text and images than the method presented by Sakaki et al. (2014). We assume that our method handles the combination appropriately to infer male or female gender using logistic regression.

The difference between our method and that presented by Sakaki et al. (2014) in C was the second largest (+16 users). Actually, C includes users whose gender was inferred correctly using the hybrid-based and the image-based method, but misjudged using the text-based method. Therefore, we assumed that our proposed method handled the image source more appropriately than the method presented by Sakaki et al. (2014).

6.3 Logistic Regression Weights

Figure 4 shows the logistic regression weights. From this figure, we observed that the weights for female users were all positive, the weights for male users were almost all negative. The weights for unknown were nearly zero, which indicates that the probability scores of text-based and image-based methods are not competing.

Presumably, the logistic regression weights obtained by training indicate the rate of the contribution to the inference. Table 4 presents the top three image content categories according to their absolute weights. The table shows that person, outdoor, and food contents are clues to male gender, but famous people, food contents, and consumer goods imply female gender.

Consequently, through analysis of the logistic regression weights, we confirmed that the rates of image contents' contributions to inference mutually differed. We therefore conclude that the rate of each image content's contribution to the inference is expected to be different for different genders. Our proposed method performs significantly better than the existing combination-based method.

7 Conclusion

This paper presented a proposal for a novel hybrid approach. The salient benefit of our system is that features provided from a text classifier and from an image classifier are combined appropriately to detect male or female gender using logistic regression. Experimental results show that our approach achieved accuracy of 80.25 [%], which was 1.35 pt higher than the conventional combination approach. In addition, through analysis of logistic regression weights, we confirmed that the rate of each image content's contribution to the inference should be different for different genders. Person, outdoor, and food contents are clues to male gender, but famous people, food contents, and consumer goods imply female gender. We therefore conclude that our proposed method using weighted combination of text and image classifiers performs markedly better than existing combination method.

Our approach is applicable to other attributes that might be inferred for SNS users, such as age, career, and residence, which were investigated by Ikeda et al. (2013) and by Rao and Yarowsky (2010). Because it is presumed that posted image contents clearly reflect SNS user hobbies and lifestyles, our approach is suitable for inferring those attributes as well. As a subject for future work, we intend to apply our approach to the inference of various SNS user attributes.

References

Adrian Ulges, Markus Koch and Damian Borth. 2012. Linking visual concept detection with viewer demographics. In *Proceedings of the ACM International Conference on Multimedia Retrieval*.

Alex Krizhevsky, Ilya Sutskever and Geoffrey E. Hinton. 2012. Imagenet classification with deep convolutional neural networks. In *Advances in Neural Information Processing Systems*, pages 1106-1114.

Chin-Chung Chang and Chin-Jen Lin. 2001. LIBSVM: a library for support vector machines. Software available at `http://www.csie.ntu.edu.tw/~cjlin/libsvm/`.

Delip Rao and David Yarowsky. 2010. Detecting latent user properties in social media. In *Proceedings of the Neural Information Processing Systems Workshop on Machine Learning for Social Networks*.

John D. Burger, John Henderson, George Kim and Guido Zarrella. 2011. Discriminating gender on Twitter. In *Proceedings of the Conference on Empirical Methods in Natural Language Processing*, pages 1301-1309.

Karen Simonyan and Andrew Zisserman. 2014. Very deep convolutional networks for large-scale visual recognition. Software available at `http://www.robots.ox.ac.uk/~vgg/research/very_deep/`.

Kazushi Ikeda, Gen Hattori, Chihiro Ono, Hideki Asoh and Teruo Higashino. 2013. Twitter user profiling based on text and community mining for market analysis. In *Knowledge Based Systems*, pages 35-47.

Rong-En Fan, Kai-Wei Chang, Cho-Jui Hsieh, Xiang-Rui Wang and Chin-Jen Lin. 2008. LIBLINEAR: A library for large linear classification. Software available at `http://www.csie.ntu.edu.tw/~cjlin/liblinear/`.

Ryosuke Shigenaka, Yukihiro Tsuboshita and Noriji Kato. Image-based user gender inference using deep learning on SNS. In *Proceedings of the Meeting on Image Recognition and Understanding*, in Japanese.

Shigeyuki Sakaki, Yasuhide Miura, Xiaojun Ma, Keigo Hattori and Tomoko Ohkuma. 2014. Twitter user gender inference using combined analysis of text and image processing. In *Proceedings of the workshop of the International Conference on Computational Linguistics*, page 54-61.

Wendy Liu, Faiyaz Al Zamal and Derek Ruths. 2012. Using social media to infer gender composition of commuter populations. In *Proceedings of the International Association for the Advancement of Artificial Intelligence Conference on Weblogs and Social Media*.

Xiaojun Ma, Yukihiro Tsuboshita and Noriji Kato. 2014. Gender estimation for SNS user profiling automatic image annotation. In *Proceedings of the International Workshop on Cross-media Analysis for Social Multimedia*.

Coupling Natural Language Processing and Animation Synthesis in Portuguese Sign Language Translation

Inês Almeida and Luísa Coheur
INESC-ID
Instituto Superior Técnico, Universidade de Lisboa
name.surname@tecnico.ulisboa.pt

Sara Candeias
Microsoft Language Development Center
Lisbon, Portugal
t-sacand@microsoft.com

Abstract

In this paper we present a free, open source platform, that translates in real time (written) European Portuguese into Portuguese Sign Language, being the signs produced by an avatar. We discuss basic needs of such a system in terms of Natural Language Processing and Animation Synthesis, and propose an architecture for it. Moreover, we have selected a set of existing tools that couple with our free, open-source philosophy, and implemented a prototype with them. Several case studies were conducted. A preliminary evaluation was done and, although the translation possibilities are still scarce and some adjustments still need to be done, our platform was already much welcomed by the deaf community.

1 Introduction

Several computational works dealing with the translation of sign languages from and into their spoken counter-parts have been developed in the last years. For instance, (Barberis et al., 2011) describes a study targeting the Italian Sign Language, (Lima et al., 2012) targets LIBRAS, the Brazilian Sign Language, and (Zafrulla et al., 2011) the American Sign Language. Some of the current research focus on sign language recognition (as the latter), some in translating text (or speech) into a sign language (like the previously mentioned work dedicated to Italian). Some works aim at recognising words (again, like the latter), others only letters (such as the work about LIBRAS). Only a few systems perform the two-sided translation, which is the case of the platform implemented by the Microsoft Asia group system (Chai et al., 2013), and the Virtual Sign Translator (Escudeiro et al., 2013).

Unfortunately, sign languages are not universal or a mere mimic of its country's spoken counterpart. For instance, Brazilian Sign Language is not related with the Portuguese one. Therefore, none or little resources can be re-used when one moves from one (sign) language to another.

There is no official number for deaf persons in Portugal, but the 2011 census (Instituto Nacional de Estatística (INE), 2012) mentions 27,659 deaf persons, making, however, no distinction in the level of deafness, and on the respective level of Portuguese and Portuguese Sign Language (LGP) literacy. The aforementioned Virtual Sign Translator targets LGP, as well as the works described in (Bento, 2103) and (Gameiro et al., 2014). However, to the best of our knowledge, none of these works explored how current Natural Language Processing (NLP) tasks can be applied to help the translation process of written Portuguese into LGP, which is one of the focus of this paper. In addition, we also study the needs of such translator in terms of Animation Synthesis, and propose a free, open-source platform, integrating state of the art technology from NLP and 3D animation/modelling . Our study was based on LGP videos from different sources, such as the Spread the Sign initiative[1], and static images of hand configurations presented in an LGP dictionary (Baltazar, 2010). The (only) LGP grammar (Amaral et al., 1994) was also widely consulted. Nevertheless, we often had to recur to the help of an interpreter.

Based on this study we have implemented a prototype, and examined several case studies. Finally, we performed a preliminary evaluation of our prototype. Although much work still needs to be done, the feedback from deaf associations was very positive. Extra details about this work can be found in (Almeida, 2104) and (Almeida et al.,

[1] http://www.spreadthesign.com

Proceedings of the 2015 Workshop on Vision and Language (VL'15), pages 94–103,
Lisbon, Portugal, 18 September 2015.

2015). The whole system is freely available[2].

This paper is organised as follows: Section 2 describes the proposed architecture, and Section 3 its implementation. In Section 4 we present our prototype and, in Section 5, a preliminary evaluation. Section 6 surveys related work and Section 7 concludes, pointing directions for future work.

2 Proposed architecture

Figure 1 presents the envisaged general architecture.

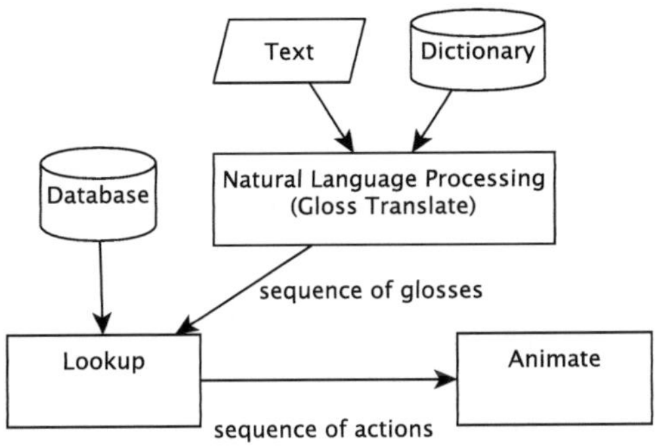

Figure 1: Proposed architecture

We followed a gloss-based approach, where words are associated to their 'meaning' through a dictionary. The order of the glosses is calculated according with the LGP grammar (structure transfer). Then, glosses are converted into gestures by retrieving the individual actions that compose it. In the last and final stage, the animation is synthesised by placing each action in time and space in a non-linear combination. The current platform is based on hand-crafted entries/rules, as there is no large-scale parallel corpus available that would allow us to follow recent tendencies in Machine Translation.

In the next sections we detail the three main components of this platform, namely the NLP, the Lookup and the Animate components, by focusing on the needs of the translation system and how these components contribute to it.

2.1 The Natural Language Processing component

As usual, the first step consists in splitting the input text into sentences. These are *tokenised* into words and punctuation. Then, possible orthographic errors are corrected. After this step, a basic approach could directly consult the dictionaries, find the words that are translated into sign language, and return the correspondent actions, without further processing. However, other NLP tools can still contribute to the translation process.

Some words in European Portuguese are signed in LGP as a sequence of signs, related with the stem and affixes of the word. Therefore, a *stemmer* can be used to identify the stem and relevant suffixes (and prefixes), which allows to infer, for instance, the gender and number of a given word. Thus, we still might be able to properly translate a word that was not previously translated into LGP (or, at least, produce something understandable), if we are able to find its stem and affixes. To illustrate this, take as example the word 'coelhinha' ('little female rabbit'). If we are able to identify its stem, 'coelho' (rabbit), and the suffix 'inha' (meaning, roughly, female (the 'a') and small (the 'inho')), we can translate that word into LGP by signing the words 'female' + 'rabbit' + 'small', in this order (which, in fact, is how it should be signed).

A *Part-of-Speech (POS) tagger* can also contribute to the translation process:

- It can couple with the stemmer in the identification of the different types of affixes (for instance, in Portuguese, a common noun that ends in 'ões' is probably a plural).

- As there are some morphosyntactic categories that have a special treatment in LGP, it is important to find the correspondent words. For instance, according with (Bento, 2103), articles are omitted in LGP ((Amaral et al., 1994) reports doubts in the respect of their existence), and thus could be ignored when identified. Also, the Portuguese grammar (Amaral et al., 1994) refers a temporal line in the gesturing space with which verbs should concord with in past, present and future tenses. Thus, to be able to identify the tense of a verb can be very important.

- A POS tagger usual feeds further processing, as for instance named entity recognisers and syntactic analysers.

A *Named Entity Recognizer* allows to identify names of persons. It is usual, among the deaf, to

[2]http://web.ist.utl.pt/~ist163556/pt2lgp

name a person with a sign (his/her *gestural name*), often with a meaning in accordance to his/her characteristics. For instance, names of public personalities, such as the current Portuguese prime minister, usually have a gestural name. However, if this name is unknown, fingerspelling the letters of his/her name is what should be done.

A *Syntactic Analyser* if fundamental to identify the syntactic components of the sentence, such as subject, and object, as LGP is usually Object–Subject–Verb (OSV), while spoken Portuguese is predominantly Subject–Verb–Object (SVO). It does not matter if it is a dependency parser or a constituents-based one. The only requirement is that, at the end, it allows structure transfer rules to be applied to the glosses. Finally, a sentiment analyser would allow to infer subjective information towards entities and the generality of the sentence, so that emotional animation layers and facial expression reinforcement can be added to the result.

After all this processing, a bilingual dictionary (glosses) is consulted, so that meaningful sequences of words (glosses) are identified (lexical transfer), and a set of syntactic rules applied, so that the final order of the set of glosses is identified.

2.2 Lookup stage

Being given a sequence of glosses, the goal of the Lookup stage is to obtain a set of actions' identifiers for the animation.

The difficulty in designing this step is derived from the fact that many Portuguese words and concepts do not have a one-to-one matching in LGP. Also, gestures may be composed of several actions, which in turn, may be compound of several actions (the gestures subunits). Finally, some contexts need to be added to the database in order to help this step.

2.3 Animate

This stage receives a sequence of actions to be composed into a fluid animation, along with a set of hints on how best to do so, for example, if the gestures are to be fingerspelled or not. The animation stage is responsible for the procedural synthesis of the animation by blending gestures and gesture subunits together.

We propose an approach where gestures are procedurally built and defined from an high-level description, based on the following parameters identified in other works (Liddell and Johnson, 1989; Liddell, 2003) as gesture subunits: a) hand configuration, orientation, placement, and movement, and; b) non manual (facial expressions and body posture).

The base hand configurations are Sign Language (SL) dependent. The parameter definition for orientation, placement and movement is often of relative nature. For example, gestures can be signed 'fast', 'near', 'at chest level', 'touching the cheek' and so on. The definition of speed is dependent on the overall speed of the animation, and the definition of locations is dependent on the avatar and its proportions.

2.3.1 Rig

To setup the character, an humanoid mesh with appropriate topology for animation and real-time playback is needed. Then, we need to associate it with the mechanism to make it move, the *rig*. We suggest a regular approach with a skinned mesh to a skeleton and bones.

Bones should be named according to a convention for symmetry and easy identification in the code. For the arms and hands, the skeleton can approximately follow the structure of a human skeleton. The rig ideally should have an Inverse Kinematics (IK) tree chain defined for both arms, rooting in the spine and ending in the hands. All fingers should also be separate IK chains, allowing for precise posing of contacts. Ideally, the IK chains should consider weight influence so that bones closer to the end-effector (hands and fingertips) are more affected, and the bones in the spine and shoulder nearly not so. The rig should also provide a hook to control the placing of the shoulder, and should make use of angle and other constraints for the joints, so as to be easier to pose and harder to place in an inconsistent position.

Finally, the rig should have markers for placement of the hands in the signing space and in common contact areas in the mesh. These markers ensure that gestures can be defined with avatar dependent terms (eg. 'near', 'touching the nose').

The markers in the signing space can be inferred automatically using the character's skeleton measures (Kennaway, 2002; Hanke, 2004), forming a virtual 3D grid in front of the character (Figure 2).

The markers in the mesh need to be defined manually and skinned to the skeleton in a consistent manner with the nearby vertices. Figure 3 shows a sample rig, with key areas in the face

Figure 2: Virtual 3D marker grid defining the signing space in front of the character

and body identified by a bone with a position and orientation in space.

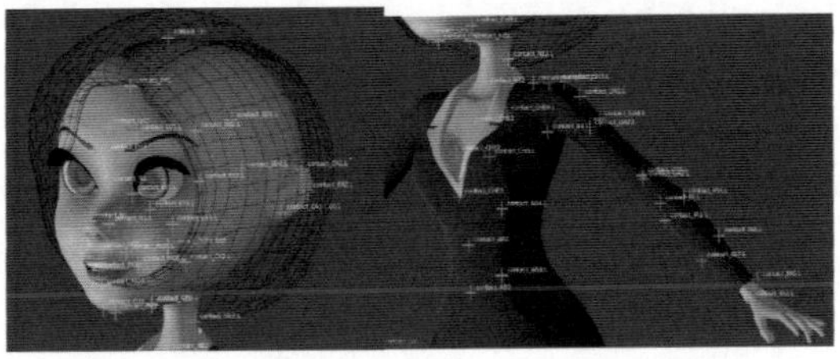

Figure 3: Definition of key contact areas in the rig

2.3.2 Building the gestures

It is now necessary to record (*key*) the poses in a good timing to build a gesture. Whichever the keying methodology, all basic hand poses and facial expressions should be recorded and can then be combined given the high level description of the gesture. The description should specify the gesture using the mentioned parameters: keyed hand configurations, placement and orientation using the spatial marks, and movement also using the marks and the overall speed of the animation.

The intersections defined by the grid from Figure 2, in conjunction with marks from Figure 3 define the set of avatar relative locations where the hands can be placed. Knowing the location where the hand should be, it can be procedurally placed with IK, guarantying physiologically possible animation with the help of other constraints.

Figure 4 shows the result of hand placement in a key area using two distinct avatars with significantly different proportions.

While this approach works well for static gestures, several problems appear when introducing movement. Gestures can change any of its parameters during the realisation, requiring a blending from the first definition (of location, orienta-

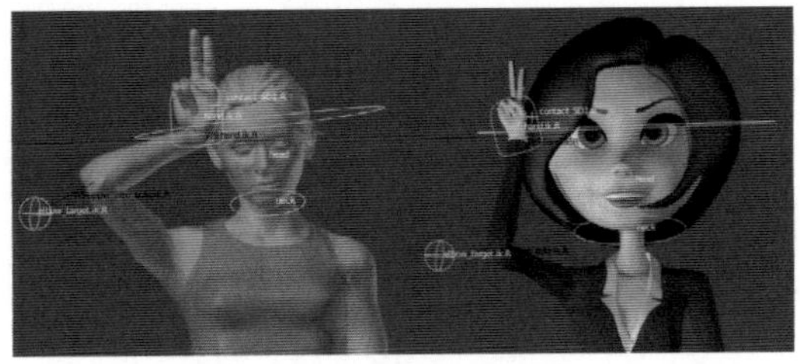

Figure 4: Avatars using the key areas

tion, configuration...) to the second. The type of blending is very important for the realism of the animation. Linear blending between two keys would result in robotic movements. Linear movement in space from one key location to another will also result in non realistic motions and even in serious collision problems (Elliott et al., 2007). For example, making a movement from an ear to the other. This is a problem of arcs. Additionally, more movements need to be defined in order to accommodate other phenomena, such as finger wiggling and several types of hand waving.

2.3.3 Blending the gestures

Moving to the sentence level, synthesising the final fluid animation is now a matter of agreeing the individual gestures in space, of realistic interpolation of keys in time, and of blending actions with each other in a non-linear way.

A reasoning module, capable of placing gestures grammatically in the signing space, and making use of the temporal line, entity allocation in space and other phenomena typically observed in SLs (Liddell, 2003) is needed.

The interpolation between animation keys is given by a curve that can be modeled to express different types of motion. The individual actions for each gesture should be concatenated with each other and with a 'rest pose' at the beginning and end of the utterance. The animation curves should then be tweaked, following the principles of animation.

Counter animation and secondary movement is also very important for believability and perceptibility. For example, when one hand contacts the other or some part of the head, it is natural to react to that contact, by tilting the head (or hand) against the contact and physically receiving the impact. Besides the acceleration of the dominant hand, the contact is mainly perceived in how it is received, being very different in a case of gentle brushing, slapping or grasping. This may be the only detail that allows distinguishing of gestures that otherwise may convey the same meaning.

Finally, actions need to be layered for expressing parallel and overlapping actions. This is the case for facial animation at the same time as manual signing and of secondary animation, such as blinking or breathing, to convey believability. The channels used by some action may be affected by another action at the same time. Thus, actions need to be prioritised, taking precedence in the blending with less important, or ending actions.

3 Implementation

We have chosen to use the Natural Language ToolKit (NLTK)[3] for NLP tasks and Blender[4] as the 3D package for animation.

The NLTK is widely used by the NLP community and offers taggers, parsers, and other tools in several languages, including Portuguese. Thus, it was chosen for all the tasks concerning NLP.

Blender is an open-source project, which allows accessing and operating on all the data (such as animation and mesh) via scripting. It offers a Python API for scripts to interact with the internal data structures, operators on said data, and with the interface. Moreover, Blender also offers the infrastructure to easily share and install addons. Therefore, the prototype was implemented as an addon, with all the logic, NLP and access to the rig and animation data done in Python. The interface is a part of Blender using the pre-existing widgets, and the avatar is rendered in real-time using the viewport renderer.

3.1 The Natural Language Processing step

The modules implemented in our system can be seen in Figure 5.

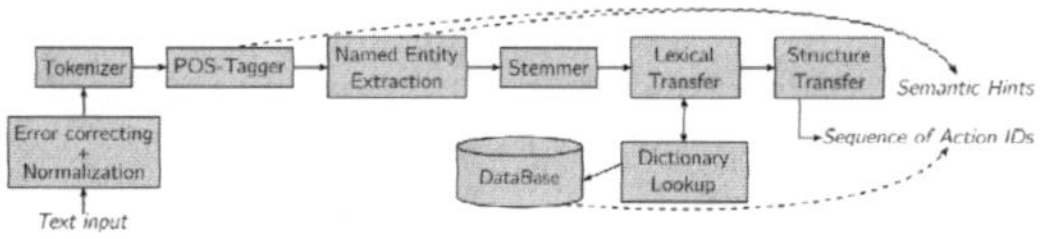

Figure 5: NLP pipeline

We also use the concept of "hint", that is, a tag that suggests if a word should be signed or spelled. Three different types of hints are possible: GLOSS (words that are not numeric quantities and have a specific gesture associated), FGSPELL (for words that should be fingerspelled), and NUMERAL (for numeric quantities). The NLP module tries to attribute a label to each word (or sequences of words), which are then used when consulting the dictionary ('Lexical Transfer').

In what concerns the NLP pipeline, we start with an 'Error correcting and normalization' step, which enforces lowercase and the use of latin characters. Common spelling mistakes should be corrected at this step. Then, the input string is split into sentences and then into words (tokenization). As an example, the sentence 'o joão come a sopa' ('João eats a soup'), becomes ['o', 'joão', 'come', 'a', 'sopa']. A stemmer identifies suffixes and prefixes. Thus, the word 'coelhinha' (as previously said, 'little female rabbit'), is understood, by its suffix ('inha'), to be a female and small derivation of the root *coelh(o)*. Therefore, 'coelhinha' is converted into [MULHER, COELHO, PEQUENO], hinted to be all part of the same gloss.

We have used the treebank 'floresta sintática' (Afonso et al., 2002) for training our 'POS-tagger'. The output of the POS-tagger for the sentence 'o joão come a sopa' is now [('o', 'art'), ('joão', 'prop'), ('come', 'v-fin'), ('a', 'prp'), ('sopa', 'n')].

We have used a Named Entity Recognizer to find proper names of persons. Our system further supports a list of portuguese names and public personalities names with their matching gestural name. For these specific entities, the system uses the known gesture instead of fingerspelling the name.

The POS-tags and recognised entities also contribute with hints. These hints are then confirmed (or not) in the next step, the 'Lexical Transfer', where we converted all the words to their corresponding gloss, using the dictionary, where the word conversions are stored. As an example, the word 'sopa' would lead to ['GLOSS', ['SOPA']], 'joao' to ['FGSPELL', ['J', 'O', 'A', 'O']] and 'two' to ['NUMERAL', ['2']] (notice that articles were discarded). Also, we provide the option of fingerspelling all the unrecognised words.

Finally, in what respects *Structure Transfer*, the current implementation only supports basic re-ordering of sequences of 'noun - verb - noun', in an attempt to convert the SVO ordering used in Portuguese to the more common structure of OSV used in LGP. We have also im-

[3]`http://www.nltk.org`
[4]`http://www.blender.org`

plement another type of re-ordering, which regards the switching of adjectives and quantities to the end of the affected noun. Following this process, [['GLOSS', ['SOPA']], ['FGSPELL', ['J','O','A','O']], ['GLOSS', ['COMER-SOPA']]] is the final output for the sentence *O João come a sopa*, and the input *dois coelhos* ('two rabbits') results in [['GLOSS', ['COELHO']], ['NUMERAL', ['2']].

3.2 The Lookup step

The Lookup step, given a gloss, is done via a JSON file mimicking a database constituted of a set of *glosses* and a set of *actions*. Action ids are mapped to blender actions, that are, in turn, referenced by the glosses. One gloss may link to more than one action, which are assumed to be played sequentially.

Figure 6 shows that *coelho* ('rabbit') has a one-to-one mapping, that *casa* ('house') corresponds to one action and that *cidade* ('city') is a composed word, formed by *casa* and a morpheme with no isolated meaning.

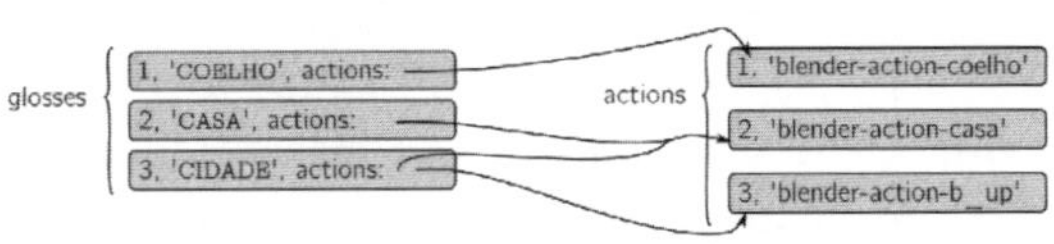

Figure 6: Database design

Knowing that gestures in LGP can be heavily contextualised, we added to the gloss structure an array of contexts with associated actions. Figure 7 shows the case of the verb *comer* ('to eat') that is classified with what is being eaten. When no context is given by the NLP module, the default is considered to be the sequence in 'actions'.

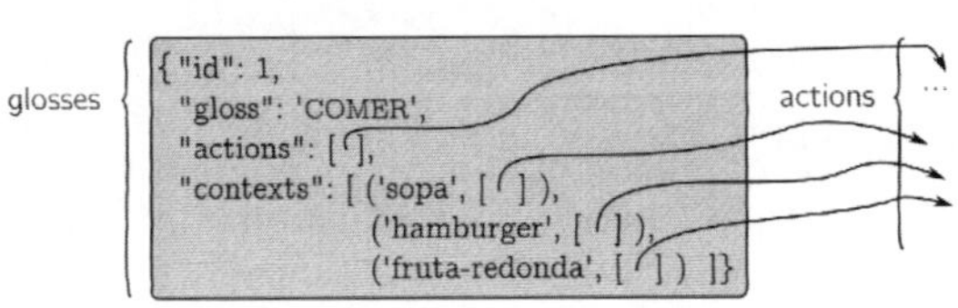

Figure 7: Supporting gloss contextualisation

3.3 The animation step

We start by setting the avatar by rigging and skinning. We chose *rigify* as a base for the rig, that needs to be extended with the spatial marks, to be used when synthesising the animation. The animation is synthesised by directly accessing and modifying the action and f-curve data. We always start and end a sentence with the rest pose, and, for concatenating the actions, we *blend* from one to the other in a given amount of frames by using Blender's Non Linear Action (NLA) tools that allow action layering. Channels that are not used in the next gesture, are blended with the rest pose instead. Figure 8 illustrates the result for the gloss sentence 'SOPA J-O-A-O COME'.

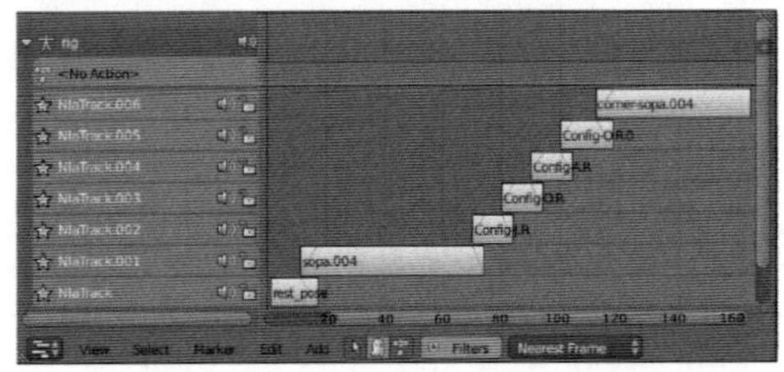

Figure 8: Action layering resulting of a translation

We adjust the number of frames for blending according to the hints received. For fingerspelling mode, we expand the duration of the hand configuration (that is originally just one frame) and blend it with the next fingerspelling in less frames than when blending between normal gloss actions. We also expand this duration when entering and leaving the fingerspell.

3.4 The interface

The interface consists of an input text box, a button to translate, and a 3D view with the signing avatar, which can be rotated and zoomed, allowing to see the avatar from different perspectives. Figure 9 shows the main translation interface (blue). Additionally, we provide an interface for exporting video of the signing (orange) and a short description of the project (green).

Figure 9: User Interface for the prototype

In what concerns the choice of the avatar, the character only needs to be imported into Blender and skinned to a *rigify* armature. Several characters were tested with success, with examples in

Figure 10.

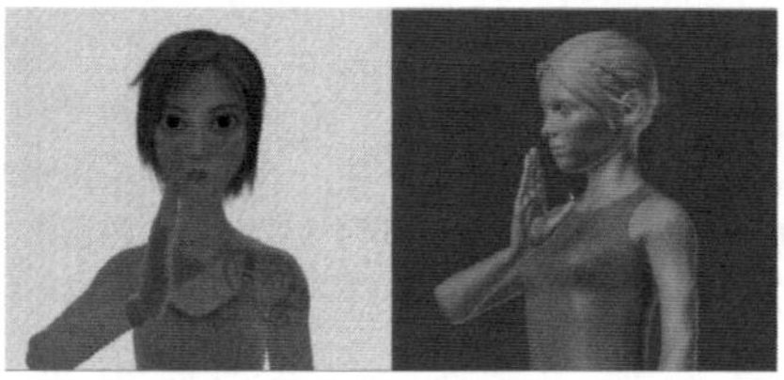

Figure 10: Example of some of the supported avatars

4 Case studies

Parallel to the development of the prototype, we devised a series of case studies to test the flexibility of the architecture and technology choices. We started with posing base hand configurations in a limited context case, passing then to full words, their derivations and blending between them. Finally, we tested the prototype with full sentences.

4.1 Basic gestures

All the 57 different hand configurations for LGP were manually posed and keyed from references gathered from (Baltazar, 2010; Amaral et al., 1994; Ferreira, 1997), and also from the Spread the Sign project videos. These hand configuration are composed of 26 hand configurations for letters, 10 for numbers, 13 for named configurations and 8 extra ones matching greek letters. This task posed no major problem.

4.2 Numbers

Numbers can be used as a quantitative qualifier, as the isolated number (cardinal), as an ordinal number, and as a number that is composed of others (eg. 147). Gestures associated with each number also vary their forms if we are expressing a quantity, a repetition or a duration, and if we are using them as an adjective or complement to a noun or verb.

Reducing the test case to ordinal numbers, the main difficulty is to express numbers in the order of the tens and up. Most cases seem to be "fingerspelt", for example, '147' is signed as '1', followed by '4' and '7' with a slight offset in space as the number grows. Numbers from '11' to '19' can be signed with a blinking movement of the units' number. Some numbers, in addition to these system, have a totally different gesture as an abbreviation, as is the example of the number '11'.

Doing a set of base hand configurations to start, proved to be a good choice as it allowed to test the hand rig and basic methodology. The ten (0 to 9) hand configurations are shown in Figure 11.

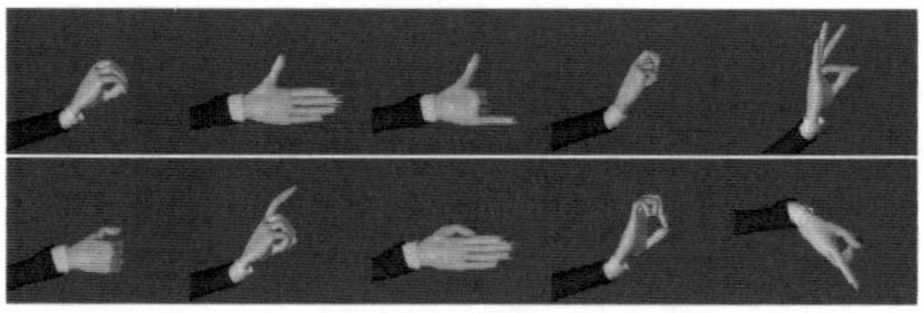

Figure 11: Hand configurations for numbers (0-9)

4.3 Common nouns and adjectives

A couple of words were chosen, such as 'coelho' ('rabbit'), with no serious criteria. Several words deriving from the stem 'coelho' were implemented, such as 'coelha' ('female rabbit') and 'coelhinho' ('little rabbit'). In the former, the gesture for "female" is performed before the gesture for "rabbit". In the latter, the gesture for the noun is followed with the gesture for the adjective (thus, 'coelho pequeno' ('little rabbit') and 'coelhinho' result in the same translation). Figure 12 illustrates both cases.

Figure 12: Gestures for 'coelha' and 'coelhinho'

4.4 Proper Nouns

As previously said, if the person does not have a gestural name that is known by the system, the letters of his/her name should be fingerspelled. This morpho-syntactic category posed no major problem.

4.5 Verbs

When the use of the verb is plain, with no past or future participles, the infinitive form is used in LGP. For instance, for the regular use of the verb 'to eat', the hand goes twice to the mouth, closing from a relaxed form, with palm up. However, this verb in LGP is highly contextualised with what is being eaten. The verb should be signed recurring to different hand configurations and expressiveness, describing *how* the thing is being eaten.

4.6 Sentences

After testing isolated words, we proceed to the full sentence: 'O João come a sopa', an already seen example, often used as a toy example in Portuguese studies. The verb gesture had to be extended, as for eating soup, it is done as if handling a spoon (for instance, for eating apples, the verb is signed as if holding the fruit)[5]. Considering the previous mentioned re-ordering from SVO (spoke Portuguese) to OSV (LGP), Figure 13 shows the resulting alignments.

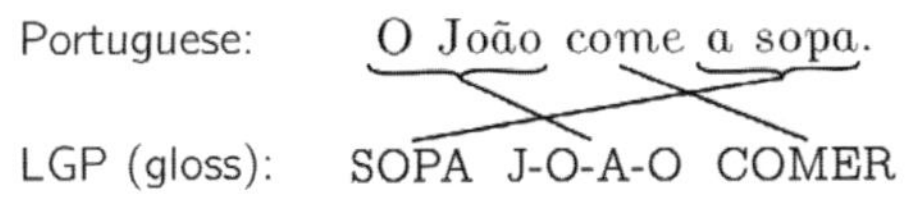

Figure 13: Alignment for European Portuguese and LGP of the sentence 'John eats the soup'

5 Evaluation

A preliminary evaluation was conducted by collecting informal feedback from the deaf communities of two Portuguese deaf associations.

5.1 Usefulness

Both associations were asked for comments on the whole idea behind this work, and if and how such application would be useful. Both were skeptical towards the possibility of achieving accurate translations, or of animating enough vocabulary for a final product, but the feedback was positive for the idea of an application that would translate to LGP, even if just isolated words were considered.

5.2 Translation Quality

The correctness and perceptibility was evaluated by six adult deaf persons and interpreters. The avatar was set to play the translations for *coelha* ('female rabbit'), *casa* ('house') and *coelhinho* ('small rabbit'). The viewers were asked, individually, to say or write in Portuguese what was being signed, with no previous information about the possibilities. In the second interaction of the system, a full sentence was added with limited variability of the form 'A eats B', where the verb 'to eat' is signed differently according to 'B'. All the gestures were recognised as well as the sentence's meaning, except for the inflection of the verb with a 'soup' object, that is signed as if handling a spoon. All of the testers recognised correctly the results, without hesitations, saying that the signs were all very clear and only lacking facial reinforcement to be more realistic.

5.3 Adequacy of the Avatar

The feedback from the deaf testers regarding the avatar looks was also very positive. There were no negative comments besides the observation that there is no facial animation. All hearing testers were also highly engaged with the system, testing multiple words and combinations, frequently mimicking the avatar.

The interest and attention observed, indicates that users had no difficulty in engaging with the avatar and found it either neutral or appealing. When asked about it, the answers were positive and the gesture blending and transitions, when noticed, was commented to be very smooth. However, sometimes the animation was deemed too slow or too fast. The animation generation should take play speed in consideration according to the expertise of the user.

6 Related Work

As ours, several systems also target the mapping of text (or speech) in one language into the correspondent signed language. Some of these systems resulted from local efforts of research groups or from local projects, and are focused in one single pair of languages (the spoken and the correspondent sign language); others aggregate the efforts of researchers and companies from different countries, and, thus, aim at translating different languages pairs (some using an interlingua approach). For instance, Virtual Sign (Escudeiro et al., 2013) is a Portuguese funded project that focus in the translation between European

[5]These contextualisations are not evident in the most recent and complete LGP dictionary (Baltazar, 2010).

Portuguese and LGP, while eSIGN[6] was an EU-funded project built on a previous project, ViSiCAST[7], whose aim was to provide information in sign language, using avatar technology, in the German and British sign languages, as well as in Sign Language of the Netherlands.

Our proposal follows in a traditional transfer machine translation paradigm of text-to-gloss/-avatar. Due to the lack of parallel corpora between European Portuguese and LGP, a data-driven method, example- and statistical-based approaches were not an option (see (Morrissey, 2008) for a study on this topic). Approaches such as the one of VISICAST (and eSIGN) (Elliott et al., 2008), which rely on formalisms, such as Discourse Representation Structures (DRS), used as intermediate semantic representations, were also not a solution, as, to the best of our knowledge, there are no free, open-source tools to calculate these structures for the Portuguese language. Thus, we focused in a simpler approach, that could profit from existing open-source tools, which could be easily used for Portuguese (and for many other languages).

We should also refer recent work concerning LGP, namely the works described in (Bento, 2103), (Gameiro et al., 2014) and (Escudeiro et al., 2013). The first focus on the mapping of human gestures into the ones of an avatar. The second targets the teaching of LGP, which the previously mentioned Virtual Sign also does (Escudeiro et al., 2014). The third contributes with a bidirectional sign language translator, between written portuguese and LGP, although it is not clear their approach in what respects text to sign language translation.

7 Conclusions and future work

We have presented a prototype that couples different NLP modules and animation techniques to generate a fluid animation of LGP utterances, given a text input in European Portuguese. We have further conducted a preliminary evaluation with the deaf community, which gave us positive feedback. Although a working product would be highly desirable and would improve the lives of many, there is still much to be done before we can reach that stage.

[6] http://www.sign-lang.uni-hamburg.de/esign/

[7] See, for instance, http://www.visicast.cmp.uea.ac.uk/Visicast_index.html

As future work we intend to perform a formal evaluation of our system, so that we can properly assess its impact. Also, we intend to extend the existing databases. Particularly inspiring is ProDeaf[8], a translation software for LIBRAS, the Brasilian Sign Language, that, besides several features, allows the crowd to contribute by adding new word/sign pairs. In our opinion, this is an excellent way of augmenting the system vocabulary, although, obviously, filters are needed in this type of scenarios. In the current version of the system, words that are not in the dictionary are simply ignored. It could be interesting to have the avatar fingerspelling them. Nevertheless, the system will probably have to be extended in other dimensions, as a broader coverage will lead to finer semantic distinctions, and a more sophisticated NLP representation will be necessary. We will also need to explore a way of simplifying the information concerning the contextualisation of a verb. For example, by storing categories of objects rather than the objects themselves. Moreover, we intent to move to the translation from LGP to European Portuguese. Here, we will follow the current approaches that take advantage of Kinect in the gesture recognition step.

Acknowledgements

We would like to thank to Associação Portuguesa de Surdos and Associação Cultural de Surdos da Amadora for all their help. However, the responsibility for any imprecision lies with the authors alone. This work was partially supported by national funds through FCT – Fundação para a Ciência e a Tecnologia, under project PEst-OE/EEI/LA0021/2013. Microsoft Language Development Center is carrying this work out in the scope of a Marie Curie Action IRIS (ref. 610986, FP7-PEOPLE-2013-IAPP).

References

S Afonso, E Bick, R Haber, and D Santos. 2002. Floresta Sintáctica: A treebank for Portuguese. *LREC*, pages 1698–1703.

Inês Almeida, Luísa Coheur, and Sara Candeias. 2015. From european portuguese to portuguese sign language. In *6th Workshop on Speech and Language Processing for Assistive Technologies (accepted for publication – demo paper)*, Dresden, Germany.

[8] http://web.prodeaf.net/

Inês Rodrigues Almeida. 2104. Exploring challenges in avatar-based translation from european portuguese to portuguese sign language. Master's thesis, Instituto Superior Técnico, Universidade de Lisboa, Lisbon, Portugal.

M.A. Amaral, A. Coutinho, and M.R.D. Martins. 1994. *Para uma gramática da Língua Gestual Portuguesa*. Colecção universitária. Caminho.

Ana Bela Baltazar. 2010. *Dicionário de Língua Gestual Portuguesa*. Porto Editora.

Davide Barberis, Nicola Garazzino, Paolo Prinetto, and Gabriele Tiotto. 2011. Improving accessibility for deaf people: An editor for computer assisted translation through virtual avatars. In *The Proceedings of the 13th International ACM SIGACCESS Conference on Computers and Accessibility*, ASSETS '11, pages 253–254, New York, NY, USA. ACM.

José Bento. 2103. Avatares em língua gestual portuguesa. Master's thesis, Faculdade de Ciências, Universidade de Lisboa, Lisbon, Portugal.

Xiujuan Chai, Guang Li, Xilin Chen, Ming Zhou, Guobin Wu, and Hanjing Li. 2013. Visualcomm: A tool to support communication between deaf and hearing persons with the kinect. In *ASSETS 13: Proceedings of the 15th International ACM SIGACCESS Conference on Computers and Accessibility*, New York, NY, USA. ACM.

R. Elliott, John Glauert, J. R. Kennaway, I. Marshall, and E. Safar. 2007. Linguistic modelling and language-processing technologies for Avatar-based sign language presentation. *Universal Access in the Information Society*, 6(4):375–391, October.

R. Elliott, J.R.W. Glauert, J.R. Kennaway, I. Marshall, and E. Safar. 2008. Linguistic modelling and language-processing technologies for avatar-based sign language presentation. *Universal Access in the Information Society*, 6(4):375–391.

Paula Escudeiro, Nuno Escudeiro, Rosa Reis, Maciel Barbosa, José Bidarra, Ana Bela Baltazar, and Bruno Gouveia. 2013. Virtual sign translator. In Atlantis Press, editor, *International Conference on Computer, Networks and Communication Engineering (ICCNCE)*, Chine.

Paula Escudeiro, Nuno Escudeiro, Rosa Reis, Maciel Barbosa, José Bidarra, Ana Bela Baltasar, Pedro Rodrigues, Jorge Lopes, and Marcelo Norberto. 2014. Virtual sign game learning sign language. In *Computers and Technology in Modern Education*, Proceedings of the 5th International Conference on Education and Educational technologies, Malaysia.

A.V. Ferreira. 1997. *Gestuário: língua gestual portuguesa*. SNR.

João Gameiro, Tiago Cardoso, and Yves Rybarczyk. 2014. Kinect-sign, teaching sign language to listeners through a game. *Procedia Technology*, 17(0):384 – 391.

Thomas Hanke. 2004. HamNoSys-representing sign language data in language resources and language processing contexts. *LREC*.

Instituto Nacional de Estatística (INE). 2012. Census 2011, xv recenceamento geral da população, v recenceamento geral da habitação, resultados definitivos – portugal. Technical report, INE.

J. R. Kennaway. 2002. Synthetic animation of deaf signing gestures. In *Gesture and Sign Language in Human-Computer Interaction*, pages 146 – 157. Springer.

Scott K Liddell and Robert E Johnson. 1989. American Sign Language: The Phonological Base. *Sign Language Studies*, 1064(1):195–277.

Scott K Liddell. 2003. *Grammar, gesture, and meaning in American Sign Language*. Cambridge University Press, Cambridge.

M. A. S. Lima, P. F. Ribeiro Neto, R. R. Vidal, G. H. E. L. Lima, and J. F. Santos. 2012. Libras translator via web for mobile devices. In *Proceedings of the 6th Euro American Conference on Telematics and Information Systems*, EATIS '12, pages 399–402, New York, NY, USA. ACM.

Sara Morrissey. 2008. *Data-driven machine translation for sign languages*. Ph.D. thesis, Dublin City University.

Zahoor Zafrulla, Helene Brashear, Thad Starner, Harley Hamilton, and Peter Presti. 2011. American sign language recognition with the kinect. In *Proceedings of the 13th International Conference on Multimodal Interfaces*, ICMI '11, pages 279–286, New York, NY, USA. ACM.

Describing Spatial Relationships between Objects in Images in English and French

Anja Belz
Computing, Engineering and Maths
University of Brighton
Lewes Road, Brighton BN2 4GJ, UK
a.s.belz@brighton.ac.uk

Adrian Muscat
Communications & Computer Engineering
University of Malta
Msida MSD 2080, Malta
adrian.muscat@um.edu.mt

Maxime Aberton and **Sami Benjelloun**
INSA Rouen
Avenue de l'Université
76801 Saint-Étienne-du-Rouvray Cedex, France
{maxime.aberton,sami.benjelloun}@insa-rouen.fr

Abstract

The context for the work we report here is the automatic description of spatial relationships between pairs of objects in images. We investigate the task of selecting prepositions for such spatial relationships. We describe the two datasets of object pairs and prepositions we have created for English and French, and report results for predicting prepositions for object pairs in both of these languages, using two methods: (a) an existing approach which manually fixes the mapping from geometrical features to prepositions, and (b) a Naive Bayes classifier trained on the English and French datasets. For the latter we use features based on object class labels and geometrical measurements of object bounding boxes. We evaluate the automatically generated prepositions on unseen data in terms of accuracy against the human-selected prepositions.

1 Introduction

Automatic image description is important not just for assistive technology, but also for applications such as text-based querying of image databases. A good image description will, among other things, refer to the main objects in the image and the relationships between them. Two of the most important types of relationships for image description are activities (e.g. a child *riding* a bike), and spatial relationships (e.g. a dog *in* a car).

The task we investigate is predicting the prepositions that can be used to describe spatial relationships between pairs of objects in images. This is an important subtask in image description, but it is rarely addressed as a subtask in its own right. If an image description method produces spatial prepositions it tends to be as a side-effect of the overall method (Mitchell et al., 2012; Kulkarni et al., 2013), or else relationships are not between objects, but e.g. between objects and the 'scene' (Yang et al., 2011). An example of preposition selection as a separate subtask is Elliott & Keller (2013) where the mapping is rule-based.

Spatial relations also play a role in referring expression generation (Viethen and Dale, 2008; Golland et al., 2010) where the problem is, however, often framed as a content selection problem from known abstract representations of the objects and scene, and the aim is to enable unique identification of the object referred to.

Our main data source is a corpus of images (Everingham et al., 2010) in which objects have been annotated with rectangular bounding boxes and object class labels. For a subset of 1,000 of the images we also have five human-created descriptions of the whole image (Rashtchian et al., 2010).

We collected additional annotations for the images listing, for each object pair, a set of prepositions that have been selected by human annotators as correctly describing the spatial relationship between the given object pair (Section 2.3). We did this in separate experiments for both English and French.

The overall aim is to create models for the mapping from image, bounding boxes and labels to spatial prepositions as indicated in Figure 1. We compare two approaches to modelling the mapping. One is taken from previous work (Elliott and Keller, 2013) and defines manually constructed rules to implement the mapping from image ge-

Proceedings of the 2015 Workshop on Vision and Language (VL'15), pages 104–113,
Lisbon, Portugal, 18 September 2015.

$\longrightarrow$ beside(person(Obj_1), person(Obj_2));
beside(person(Obj_2), dog(Obj_3));
in_front_of(dog(Obj_3), person(Obj_1))

Figure 1: Image from PASCAL VOC 2008 with annotations and prepositions representing spatial relationships (objects numbered in descending order of size of area of bounding box).

la personne	le chien	la voiture	la chaise	le cheval	le chat	l'oiseau	le vélo	la moto	l'écran	l'avion	la bouteille	le bateau	le canapé	le train	la plante	le mouton	la vache	la table	le bus
person	dog	car	chair	horse	cat	bird	bicycle	motorbike	tv/monitor	aeroplane	bottle	boat	sofa	train	pottedplant	sheep	cow	diningtable	bus
783	123	112	92	92	88	86	79	77	63	60	59	58	57	44	43	33	27	15	9

Table 1: Object class label frequencies.

ometries to prepositions (Section 3.1). The other is a Naive Bayes classifier trained on a range of features to represent object pairs, computed from image, bounding boxes and labels (Section 3.2). We report results for English and French, in terms of two measures of accuracy (Section 5).

2 Data

2.1 VOC'08

The PASCAL VOC 2008 Shared Task Competition (VOC'08) data consists of 8,776 images and 20,739 objects in 20 object classes (Everingham et al., 2010). In each image, every object in one of the 20 VOC'08 object classes is annotated with six types of information of which we use the following three:

1. *Class*: one of: aeroplane, bird, bicycle, boat, bottle, bus, car, cat, chair, cow, dining table, dog, horse, motorbike, person, potted plant, sheep, sofa, train, tv/monitor.
2. *Bounding box*: an axis-aligned bounding box surrounding the extent of the object visible in the image.
3. *Occlusion:* a high level of occlusion is present.

Examples of all six types of annotation can be seen in Figure 2. We use the object class labels in predicting prepositions, and for the French experiments we translated them as follows (in the same order as the English labels above):

> l'avion, l'oiseau, le vélo, le bateau, la bouteille, le bus, la voiture, le chat, la chaise, la vache, la table, le chien, le cheval, la moto, la personne, la plante, le mouton, le canapé, le train, l'écran

2.2 VOC'08 1K

Using Mechanical Turk, Rashtchian et al. (2010) collected five descriptions each for 1,000 VOC'08 images selected randomly but ensuring even distribution over the VOC'08 object classes. Turkers had to have high hit rates and pass a language competence test before creating descriptions, leading to relatively high quality.

We obtained a set of candidate prepositions from the VOC'08 1K dataset as follows. We parsed the 5,000 descriptions with the Stanford

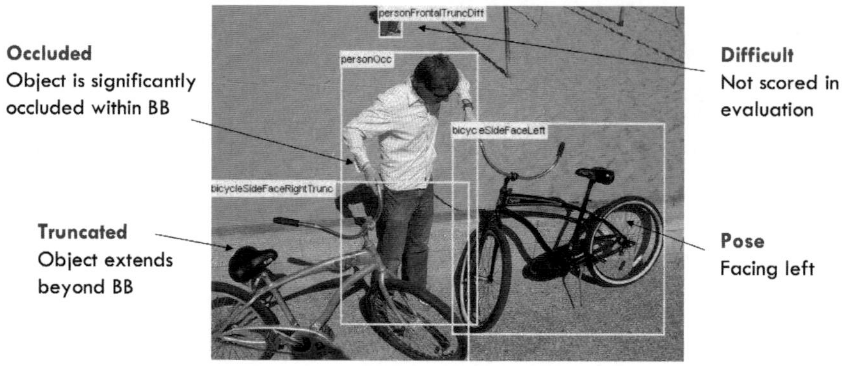


```
A main holds two bikes near a beach.
A young man wearing a striped shirt is holding two bicycles.
Man with two bicycles at the beach, looking perplexed.
Red haired man holding two bicycles.
Young redheaded man holding two bicycles near beach.
```

Figure 2: Image 2008_008320 from PASCAL VOC 2008 with annotations and image descriptions obtained by Rashtchian et al. (2010). (BB = bounding box; image reproduced from http://lear.inrialpes.fr/RecogWorkshop08/documents/everingham.pdf.)

Parser version 3.5.2[1] with the PCFG model, extracted the nmod:*prep* prepositional modifier relations, and manually removed the non-spatial ones. This gave us the following set of 38 prepositions:

$\mathbf{V_E}$ = { *about, above, across, against, along, alongside, around, at, atop, behind, below, beneath, beside, beyond, by, close_to, far_from, in, in_front_of, inside, inside_of, near, next_to, on, on_top_of, opposite, outside, outside_of, over, past, through, toward, towards, under, underneath, up, upon, within* }

For the list of French prepositions we started by compiling the list of possible translations of the English prepositions, after which we checked the list against 200 example images which resulted in a few additions and deletions. The final list for French has the following 21 prepositions (note there is no 1-to-1 correspondence with the English prepositions):

$\mathbf{V_F}$ = { *à côté de, a l'interieur de, a l'éxterieur de, au dessus de, au niveau de, autour de, contre, dans, derrière, devant, en dessous de, en face de, en haut de, en travers de, le long de, loin de, par delà, parmi, près de, sous, sur* }

[1] http://nlp.stanford.edu/software/lex-parser.shtml

2.3 Human-Selected Spatial Prepositions

We are in the process of extending the VOC'08 annotations with human-selected spatial prepositions associated with pairs of objects in images. So far we have collected spatial prepositions for object pairs in images that have exactly two objects annotated (1,020). Annotators were presented with images from the dataset where in each image presentation the two objects, Obj_1 and Obj_2, were shown with their bounding boxes and labels. If there was more than one object of the same class, then the labels were shown with indices (numbered in order of decreasing size of bounding box).

2.3.1 English data

Next to the image was shown the template sentence "The Obj_1 is ___ the Obj_2", and the list of possible prepositions extracted from VOC 1K (see last section). The option 'NONE' was also available in case none of the prepositions was suitable (but participants were discouraged from using it).

Table 1 shows occurrence counts for the 20 object class labels, while the two columns on the left of Table 2 show how many times each preposition was selected by the annotators in the English version of the experiment. The average number of prepositions per object pair chosen by the English annotators was 2.01.

Each pair of objects was presented twice, the template incorporating the objects once in each or-

English				French			
next to	304	in	16	à côté de	274	en haut de	2
beside	211	inside	15	près de	183	parmi	0
near	156	inside of	10	devant	177		
close to	149	above	7	contre	161		
in front of	141	around	6	derrière	161		
behind	129	at	5	sur	117		
on	115	past	5	au niveau de	110		
on top of	103	towards	5	sous	95		
underneath	90	within	5	au dessus de	82		
beneath	84	below	4	en face de	79		
far from	74	over	4	en dessous de	74		
under	68	toward	1	loin de	57		
NONE	64	about	0	par delà	42		
alongside	56	across	0	le long de	40		
by	50	along	0	dans	23		
upon	44	outside	0	autour de	21		
against	26	outside of	0	en travers de	14		
opposite	26	through	0	à l'interieur de	10		
beyond	20	up	0	AUCUN	6		
atop	18			à l'éxterieur de	3		

Table 2: Number of times each preposition was selected by the English and French annotators.

der, "The Obj_1 is ___ the Obj_2" and "The Obj_2 is ___ the Obj_1".[2] Participants were asked to select all correct prepositions for each pair.

2.3.2 French Data

The experimental design and setup was the same as for the English. The template sentence for the French data collection was "Obj_1 est ___ Obj_2", with the determiners included in the labels (see end of Section 2.2); e.g. "La plante est ___ l'écran".

Table 1 shows occurrence counts for the 20 object class labels, while the two columns on the right of Table 2 show how many times each preposition was selected by the annotators in the French version of the experiment. The average number of prepositions per object pair chosen by the French annotators was 1.73.

3 Predicting Prepositions

When looking at a 2-D image, people infer all kinds of information not present in the pixel grid on the basis of their practice mapping 2-D information to 3-D spaces, and their real-world knowledge about the properties of different types of objects. In our research we are interested in the extent to which prepositions can be predicted without any real-world knowledge, using just features that can be computed from the image and the objects' bounding boxes and class labels.

In this section we look at two methods for mapping language and visual image features to prepositions. Each takes as input an image in which two objects in the above object classes have been annotated with rectangular bounding boxes and object class labels, and returns as output preposition(s) that describe the spatial relationship between the two objects in the image.

3.1 Rule-based method

The rule-based method we examine is a direct implementation of the eight geometric relations defined in Visual Dependency Grammar (Elliott and Keller, 2013; Elliott, 2014). An overview is shown in Figure 3, for details see Elliott (2014, p. 13ff).

In order to implement these rules as a classifier, we pair each rule with the preposition referenced in it. In the case of *surrounds*, we use *around* instead. Two of the relations are problematic for us to implement, namely *behind* and *in front of*, because they make use of manual annotations that in fact encode whether one object is behind or in

[2]Showing objects in both orders is necessary for non-reflexive prepositions such as *under, in, on*, but also allows for other (unknown) factors that may influence preposition choice such as respective size of first and second object.

front of the other. We do not have this information available to us in our annotations.

What we do have is the 'occluded' flag (see list of VOC'08 annotations in Section 2.1 and Figure 2) which encodes whether the object tagged as occluded is partially hidden by another object. The problem is that the occluding object is not necessarily one of the two objects in the pair under consideration, i.e. the occluded object might be behind something else entirely. Nevertheless, the 'occluded' flag, in conjunction with bounding box overlap, gives us an angle on the definition of *in front of* ('the Z-plane relationship is dominant'); we define the two problematic relations as follows:

Y is tagged 'occluded' and the overlap between X and Y is more than 50% of the bounding box area of Y.

X is tagged 'occluded' and the overlap between X and Y is more than 50% of the bounding box area of X.

In pseudocode, and for English, our implementation looks as follows (a is the centroid angle, P is the output list of prepositions, and 'overlap' is the area of the overlap between the bounding boxes of Object 1 and Object 2):

```
P = {}

if overlap is 100% of Obj2 then
    P = P ∪ {around}                      ▷ Obj1 surrounds Obj2
end if

if overlap > 50% of Obj1 then
    P = P ∪ {on}                          ▷ Obj1 on Obj2
end if

if Obj2 occluded and
     overlap > 50% of Obj2 then
    P = P ∪ {in front of}                 ▷ Obj1 in front of Obj2
else if Obj1 occluded and
          overlap > 50% of Obj1 then
    P = P ∪ {behind}                      ▷ Obj1 behind Obj2
end if

if 225 < a < 315 then
    P = P ∪ {above}                       ▷ Obj1 above Obj2
else if 45 < a < 135 then
    P = P ∪ {below}                       ▷ Obj1 below Obj2
else if opposite conditions are met then
    P = P ∪ {opposite}                    ▷ Obj1 opposite Obj2
else
    P = P ∪ {beside}                      ▷ Obj1 beside Obj2
end if

return P
```

This algorithm returns between 1 and 4 prepositions. The counts for multiple outputs are as follows (no different for English and French):

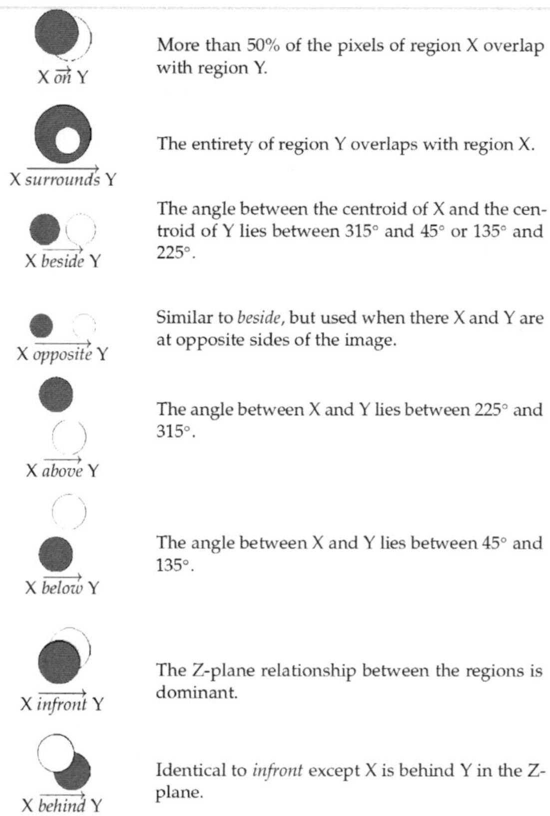

Figure 3: Overview of the eight geometric relations defined in VDR, figure copied from Elliott (2014, p. 13).

$\|P\|$	Returned in n cases
1	580
2	159
3	247
4	14

For evaluating the rule-based classifier against the French human-selected prepositions we translated the eight English prepositions as follows (listed in the same order as in Figure 3):

> sur, autour de, à côté de, en face de, au dessus de, en dessous de, devant, derrière

3.2 Naive Bayes Classifier

Our second preposition selection method is a Naive Bayes Classifier. Below we describe how we model the prior and likelihood terms, before describing the whole model. The terms come together as follows under Naive Bayes:

$$P(v_j|\mathbf{F}) \propto P(v_j)P(\mathbf{F}|v_j) \qquad (1)$$

Model	ENGLISH				FRENCH			
	$Acc_A(1..n)$				$Acc_A(1..n)$			
	$n=1$	$n=2$	$n=3$	$n=4$	$n=1$	$n=2$	$n=3$	$n=4$
v_{RB}	21.2%	28.1%	32.7%	32.8%	30.4%	38.1%	42.1%	42.2%
v_{OL}	34.4%	46.1%	51.2%	53.1%	41.4%	49.2%	57.5%	57.9%
v_{ML}	30.9%	46.2%	55.7%	58.4%	25.6%	42.6%	51.7%	52.7%
v_{NB}	51.0%	64.5%	67.4%	68.1%	46.7%	64.2%	72.4%	72.4%
	$Acc_A^{Syn}(1..n)$				$Acc_A^{Syn}(1..n)$			
	$n=1$	$n=2$	$n=3$	$n=4$	$n=1$	$n=2$	$n=3$	$n=4$
v_{RB}	31.2%	41.1%	46.5%	46.7%	32.7%	41.8%	45.7%	46.0%
v_{OL}	43.9%	49.0%	55.9%	57.1%	41.8%	50.0%	57.7%	58.1%
v_{ML}	35.6%	50.5%	58.7%	60.9%	26.8%	43.3%	52.3%	53.3%
v_{NB}	57.2%	65.6%	69.9%	70.7%	47.5%	64.4%	72.6%	72.9%

Table 3: Accuracy A results for English and French.

where $v_j \in \mathbf{V}$ are the possible prepositions, and $\mathbf{F}$ is the feature vector.

3.2.1 Prior Model

The prior model captures the probabilities of prepositions given ordered pairs of object labels L_s, L_o, where the normalised probabilities are obtained through a frequency count on the training set, using add-one smoothing.

In order to test this model separately, we simply construe it as a classifier to give us the most likely preposition v_{OL}:

$$v_{OL} = \underset{v \in \mathbf{V}}{argmax} \; P(v_j | L_s, L_o) \qquad (2)$$

where v_j is a preposition in the set of prepositions $\mathbf{V}$, and L_s and L_o are the object class labels of the first and second objects.

3.2.2 Likelihood Model

The likelihood model is based on a set of six geometric features computed from the image size and bounding boxes:

- F_1: Area of Obj_1 (Bounding Box 1) normalized by Image size.
- F_2: Area of Obj_2 (Bounding Box 2) normalized by Image Size.
- F_3: Ratio of area of Obj_1 to area of Obj_2.
- F_4: Distance between bounding box centroids normalized by object sizes.
- F_5: Area of overlap of bounding boxes normalized by the smaller bounding box.
- F_6: Position of Obj_1 relative to Obj_2.

F_1 to F_5 are real-valued features, whereas F_6 is a categorical variable over four values (N, S, E, W). For each preposition, the probability distributions for each feature is estimated from the training set. The distributions for F_1 to F_4 are modelled with a Gaussian function, F_5 with a clipped polynomial function, and F_6 with a discrete distribution.

For separate evaluation, a maximum likelihood model, which can also be derived from the Naive Bayes model described in the next section by choosing a uniform $P(v)$ function, is given by:

$$v_{ML} = \underset{v \in \mathbf{V}}{argmax} \prod_{i=1}^{6} P(F_i | v_j) \qquad (3)$$

3.2.3 Complete Naive Bayes Model

The Naive Bayes classifier is derived from the maximum-a-posteriori Bayesian model, with the assumption that the features are conditionally independent. A direct application of Bayes' rule gives the classifier based on the posterior probability distribution as follows:

$$\begin{aligned} v_{NB} &= \underset{v \in \mathbf{V}}{argmax} \; P(v_j | F_1, ...F_6, L_s, L_o) \\ &= \underset{v \in \mathbf{V}}{argmax} \; P(v_j | L_s, L_o) \prod_{i=1}^{6} P(F_i | v_j) \end{aligned} \qquad (4)$$

Intuitively, $P(v_j | L_s, L_o)$ weights the likelihood with the prior or *state of nature* probabilities.

4 Evaluation Measures

We use two methods (Acc_A and Acc_B) of calculating accuracy (the percentage of instances for

ENGLISH												
Preposition	v_{NB}						v_{RB}					
	$Acc_B(1..n)$				$Acc_B^{Syn}(1..n)$		$Acc_B(1..n)$				$Acc_B^{Syn}(1..n)$	
	n=1	n=2	n=3	n=4	n=1	n=4	n=1	n=2	n=3	n=4	n=1	n=4
next to	23.0	77.0	89.8	93.1	73.7	94.7						
beside	58.3	81.5	85.8	91.9	75.8	96.2	70.1	76.3	78.7	78.7	100	100
near	43.6	55.1	74.4	82.7	44.2	96.8						
close to	4.7	14.8	51.7	87.9	16.1	94.0						
in front of	29.1	39.7	48.2	52.5	29.1	52.5	11.3	22.0	26.2	26.2	10.6	26.2
behind	31.0	38.0	50.4	73.6	31.0	73.6	8.5	14.0	22.5	24.0	8.5	24.0
on	72.2	83.5	85.2	86.1	80.0	86.1	20.9	55.7	77.4	78.3	35.4	85.2
on top of	10.7	76.7	81.6	82.5	80.6	84.5						
underneath	53.3	68.9	84.4	86.7	68.9	90.0						
beneath	15.5	73.8	79.8	85.7	15.5	85.7						
far from	44.6	62.2	66.2	68.9	44.6	68.9						
under	22.1	27.9	82.4	83.8	67.6	83.8						
NONE	34.4	53.1	67.2	73.4	34.4	73.4						
alongside	0.0	5.4	8.9	12.5	0.0	10.7						
by	4.0	8.0	10.0	38.0	72.0	86.0						
upon	0.0	4.5	75.0	77.3	81.8	86.4						
against	7.7	11.5	19.2	26.9	7.7	26.9						
opposite	19.2	34.6	42.3	50.0	19.2	46.2	26.9	26.9	26.9	26.9	26.9	26.9
beyond	15.0	25.0	25.0	30.0	15.0	30.0						
around	33.3	33.3	50.0	66.7	33.3	66.7	33.3	50.0	66.7	66.7	33.3	66.7
above	14.3	14.3	14.3	57.1	14.3	57.1	0.0	0.0	0.0	0.0	14.3	14.3
below	0.0	25.0	75.0	75.0	0.0	75.0	25.0	25.0	25.0	25.0	25.0	25.0
Mean	24.3	41.6	57.6	67.4	41.1	71.2	24.5	33.7	40.4	40.7	31.8	46.0

Table 4: English Acc_B results: $Acc_B(1..n)$, $n \leq 4$; $Acc_B^{Syn}(1)$; and $Acc_B^{Syn}(1..4)$ for v_{NB} and v_{RB} models. Shown: all prepositions of frequency 20 and above, in order of frequency. Also included are less frequent words if they are in the set of eight prepositions produced by the v_{RB} method.

which a correct output is returned). The notation $Acc_A(1..n)$ or $Acc_B(1..n)$ is used to indicate that in this version of the evaluation method at least one of the top n most likely outputs (prepositions) returned by the model needs to match one of the human-selected reference prepositions for the model output to count as correct.

Furthermore, we use the notation $Acc_A^{Syn}(1..n)$ or $Acc_B^{Syn}(1..n)$ to indicate that in this version, at least one of the top n most likely outputs (prepositions) returned by the model, or one of its near synonyms, needs to match one of the human-selected reference prepositions for the model output to count as correct.

The near synonym sets used for English are: {*above, over*}, {*along, alongside*}, {*atop, upon, on, on_top_of*}, {*below, beneath*}, {*beside, by, next_to*}, {*beyond, past*}, {*close_to, near*}, {*in, inside, inside_of, within*} {*outside, outside_of*}, {*toward, towards*}, {*under, underneath*}, plus 11 singleton sets.

For French we used: {*a_l'interieur_de, dans*}, {*au_dessus_de, en_haut_de*}, {*en_dessous_de, sous*}, plus 15 singleton sets. This gives us 18 sets for French, and 22 for English.

For the rule-based selection method we do not have the ranked outputs needed to compute Acc_A and Acc_B. Interpreting the output set P directly as ranked would mean preserving the order in which prepositions are selected by rules which is likely to be unfair to this method. Instead we randomly shuffle P and then interpret it as ranked, with the first in this shuffled list giving the highest ranked output v_{RB}. To be on the safe side we average all results over 10 different random shuffles. Note that from $n = 4$ upwards, it makes no difference whether the outputs are truly ranked or not.

FRENCH												
Preposition	v_{NB}						v_{RB}					
	$Acc_B(1..n)$				$Acc_B^{Syn}(1..n)$		$Acc_B(1..n)$				$Acc_B^{Syn}(1..n)$	
	n=1	n=2	n=3	n=4	n=1	n=4	n=1	n=2	n=3	n=4	n=1	n=4
à côté de	40.1	65.0	80.7	91.2	40.1	91.2	66.7	72.6	74.1	74.1	65.1	74.1
près de	23.5	49.2	75.4	83.6	23.5	83.6						
devant	23.2	38.4	46.9	53.7	23.2	53.7	5.2	13.1	15.8	15.8	6.2	15.8
contre	41.0	63.4	78.3	83.2	41.0	83.2						
derrière	16.1	29.8	46.0	70.8	16.1	70.8	4.3	11.2	16.1	16.8	7.1	16.8
sur	53.0	70.9	85.5	88.9	53.0	88.9	27.2	60.7	77.8	77.8	28.1	77.8
au niveau de	28.2	59.1	71.8	78.2	28.2	78.2						
sous	78.9	90.5	90.5	92.6	89.5	95.8						
au dessus de	19.5	56.1	62.2	69.5	19.5	69.5	24.4	39.2	52.1	52.4	28.2	52.4
en face de	20.3	34.2	48.1	54.4	20.3	54.4	35.4	35.4	35.4	35.4	35.4	35.4
en dessous de	12.2	59.5	70.3	81.1	56.8	81.1	30.1	43.7	48.6	48.6	59.4	100
loin de	38.6	56.1	63.2	66.7	38.6	66.7						
par delà	16.7	35.7	40.5	45.2	16.7	45.2						
le long de	7.5	20.0	22.5	22.5	7.5	22.5						
dans	56.5	78.3	82.6	91.3	56.5	91.3						
autour de	28.6	28.6	42.9	42.9	28.6	42.9	24.4	42.3	57.1	57.1	23.6	57.1
en travers de	28.6	42.9	50.0	57.1	28.5	57.1						
à l'interieur de	20.0	80.0	90.0	90.0	80.0	100						
Mean	30.7	53.2	63.7	70.1	37.1	70.9	27.2	39.8	47.1	47.3	31.6	53.7

Table 5: French Acc_B results: $Acc_B(1..n)$, $n \leq 4$; $Acc_B^{Syn}(1)$; and $Acc_B^{Syn}(1..4)$ for v_{NB} and v_{RB} models. Shown: all prepositions of frequency 10 and above, in order of frequency. Also included are less frequent words if they are in the set of eight prepositions produced by the v_{RB} method.

Accuracy measure A: $Acc_A(1..n)$ returns the proportion of times that at least one of the top n prepositions returned by a model for an ordered object pair is in the set of all human-selected prepositions for the same object pair. Acc_A can be seen as a system-level Precision measure.

Accuracy measure B: $Acc_B(1..n)$ computes the mean of preposition-level accuracies. Accuracy for each preposition v is the proportion of times that v is returned as one of the top n prepositions out of all cases where v is in the human-selected set of reference prepositions. Acc_B can be seen as a preposition-level Recall measure.

5 Results

The current French and English data sets each comprise 1,000 images/object-pair items, each of which is labelled with one or more prepositions. For training purposes, we create a separate training instance (Obj_s, Obj_o, v) for each preposition v selected by our human annotators for the context 'The Obj_s is v the Obj_o' (or the French equivalent). The models are trained and tested with leave-one-out cross-validation.

Table 3 shows English and French Acc_A and Acc_A^{Syn} results for the rule-based method (v_{RB}), the prior model (v_{OL}), the likelihood model (v_{ML}), and the Naive Bayes model (v_{NB}). The main results are the $Acc_A(1)$ results, because after all a method needs to select a single preposition in order to be usable, e.g. in image description.

$Acc_A^{Syn}(1)$ gives an idea of how much greater a proportion of a method's outputs would be considered correct by human evaluators.

The remaining measures give various perspectives on the proportion of times a method came close to getting it right, for four degrees of 'close'. E.g. $Acc_A^{Syn}(1..4)$ shows what proportion of times one of the top 4 prepositions generated by a method, or one of their near synonyms, was in the reference set.

It is clear that the English results are more affected by synonym effects. E.g. $Acc_A(1..n)$ for English is nearly 10 percentage points lower than for French for all n, whereas this difference all but disappears for $Acc_A^{Syn}(1..n)$.

Overall, the v_{NB} method always achieves the best result, as expected. The v_{ML} model seems to be better at English than French, whereas for v_{OL} it is the other way around.

Generally, once synonyms are taken into account, the results are strikingly similar for English and French, with the exception of the V_{ML} model which does worse for French.

Tables 4 and 5 list the $Acc_B(1..n), n \leq 4$ and $Acc_A^{Syn}(1..n), n \in \{1, 4\}$ results for the v_{NB} and v_{RB} models; values are shown for the most frequent prepositions (in order of frequency) and for the mean of all preposition-level accuracies. We are not showing all prepositions partly for reasons of space, but also because for the low frequency prepositions, the models tend to underfit or overfit noticeably.

Note that here too we consider the $Acc_A(1)$ and $Acc_A^{Syn}(1)$ figures to be the main results. Among the English prepositions that v_{NB} does well with (considered under the main $Acc_B(1)$ measure) are *beside, near, underneath, far from*, and results for *on* are particularly good; v_{RB} does well for *beside*.

As for French, v_{NB} does well with *à côté de, contre, sur, loin de*, while results for *sous* are particularly good. v_{RB} does well for *à côté de*. Apart from *near, underneath* and *contre*, these are the same prepositions, semantically, as the English ones the methods do well with.

6 Conclusion

We have described (i) English and French datasets in which object pairs are annotated with prepositions that describe their spatial relationship, and (ii) methods for automatically predicting such prepositions on the basis of features computed from image and object geometry (visual information) and from object class labels (language information).

The main method we tested, a Naive Bayes classifier which takes both language and vision information into account, does best in terms of all evaluation methods we used, and it does better on English than on French. When evaluated separately, the prior model which is based on language information only, outperforms the likelihood model which is based on visual information only, in terms of the main evaluation measures $Acc_A(1)$ and $Acc_A^{Syn}(1)$.

Main results in the region of 50% leave room for improvement; the fact that these go up to around 70% when the top 4 results are taken into account indicates that the method gets it nearly right a lot of the time and that for a smaller set of prepositions, and with more sophisticated machine learning methods, better results will be obtained.

It seems clear from the results, and intuitively obvious, that a greater presence of near synonyms in the data makes for a harder modelling task. We had a principled reason for using this particular set of English prepositions: it is the set observed in the human-authored descriptions we used (see Section 2.2). In our future work we will also work with the single *best* prepositions chosen by annotators to describe spatial relationships. This seems likely to result in a smaller list of prepositions overall and an easier modelling task. In order to get a truer impression of the quality of results we will also carry out human evaluation.

Acknowledgments

The research reported in this paper was supported by a Short-term Scientific Mission grant under European COST Action IC1307 (The European Network on Integrating Vision and Language).

References

Desmond Elliott and Frank Keller. 2013. Image description using visual dependency representations. In *Proceedings of the 18th Conference on Empirical Methods in Natural Language Processing (EMNLP'13)*, pages 1292–1302.

Desmond Elliott. 2014. *A Structured Representation of Images for Language Generation and Image Retrieval*. Ph.D. thesis, University of Edinburgh.

Mark Everingham, Luc Van Gool, Christopher KI Williams, John Winn, and Andrew Zisserman. 2010. The PASCAL Visual Object Classes (VOC) Challenge. *International Journal of Computer Vision*, 88(2):303–338.

Dave Golland, Percy Liang, and Dan Klein. 2010. A game-theoretic approach to generating spatial descriptions. In *Proceedings of the 15th Conference on Empirical Methods in Natural Language Processing (EMNLP'10)*, pages 410–419. Association for Computational Linguistics.

Gaurav Kulkarni, Visruth Premraj, Vicente Ordonez, Sudipta Dhar, Siming Li, Yejin Choi, Alexander C Berg, and Tamara Berg. 2013. Babytalk: Understanding and generating simple image descriptions. *Pattern Analysis and Machine Intelligence, IEEE Transactions on*, 35(12):2891–2903.

Margaret Mitchell, Xufeng Han, Jesse Dodge, Alyssa Mensch, Amit Goyal, Alex Berg, Kota Yamaguchi, Tamara Berg, Karl Stratos, and Hal Daumé III. 2012. Midge: Generating image descriptions from computer vision detections. In *Proceedings of EACL'12*.

Cyrus Rashtchian, Peter Young, Micah Hodosh, and Julia Hockenmaier. 2010. Collecting image annotations using Amazon's Mechanical Turk. In *Proceedings of the NAACL HLT 2010 Workshop on Creating Speech and Language Data with Amazon's Mechanical Turk*, pages 139–147. Association for Computational Linguistics.

Jette Viethen and Robert Dale. 2008. The use of spatial relations in referring expression generation. In *Proceedings of the Fifth International Natural Language Generation Conference (INLG'08)*, pages 59–67. Association for Computational Linguistics.

Yezhou Yang, Ching Lik Teo, Hal Daumé III, and Yiannis Aloimonos. 2011. Corpus-guided sentence generation of natural images. In *Proceedings of the 16th Conference on Empirical Methods in Natural Language Processing (EMNLP'11)*, pages 444–454. Association for Computational Linguistics.

Author Index

Association for Computational Linguistics
209 N. Eighth Street
Stroudsburg, Pennsylvania 18360

ISBN 978-1-5108-1190-4
9 781510 811904

Baltic Polymer Symposium 2019

Vilnius, Lithuania
18-20 September 2019